The Art of Software Architecture
Design Methods and Techniques

Stephen T. Albin

WILEY

Wiley Publishing, Inc.

Executive Publisher: Joe Wikert
Executive Editor: Robert M. Elliott
Assistant Developmental Editor: Emilie Herman
Editorial Manager: Kathryn A. Malm
Assistant Managing Editor: Vincent Kunkemueller
Text Design & Composition: Wiley Composition Services

Library of Congress Cataloging-in-Publication Data:

Albin, Stephen, 1967-
  The art of software architecture : design methods and techniques / Stephen T. Albin.
      p. cm.
Includes bibliographical references and index.
  ISBN 0-471-22886-9
1. Computer software—Development.
2. Computer architecture. I. Title.
QA76.76.D47 A398 2003
005.1—dc21
                          2002155539

10 9 8 7 6 5 4 3 2 1

To Jessie, Morgan, and Hannah
for their love and inspiration.

Contents

Acknowledgments

I would like to thank Scott Seaton, Steve Richard, and Stuart Thompto at ListenPoint for allowing me the time to complete this project.

I would also like to thank the staff at Wiley Publishing, Inc., and especially Emilie Herman for her excellent assistance reviewing and revising the manuscript.

Finally, I wish to thank my wife, Jessie, for her patience and support, and my daughters, Morgan and Hannah, for sharing me with this project.

About the Author

Stephen T. Albin is a software engineer and consultant in northern California and has developed commercial enterprise software applications, platforms, and technologies. He is a member of the ACM and IEEE Computer and Engineering Management Societies. He can be reached at stevealbin@computer.org.

Introduction

Software architecture is often confused with low-level design and the technology stack. Technology vendors and popular technology-focused journals tend to propagate this misunderstanding. As a result, many software engineers produce architecture descriptions that are nothing more than regurgitated diagrams of technology layers. The classic enterprise application architecture is often a diagram of so-called architectural layers depicting a presentation layer on top of a business logic layer (or middle-tier) on top of a persistence layer. This representation communicates nothing about how the system handles the functional or nonfunctional requirements of the system. It merely shows the technology to be used and how that technology will be integrated.

There is a temptation to assume that the layers of an application architecture map directly to individual technologies: Presentation is composed of Java Servlets and Java Server Pages (JSP); the business layer is composed of Enterprise JavaBeans (EJB); and the persistence layer is a relational database management system (RDBMS). For some simple systems, there is a one-to-one correspondence between the architectural layers and individual technologies. Those assumptions quickly become fallacies when the system becomes functionally more complex. Presentation logic may be composed not only of the servlets and JSP but also of EJBs and data stored in a relational database (for example, user preferences). Business logic may be composed not only of middle-tier EJB objects but also stored procedures and database triggers as well as other component technologies such as business rules engines and workflow engines.

For one system that I had to redesign, the only architectural description that existed was just such a technology stack. It depicted how eXtensible Markup Language (XML) documents would be passed between Java Servlets and

Enterprise JavaBeans as a flexible approach to creating the middle-tier application programming interface (API). It said nothing about how the system was composed of a main business logic subsystem, a security subsystem, and a reporting subsystem. Instead, it focused on how XML documents would be mapped to and from the relational database tables. Engineers on the project would often draw whiteboard diagrams of the system to include these three subsystems, as well as several other functional modules. The reality was that these were not modules. There was no separation or decoupling between any of them. The reporting module was composed of some user interface code that queried data from the same database tables that the other functions of the system operated on. The security logic was just an aspect of the system. There was no discernable security module; instead, the security logic was embedded in many objects throughout the system. The development organization structured itself around the presentation layer and everything else, treating the user interface as if it were a true module. The resulting system was difficult and costly to develop and maintain.

Software architecting involves the design of a system from multiple viewpoints. The common viewpoints used in software engineering are the technology stack (or physical) view, the object (or data) model, and the use case (or behavioral) view. These viewpoints are useful and necessary because they capture many types of design decisions and represent many system qualities such as functionality, information, and physical construction. They do not represent many other important system quality attributes such as modifiability, buildability, security, reliability, and performance, nor do they represent non-operational or business-oriented qualities such as the ability to reduce development and maintenance costs.

The problem with representing an architecture with this single technology-focused view is that we only see a vertical slice through a multidimensional system. Many architectural decisions cannot be represented in this view. If this is the only view we create, then we will probably neglect the other views to the detriment of the system itself.

An often ignored architectural viewpoint is the component or subsystem view of a system. By definition, a system is an aggregation of cooperating components. Without this view the system appears as a single module, despite the fact that engineers may talk about the security subsystem or the reporting system. It's easy to draw a few boxes and arrows on a whiteboard, but if these boxes and arrows don't mean anything, then we shouldn't bother.

A module has a clear interface that other modules import. The internals of the module are free to change. A Java Database Connectivity (JDBC) driver is an example. Applications rely on the published JDBC Java interfaces. Many vendors produce implementations, but they all conform to the same interface and therefore can be replaced. If an element of code cannot be replaced by another implementation without causing other elements to change, then that element of code is not a module. What makes a system modular is the relatively small amount of information shared between the modules and the development teams designing and implementing those modules. Treating something as if it were a module will only frustrate the developers and managers.

In the above system, one of the first true decompositions of the system was the separation of the reporting system from the operational (or transactional) system. The results were tremendous, especially given the simplicity of the decomposition. No longer were there performance problems with running queries against the operational tables. No longer were operational and reporting use cases intertwined. The system was much easier to develop and maintain. In hindsight, the separation of the system into these two modules seems obvious and trivial. Yet when no one was looking at the system from this point of view, it was far from obvious, and the problems incurred were great. This little design decision can even be expressed as a software architecture pattern: *Separate operational data from analytic data* so that the two are loosely coupled such that they may be designed, developed, and maintained fairly independently and so that the system may have better performance.

Software architecture is emerging as a new discipline in software development in response to the growing complexity of software systems and the problems they are attempting to solve. Software is becoming the dominant component of many systems, and it is necessary for the community to develop new practices, principles, and standards so that we may somehow manage the growing complexity.

There are a couple of philosophies concerning how to improve the software crisis. One approach is to improve the quality of the software development process. In this school of thought, quality can be improved by using iterative development techniques, rapid application development (RAD) tools, frequent integration and testing, and keeping careful records so that an organization can build up historical data that will aid in improving the process in future product cycles. It uses iterative/increment development processes like the Rational Unified Process and the Capability Maturity Model (CMM). Another approach for improving software quality is to stay away from the heavyweight planning-oriented processes and instead adopt agile processes and use of techniques such as RAD and eXtreme Programming (XP).

Most software engineers in the role of software architect have little or no training in the discipline of software architecture, mostly because there is no well-developed theory or standard university curriculum. As for prior generations of untrained software programmers who developed their craft through trial and error, a lot of rediscovery of principles, patterns, and techniques occurs. Practitioners and researchers began to document reusable patterns of software design and engineering processes. There is a body of knowledge accumulating in the industry and being documented as principles and patterns in books, conference proceedings, and technical journals. However, the practicing software architect scarcely has time to keep up with the flow of information, let alone enough time to synthesize it into practical knowledge. This book is an attempt to synthesize and distill much of this information so that the practicing software architect, and especially the beginning software architect, may be able to fill in the gaps in his or her understanding of software architecture design.

The Art of Software Architecture presents software architecting independently of any particular engineering process or organization maturity. It supplies the software architect with the information and tools necessary to make sound architectural decisions and create effective software architectures. The book includes thorough introductions to and applications of methodologies; design representations and models; technologies (such as object-orientation and component-orientation); reference models; architectural frameworks; and analysis, design, and architecture patterns.

No one book can serve as a software architect's handbook. The subject is broad and deep, and it is evolving. This book focuses on how software architects create software architectures. It outlines the discipline and its methodologies and gives the reader a sense of the scope of the topic. Whereas many software architecture books focus on a process or a technology-based view, this book is organized around the fundamentals, models, and techniques of software architecture design.

This book focuses on the design methods and techniques that a software architect must practice. You cannot become a good architect by simply reading about it; you must apply the things you have learned in order to understand how they *should* be applied and how best to apply them. One barrier to effectively using object-oriented design, for example, is the skill in actually defining the right objects and their relationships. UML and object-oriented programming languages only help you express your designs; they do not help you produce good designs. Another barrier is that a solution is only as good as the problem statement. If the problem statement is confusing, wrong, or missing, then the design process has no input ("garbage in/garbage out").

The Goals of This Book

The demands of software development organizations strain software designers. This is especially true of smaller development organizations that do not have standardized development processes or a lot of experience in architecting software. These organizations make up about 70 percent of the software organizations that exist today. Most of these organizations cannot implement expansive development methodologies or adopt formal software design specification methods for any number of reasons such as cost of training in time and money, cost of tools to support the methodology, cost of evangelizing the methodology in terms of time and personal energy, the risk of introducing a new methodology while trying to build software, and simply a lack of understanding of the practical importance of an effective software architecting process. Software development organizations need to implement practices that improve the software architecture without necessarily requiring the organization to change overnight. The software architects are often the persons who need to effect this change.

This book is especially for the software architect in the smaller, less mature software development organization (characterized as predominantly practicing *ad hoc* development). It provides practical guidance on the generation of effective software architectures. It will:

- Provide a sound understanding of the fundamental concepts of software architecture

- Serve as a road map through the information and schools of thought in software architecture

- Teach classic software architecting styles, patterns, heuristics, methodologies, and models

How This Book Is Organized

Most of the literature on software architecture addresses the structure of software but not the design processes and heuristics for generating them. Software pattern books provide a lot of help in this area because they not only show abstract software structures but they also provide some techniques for generating architectures based on these patterns. What seem to be missing are the fundamentals of software design, especially from the architecture perspective.

This book provides an integrated view of design methods, processes, practices, heuristics, and patterns and gives the reader a better sense of the scope of the topic of software architecture while providing practical guidance for designing software architectures from analysis through implementation.

In Chapter 1, "Introduction to Software Architecture," I explore the roots of software architecture. The fundamental problems of software development, which comprise the *software crisis*, are that software is expensive to develop, it is typically of low quality, and it is often delivered late. Software development has undergone several small revolutions or paradigm shifts to address these problems. Each new paradigm incorporates new technologies but still solves the problems the same basic way.

Software architecture is an emerging discipline that focuses on the design of software at a level higher than the programming language. It is possible to reason about many qualities of a software system before it is built, based on the architectural design models or *architectural description*.

In Chapter 2, "The Software Product Life Cycle," I address the role of software architecture in the software product development life cycle. There are many methodologies and views of software development, which we call development life-cycle models. Different stakeholders have different perspectives and concerns and need to see different information in order to assess progress and quality. Architecture provides another viewpoint of the life cycle that involves developing a system design that balances the competing concerns of all stakeholders.

Chapter 3, "The Architecture Design Process," presents a general model of the process of architectural design. A design solution to a problem may be a concrete artifact like source code, or it may be an abstract artifact like a high-level model. Software design is a progression of refining abstract problem statements to executable code. In the middle of this progression is a series of models that help the problem-solving process.

Design is the process of finding or discovering solutions to problems. Design methods help us search for these solutions. Models are one way to manage the complexity of design discovery. Models represent essential knowledge for solving a particular problem while suppressing other knowledge that may be irrelevant to the problem and the inclusion of which would only hinder the design process.

In Chapter 4, "Introduction to Software Design," I present the fundamental methods and techniques of software design. Software design can be viewed as a psychological activity in which a designer is applying design principles to problems in order to produce solutions. In a systematic design methodology, we reduce the risk of project failure by producing more than one possible solution; that is, we *search* for the solution. In Chapter 5, "Complexity and Modularity," precise definitions of complexity, modularity, and the notion of architectural levels of design are presented. Complexity is one of the main forces that we attempt to manage with our software development tools and methods. When not managed, complexity can cause a project to be delivered late, over budget, or cancelled. Complexity can be measured by the interconnectedness of things. In order for a system or process to exhibit complexity, it must be an aggregation of multiple interconnected parts. We refer to these connections as *dependencies*. A fundamental tool in representing a complex system, the design structure matrix (DSM), is presented.

The design structure matrix can help the architecture find the right modules for the system and the shared design decisions among modules, which are called *design rules*.

Design is about finding solutions to problems. In Chapter 6, "Models and Knowledge Representation," we see that problems and solutions are both forms of systems knowledge. In order to begin a search for a solution, we must understand the problem. There is a hierarchy of systems knowledge starting from the most basic knowledge of the types of attributes of a system, the values of those attributes, generative models that can generate those attribute values, and finally a physical system that implements the generative model. Models are the means by which we capture and represent knowledge about the system that we are designing.

In Chapter 7, "Architecture Representation," we learn about the problems of describing the component structure of a software system. The classic views of software have fairly mature modeling notations. However, there are no standard architecture description languages that are expressive enough to represent many types of architectural styles and yet still be practical. This chapter continues the theme of models into the more concrete realm of architecture representation.

In Chapter 8, "Quality Models and Quality Attributes," I present classic system quality attributes and how the architectural design can address them. A system is understood by understanding its quality attributes. The classic software quality attribute types include functionality, security, performance, reliability, and modifiability.

In Chapter 9, "Architectural Design Principles," we learn about specific methods and techniques that can help us discover the components of the system. Design principles are applied within the context of design methods and techniques.

Chapter 10, "Applying Architectural Styles and Patterns," presents the concept of architectural style and how it influences the architecting process. Architectural styles are generalized knowledge captured about existing system architectures. There is a small set of basic architectural styles from which an architecture may be derived.

Chapter 11, "Understanding Metamodels," continues the theme of architecture models. A metamodel is a model for creating models. Well-defined metamodels can help in the discovery and creation of architectural designs by reusing domain knowledge. Reference models are metamodels that describe domain-specific problem decompositions. A reference model may be an industry standard, such as the common warehouse metamodel or the workflow reference model or an informal model presented in the software design literature. In this chapter we see how to use metamodels in the architecture process.

In Chapter 12, "Creating Architectural Descriptions," I present the IEEE Recommended Practice for the Description of Software Intensive Systems, Std. 1471. This is a standard framework for software architectural description based on the concept of multiple views.

Chapter 13, "Using Architecture Frameworks," continues with the theme of the architectural description. In this chapter I present the 4+1 View Model of Architecture and the ISO Reference Model for Open Distributed Computing (RM-ODP) as specific frameworks for creating an architectural description. The RM-ODP is a powerful model that prescribes five standard views of architecture: the enterprise viewpoint, the information viewpoint, the computational viewpoint, the engineering viewpoint, and the technology viewpoint. By following the metamodels of each of these viewpoints, the software architect can create a series of architectural models that represent the system in various states of abstraction.

I end the book with Chapter 14, "Software Architecture Quality." In this chapter I return to the subject of quality at the architectural level of design. Quality cannot be tested into a system, so a system must be designed with quality. The candidate architecture for a system can be assessed to understand the quality attribute characteristics of the system described, before actually constructing the system. A software architecture description can be evaluated so that we may understand many potential quality attributes of the system including modifiability, performance, and reliability. Each quality attribute can be assessed using different assessment techniques.

Who Should Read This Book

Beginning software architects are usually experienced software engineers. However, the software engineer must make a mental paradigm shift when it comes to designing software systems at the architectural level. All of his or her prior knowledge about object-oriented programming is still applicable, but it must be applied on a different scale, at different levels of abstraction. This book is useful for understanding how to architect a software system and even how to design a single module. The design principles can be applied at many levels of software design. Experienced software architects will find new material to broaden their knowledge and provide them with a fresh insight into software architecting.

Technical managers will gain insight into the processes of software architecting, as well as the styles of architecture and techniques used to generate them. This will enable managers to more effectively create project teams, plans, and schedules, as well as implement reuse plans, conduct design reviews, and choose an appropriate process framework. Architecture, organization, and process are interwoven. The architecture of a system influences the structure of an organization and the process by which a system is realized. Technical managers will also learn that the architecture of a system addresses many business- and development-related requirements.

Depending on what you want out of this book, you should have experience in one or more of the following:

- Object-oriented programming with a language such as C++ or Java
- Managing object-oriented projects
- Object-oriented analysis and design
- Other systems analysis and design techniques (for example, structured analysis)

CHAPTER 1

Introduction to Software Architecture

Software architecture involves the integration of software development methodologies and models, which distinguishes it from particular analysis and design methodologies. The structure of complex software solutions departs from the description of the problem, adding to the complexity of software development. Software architecture is a body of methods and techniques that helps us to manage the complexities of software development.

Software architecture is a natural extension of the software engineering discipline. In early literature it was simply referred to as *programming in the large*. Software architecture presents a view of a software system as components and connectors. Components encapsulate some coherent set of functionality. Connectors realize the runtime interaction between components. The system design achieves certain qualities based on its composition from components and connectors. The architecture of a software system can be specified in a document called the architectural description. Software architecture design is not entirely different from existing software design methodologies. Rather it complements them with additional views of a system that have not been traditionally handled by methodologies like object-oriented design. We will learn that software architecture fits within a larger *enterprise architecture* that also encompasses business architecture, information technology architecture, and data architecture.

This chapter begins with a brief discussion of the evolution of software development, followed by the fundamental engineering techniques that comprise the discipline of software engineering. Finally, we look at the craft of software architecture as a discipline that complements software engineering.

Evolution of Software Development

Roughly every decade the software development field experiences a shift in software design paradigms. Design methodologies and tools must evolve as the problems and technologies become more complex. Software development was born around 1949 when the first stored-program computer, the Cambridge EDSAC, was created. Programs were initially created as binary machine instructions. This approach to programming proved to be slow and difficult because of the human inability to easily memorize long, complex binary strings. The notion of a human-readable shorthand for designing programs was conceived. Initially, the concept behind the programming shorthand was to allow a *program designer* to design a program and for a programmer or *coder* to manually translate the shorthand into binary code.

In the early 1950s, it became apparent that the majority of a programmer's time was spent correcting mistakes in software. One response to this situation was the creation of program subroutines that allowed programmers to reuse program fragments that had already been written and debugged, thus improving the productivity of programmers. By the late 1950s, the handcrafting of programs—even with the aid of reusable subroutines—was becoming uneconomical. Hence research in the area of *automatic programming* systems began. Automatic programming would allow programmers to write programs in a high-level language code, which was easier to read by humans, that would then be converted into binary machine instructions by use of another program. Thus, the first paradigm shift in software development was about to occur.

Experienced binary programmers were reluctant to change their habits to adopt a new method of working and resisted automatic programming. However, automatic programming became the dominant paradigm after International Business Machines (IBM) developed an automatic programming system for scientific programs called FORTRAN (the Formula Translator). Automatic programming not only improved programmer productivity but it also made programs portable across hardware platforms. Porting to new hardware prior to automatic programming required rewriting an entire program, which was too costly and a hindrance to selling hardware. By the mid-1960s, FORTRAN had established itself as the dominant language for scientific programming.

During the 1960s, there was a dramatic rise in the number of software development contractors and ready-made programs for specific vertical markets, such as banking and insurance. The term *software* was coined as an implicit recognition that software was viewed as an entity in its own right. Software was also being marketed and sold separately from hardware, which marked a departure from the earlier practices of giving software away for free as part of the hardware platform. The hiding of the internal details of an operating system using abstract programming interfaces improved programmer productivity and helped make programs more portable across hardware platforms. Programs could work with logical files instead of physical locations of bits on a tape or magnetic disk. It was also during this period that extensive research began in programming languages, which continued through the 1970s.

By the late 1960s, it was clear that software development was unlike the construction of physical structures: You couldn't simply hire more programmers to speed up a lagging development project (Brooks, 1975). Software had become a critical component of many systems, yet was too complex to develop with any certainty of schedule or quality. This imposed financial and public safety concerns. The situation became known as the *software crisis*, and in response the software development community instituted *software engineering* as a discipline. It called for software manufacturing to be based on the same types of theoretical foundations and practical disciplines that are traditional for the established branches of engineering.

In 1968, Edsger Dijkstra published a paper on the design of a multiprogramming system called "THE" (Dijkstra, 1968). This is one of the first papers to document the design of a software system using hierarchical layers, from which the phrase *layers of abstraction* was derived. Dijkstra organized the design of the system in layers in order to reduce the overall complexity of the software. Though the term *architecture* had not yet been used to describe software design, this was certainly the first glimpse of software architecture; programming in the large was a common phrase used to describe this aspect of software design.

A second paradigm shift occurred in the first half of the 1970s with the development of structured design and software development models. These were based on a more organic, evolutionary approach, departing from the waterfall-based methodologies of hardware engineering. Research into quantitative techniques for software design began but never established itself in mainstream industry, in part due to the inherent qualitative nature of software systems. During this time researchers began focusing on software design to address the problems of developing complex software systems. The premise of this work was that software design is a separate activity from implementation in software development and that it requires its own tools, techniques, and modeling languages.

In 1972 David Parnas published a paper that discussed how modularity in systems design could improve system flexibility and comprehensibility while shortening development time (Parnas, 1972). He introduced the programming world to the concept of *information hiding*, which is one of the most fundamental design principles in software development today.

In the 1980s, software engineering research shifted focus toward integrating designs and design processes into the larger context of software development process and management. Structured design methods could not scale as software systems grew in complexity, and in the latter half of the 1980s a new design paradigm began to take hold—*object-orientation*. With object-oriented programming, software engineers could (in theory) model the problem domain and solution domain within an implementation language. Research that led to object orientation can be traced back to the late 1960s with the development of Simula, a simulation programming language, and it was later refined in Smalltalk. Object-oriented programming started to become popular with C++. At this time there was also a shift in application design metaphors from text-based terminals to graphical user interfaces (GUIs). Object-oriented programming was well suited for the development of GUIs. In the late 1980s and early 1990s, the term *software architecture* began to appear in literature.

Object-oriented programming was in full swing by the mid-1990s, when the Internet became the new computing platform. At around the same time, software design was experiencing another shift. This time it was not away from the prior design paradigms, however, but rather toward an integration of methods. Object orientation was being augmented with design techniques such as Class/Responsibilities/Collaborators (CRC) cards and use case analysis. Methods and modeling notations that came out of the structured design movement were making their way into the object-oriented modeling methods. This included diagramming techniques such as state transition diagrams and processing models.

It was becoming obvious that an integrated, multiviewed approach to design was required to manage the complexity of designing and developing large-scale software systems. This multiview approach culminated in the development of the Unified Modeling Language (UML), which integrates modeling concepts and notations from many methodologists. It was also during the late 1990s that design patterns started becoming a popular way to share design knowledge.

I believe that we are experiencing a fifth paradigm shift in software development, which is the recognition that software architecture is an important aspect of software development and of the introduction of software architecture methods and activities into the software development life cycle. This shift, like the last one, is not one of divergence of design methods but rather one of the integration of new methods and activities with existing methods and activities.

Fundamentals of Software Engineering

The main task of engineers, according to Pahl (Pahl, 1996), "is to apply their scientific and engineering knowledge to the solution of technical problems, and then to optimize those solutions within the requirements and constraints set by material, technological, economical, legal, environmental, and human-related considerations." We can extend this definition to define the main task of software engineers. Informally, the main task of software engineers is to apply their logic and programming knowledge to the solution of technical and business problems. Then they optimize those solutions within the requirements and constraints set by logic (the material of software engineering); software technology; and economical, legal, environmental, and safety considerations.

The term *engineering*, as applied to software, is not always entirely appropriate. I think it assumes too broad of a specialty. I think of software development as involving many subdisciplines. These include specialties like database design and implementation, Structured Query Language (SQL), Java, and C++ programming, and eXtensible Stylesheet Language Transformations (XSLT) coding. The specialties can even be finer grained than this. Each of these technologies needs specialists just as there are specialists in established engineering disciplines such as electronic and mechanical engineering. In each of these fields there are further specializations. Yet we treat software development as if it were a single engineering discipline. It is, in fact, several related disciplines. Imagine that a competent developer of XSLT is given very clear specifications, to which a given transformation, or stylesheet, must conform, including well-defined inputs and outputs. The XSLT designer can produce a stylesheet using available tools and methods and possibly reuse parts from an existing library of XSLT. This assumes that we can provide well-defined specifications.

I think that the division of software engineering is probably necessary with some combination of technology (databases, Java) and problem domains. Of course, having specialties with individual techniques, tools, and methods still poses a problem of engineering sophisticated systems that involve integrating these technologies. This is where the software architect comes in. The software architect could be considered a type of software engineer that may not necessarily be a specialist in all of the particular software engineering domains. The software specialist is a specialist in architecture design, and understands the varieties of technology well enough to integrate them into a cohesive solution to a complex problem.

It is not uncommon in practice today to divide labor along technology lines. It is common to separate user interface (UI) or presentation development from middle-tier development or back-end development. But without architecture, even this separation of engineering specialties will not necessarily help produce high-quality systems. Some authors argue that this separation (called *horizontal slicing*) is not necessarily effective and advocates a vertical slicing where each developer owns a set of functional requirements and implements them front to back. Both approaches can be used effectively. It's more a matter of the skills of the individuals together with the technical leadership and project management techniques.

The two primary problems in software development that have yet to be solved satisfactorily are making systems cost effective and of higher quality. Improving the productivity of software engineers is an important part of making systems cost effective. Improving the quality of systems is important in order to make them safer and more effective in accomplishing business goals and objectives. Improving the quality of the design of a system also aids in achieving cost-effectiveness. A major obstacle to solving these two problems is the complexity inherent in developing software. This is a result of the complexity of the problems being solved, the wide variety of technologies that may be applied, and the fact that software development is almost purely a design activity. (As opposed to other engineering disciplines of which manufacturing is a major time and cost element of the process, in software even writing code is a design activity and cannot be managed like a manufacturing process.)

Using current methods, technologies, and programming languages, we are able to solve problems to a certain level of complexity. However, to break through the barriers established by the complexity of the problem to build larger systems, we need to evolve our methods and tools. As systems grow in complexity, certain other quality attributes become more relevant; as the size of a system grows, the number of dimensions of the system also grows. In small systems, we can focus on functional correctness and performance. In large systems, we need to address attributes such as portability, security, reliability, and modifiability.

There are several fundamental software engineering techniques that can help improve the quality and cost-effectiveness of software:

- Reusable assets
- General-purpose programming languages
- Special-purpose programming languages
- Modeling languages and notations

Reusable Assets

Code reuse improves the productivity of the programmer by shortening the amount of time required to implement some functionality. Of course, there is a trade-off of time spent discovering, learning, and integrating the reusable code, so reusable code needs to be easy to find, quick to learn, and straightforward to integrate. Code reuse manifests itself in the following:

- Source code that can be copied and modified to suit or be used as is (for example, C++ algorithms from a shareware repository or copied from a book).

- Commercial off-the-shelf (COTS) components that are available in binary (compiled) form and that can be imported or linked to other components or applications. This includes:

  - Binary code "libraries" that can be linked into a program at compile time or loaded and bound at run time (for example, a sockets library).

  - Operating environments and platforms (for example, operating systems, databases, application servers).

Reusable components, especially ones that address large problem spaces, provide a huge boost in productivity. Imagine if you had to write your own middleware, application server, and database in order to develop a distributed business application. Of course, all of those reusable technologies contain more features than any single application needs but even to develop the subset required by an application is a formidable and time-consuming task.

In order to effectively reuse components, we must be able to express our solution in terms of the abstractions of the component. There are times when a particular abstraction, such as relational entities, doesn't suit all of our needs, just as a natural language may not have words to express certain concepts. So we invent new technologies just as we invent new words. Object-oriented databases are an example of such an invention. When object-oriented programming started to supplant existing structured languages like C and Pascal, a semantic gap was introduced between the representation of information in the programming language and the representation of information in the database. Many papers and books have addressed the object-relational mapping problem. Today we have documented patterns for object-relational mapping that assist us in overcoming this obstacle.

General-Purpose Programming Languages

Powerful general-purpose programming languages like C++ and Java provide expressive power for creating solutions to many complex problems by allowing the programmer to focus on the problem at hand and worry less about specific hardware capabilities. General-purpose object-oriented languages don't solve the problem of complexity alone; they must be used in conjunction with guidelines and design patterns. How often have you seen a class that was really just a big collection of structured subroutines, such as the God Class (Riel, 1996)?

Special-Purpose Programming Languages

Some COTS components have specialized programming languages for creating applications or parts of an application. The languages can be easier to use than general-purpose programming languages for specific problems. For example, when using a relational database component a programmer uses Data Definition Languages (DDL) and SQL to implement a data storage and access solution. SQL is specialized for the domain of relational databases. Specialized languages improve productivity by allowing the developer to think in terms of the abstractions of a specific technology (which is a simpler domain to comprehend) rather than by using the same general-purpose language for all programming problems. If a programmer had to understand how the data was stored in files and how the files were indexed, the problem would become much more complex. Of course, specialized languages introduce complexities of their own. The industry addresses this by developing guidelines and design patterns for the effective use of a particular technology. In relational databases, the theory of normal forms was developed to help programmers design databases with certain quality attributes. Other examples of specialized languages are Web presentation technologies such as Active Server Pages (ASP), Java Server Pages (JSP), and Hypertext Preprocessor (PHP), and data representation and transformation languages such as Hypertext Markup Language (HTML), eXtensible Markup Language (XML), and eXtensible Stylesheet Language Transformations (XSLT).

Modeling Languages and Notations

Modeling languages and design notations emerged as methods for improving software design quality. It is argued that an expressive modeling notation can expand our capability to design software much like mathematics allows us to reason about more complex things than our minds would normally be capable of without such a language. The entity relationship diagram (ERD), for example, is a powerful modeling language and notation that allows a software engineer to design and communicate expressive data models. Without such a language, it would be difficult to think about the information design of a system, and without a notation to represent the diagrams, it would be difficult to communicate those designs to others. The formality of the language allows different people to interpret a model in a precise way.

The UML is a rich collection of modeling notations for representing many aspects or views of a software system, including the information and information flow, class structure, and object interactions. The UML and other modeling languages improve a software engineer's individual capacity to create complex solutions. Some UML tools today allow for partial code generation from UML models. It is possible that a language like UML may become a true programming language (either special-purpose or general-purpose) As we have seen in the brief history above, what begins as a notation for representing software design can become the next-generation programming language.

Elements of Software Architecture

In this section, I present an overview of software architecture. I explore the definition of software architecture and the relationship between architecture and systems followed by a discussion of architectural descriptions. I discuss the relationship between the activities of software architecture and other software design methods. In the last section of this chapter, I discuss how software application architecture fits into the context of enterprise architecture.

Components, Connectors, and Qualities

Many authors equate architecture with system quality attributes such as reliability and modifiability and how those attributes are affected by the physical decomposition of the software system in terms of components and their arrangements. Different arrangements of components can affect attributes like reliability and modifiability without necessarily affecting the functionality. Architectural Description Languages (ADLs) are languages for describing a system at this level of abstraction. An ADL is one view of the architecture of a software system. To get a more complete or comprehensive understanding of the architecture requires multiple views.

Shaw and Garlan define software architecture abstractly as involving the description of the elements that compose the system, their interactions, the patterns and principles that guide their composition and design, and the constraints on those patterns (Shaw, 1996). A system, therefore, is defined in terms of its physical (implementation) elements or components and their interactions. A system itself is also a component, and systems can be composed of other systems. Booch considers an object-oriented design to be the application's architecture (Booch, 1994). Others consider the architecture to be the global view or the high-level set of views that are commonly defined in architecture reference models, like the 4 + 1 Model View or the Reference Model for Open Distributed Processing (RM-ODP).

As defined by the Institute of Electrical and Electronics Engineers (IEEE) Recommended Practice for Architecture Description of Software-Intensive Systems (IEEE standard 1471-2000), an *architecture* is "the fundamental organization of a system embodied in its components, their relationships to each other, and to the environment, and the principles guiding its design and evolution." This definition is fairly abstract and applies to systems other than just software.

The term *software architecture* in the context of this book means the observable properties of a software system (also known as the *form* of the system). It is important to note that the structure of a system includes its static and dynamic forms. In the sense of object-oriented design, this includes not only the models of components and classes but also the models of component and object collaborations and the user-perceivable functions they enable. The term *software architecting* means the process of creating software architectures. Although the classic definition of architecture includes the processes and the artifacts, I choose to use the word architecting as defined by Rechtin (Rechtin, 1991) to differentiate between the process and the artifacts. Finally, the term software architect refers to an individual who performs architecting to produce architectures.

All of these definitions include some notion of the function and form of a system in terms of components, their static and dynamic interrelationships and environmental relationships, and the principles and guidelines for the design, evaluation, and evolution of the components and the system as a whole. All of these are begging definitions because the definitions are themselves based on abstract, ill-defined concepts. These concepts and the overall definition of software architecture shall become clear throughout the course of this book.

Software systems have architectures, regardless of how simple they are in terms of components. However, an architecture is not a system. In early systems the main attributes of real concern were functionality, portability, memory usage, and performance—basically, an architecture with relatively few dimensions of quality attributes. There was no pressing need for software architectural descriptions. Functionality could be comprehended by looking at the source code itself or executing the system with some reasonable set of test data. Portability was achieved by simply using higher-level general-purpose programming languages. Performance could be comprehended by executing the system or studying the algorithms of the program.

When systems started becoming more complex in terms of function and information, the use of structured programming techniques and data modeling methods helped with the design and comprehension of the software. It was even possible to start modeling the system abstractly as a hierarchy of functions and a graph of information structures, which made it possible to reason about some aspects of the correctness of the program before implementing the specific functions and data structures. Programmers would execute the system or portions of the system to validate the functions and to identify performance bottlenecks. They would then correct those functions or make those functions more efficient or refactor the functions if necessary. Similarly, the programmers would study the system for memory and other resource usage.

As software systems continued to grow in complexity, the structured programming and data modeling techniques could not scale in terms of number of functions or semantic complexity of data, or in terms of other attributes like modifiability and reliability that were becoming more important in software systems. In response, object orientation took over as the dominant programming methodology in new application development. Object orientation could handle the increasing complexity of information semantics and functions as well as address quality attributes that were becoming increasingly important: reusability and modifiability. As you can see, it is not enough to model the system directly in source code and reason about its properties. How do you evaluate source code for reliability, modifiability, or usability? Even the use of models such as class hierarchies and object collaboration diagrams are not enough to reason about the many quality attributes required in today's software systems. We need additional tools and techniques to design software as the architecture of software grows in complexity.

CIVIL ARCHITECTURE: A METAPHOR FOR SOFTWARE DESIGN

The field of civil architecting has become a popular metaphor for the development of software-intensive systems. In civil architecture the architect creates a representation of a building's physical structure that is limited in scale or number of dimensions. The architect identifies the constraints on the design such as the location and local building laws and integrates structural, business, and aesthetic concerns. The architect is the client's advocate and is trusted to coordinate all aspects of the building project but does not extend to all aspects of the project. The architect addresses usage, value, cost, and building risks within the client's requirements. The architect aids the client in making a build or no-build decision.

Software systems today really are more analogous to urban developments than to individual buildings. Consider how a software system evolves (albeit in condensed time compared to that of cities). If buildings evolved as drastically as software, we would see buildings where new floors are added or blocks of floors are removed, or where additional buildings are appended to the existing one. However, when compared to cities and especially urban development, we do see analogous evolution such as new housing developments sprouting up where there were none, new roads being created, many highways being widened to allow for new traffic requirements, and old neighborhoods being razed and replaced with malls. Two separate urban areas eventually merge and become indistinguishable. This is more like what is going on in software development today. Of course, with all metaphors there are areas where the two things being compared simply don't equate, and this is where we need to be careful and avoid the fallacy by analogy.

Architectural Description

Architecting is the specification of a system that, when constructed, will exhibit required properties. In other words, architecting is the creation of descriptions of a system that are suitable for evaluation and serve as plans for implementation. The description of a system must include the specification of quality attributes and the description of the design in terms of software structures that will implement those properties. However, mapping quality attributes requirements to software structures is not easy; there is a large chasm between the two. How do you transform the requirement that a system handle 100 requests per second into a set of servlets, Enterprise Java Beans (EJBs), and relational database tables?

The process of creating an architectural description requires intermediate models that help to bridge this chasm. This is the role of design methodologies. Commonly, functional and information requirements are mapped to implementation-independent data models and functional models. For example, use case models and application domain object models (both analysis models) serve as intermediate models. They formulate the requirements in terms of concepts closer to the implementation space but still expressed in terms of the problem space.

Depending on the methodology, the functional model and information model are mapped to some logical component model taking into consideration other required quality attributes such as modifiability and performance. The resulting models show more clearly the relationship between function and data and other nonfunctional quality attribute requirements. This model is closer to the solution space of computational elements and is further from the semantic space of the problem. However, it is still expressed in implementation-independent terms. In object-oriented terms, this would be another object model (class diagrams, object collaboration diagrams, and sequence diagrams in UML) that still contains the essence of the problem domain objects but transformed to an idealized computing object.

The computational view starts to show the shape of the architecture since the computational elements embody not only functional and information requirements but also the nonfunctional requirements. It is within this type of model that architectural styles are applied. Architectural styles are generalized computational models that are devoid of specific application domain functionality. Examples of architectural styles are n-tier client/server, pipes and filters, and distributed objects. The information and functional models do not take into account the architectural style (or should attempt to limit the number of constraints that might affect the selection of architectural styles). It is quite possible that the objects in the computational model no longer resemble their analytical counterparts. This is where the complexity of software architecting lies, and it is at this point where the form of the solution appears to depart from the description of the problem. This is why a clear formulation of the problem is so important. Without it, it is easy for software engineers who are focusing on the internals of the software system to lose sight of the overall problem being addressed.

The computational model may be influenced by available technologies and possibly by technology requirements. For example, the enterprise platform may be chosen in advance. It is common for an organization to adopt a platform such as Microsoft XML Web Services platform (.NET) or Java 2 Enterprise Edition (J2EE) before a full abstraction of the computational model of the system is complete. For better or for worse, the software architect must design within these constraints. A model of the technology (sometimes referred to as a physical architecture) maps the computational model to physical components such as ASP, JSP, Enterprise JavaBeans (EJBs), Component Object Model (COM) objects, database entities, and XML documents.

The mapping of elements between models must also be specified as well as the rationale for each model. The rationale captures why a decision was made given many competing choices. The larger the software system, the more formal or systematic the models, traces, and rationales should probably be. The smaller the system, the less important. The software architecture team must ultimately determine how much is actually modeled and specified and how formal or informal to be. It is these activities that form the core set of activities that the architect should perform.

Software Architecture versus Software Design Methodologies

How does software architecting differ from software design methodologies such as object orientation? Software architecting is a relatively new metaphor in software design and really encompasses design methodologies such as object orientation as well as analysis methodologies. The software architect today is a combination of roles such as systems analyst, systems designer, and software engineer. But architecting is more than just a reallocation of functions: The different aspects of architecting may still be performed by specialists but are now commonly falling under the orchestration of the *chief architect*. The concept of architecting in software is meant to subsume the activities of analysis and design into a larger, more coherent design framework. In addition, the demands of applications today are different than they were even 10 years ago when object orientation was becoming the established design paradigm. Applications tend to be larger, more integrated, and implemented by using a wide variety of technologies. Organizations are realizing that the high cost of software development needs to be brought under some control and that many of the promises or claims of methodologies have still not helped with this cost.

If architecting subsumes analysis and design, what makes it different than analysis and design? For example, why is architecting different than object-oriented analysis and design? In many ways it is the same but the scope of the analysis and design efforts is bigger. We are recognizing that object models such as class diagrams are still not expressive enough to capture all aspects of a system and that we need to integrate other methodologies and models into a coherent whole. This integration of methodologies and models is one thing that distinguishes software architecting from particular analysis and design techniques.

Just as the software development community claimed the name *software engineering* in an attempt to raise the bar of current development practices, so has the software engineering community adopted the term *software architecture* to say that we recognize that many aspects of software development really resemble systems architecting and urban planning. This is most evident in the adoption of pattern languages for software design. Originally a concept developed by Christopher Alexander, pattern languages are reusable elements of architecture wisdom for designing and constructing cities, buildings, houses, and so on, down to the smallest details, such as the placement of chairs in a room to satisfy certain desired qualities of living (Alexander, 1979).

So to identify a new profession called software architecting is to make a statement that we recognize that software development is really not scientific but rather more closely resembles the craft guilds of the Middle Ages. This is not to say that we do not strive for a scientific underpinning to what we do as software developers, but that we are realistic about the state of the art in software design. To claim the title is also to make the statement that we recognize that software development is really not a homogeneous activity relegated to a single specialty (programming) but involves many specialties and different technologies. Even though these technologies are all software, they really require different expertise and design methods. Therefore, we recognize that software architecting involves interdisciplinary software engineering methodologies from object-oriented analysis to functional decomposition; from object-oriented programming to relational database design and XML schema design, and even user interface and usability design.

Types of Architecture

In the IT industry, the term *architecture* is used to refer to several things. From an enterprise point of view, there are four types of architecture:

- Business architecture
- Information technology (IT) architecture
- Information architecture
- Application (software) architecture

Collectively, these architectures are referred to as *enterprise architecture*. A business or business process architecture defines the business strategy, governance, organization, and key business processes within an enterprise. The field of business process reengineering (BPR) focuses on the analysis and design of business processes, not necessarily represented in an IT system. The IT architecture defines the hardware and software building blocks that make up the overall information system of the organization. The business architecture is mapped to the IT architecture. The IT architecture should enable achievement of the business goals using a software infrastructure that supports the procurement, development, and deployment of core mission-critical business applications. The purpose of the IT architecture is to enable a company to manage its IT investment in a way that meets its business needs by providing a foundation upon which data and application architectures can be built. This includes hardware and a software infrastructure including database and middleware technologies. New IT technologies enable business processes and capabilities that would otherwise not be possible. The Web is an example.

The data architecture of an organization includes logical and physical data assets and data management resources. Information is becoming one of the most important assets a company has in achieving its objectives, and the IT architecture must support it. Application architecture serves as the blueprint for individual applications systems, their interactions, and their relationships to the business processes of the organization. The application architecture is commonly built on top of and utilizes the services of the IT architecture. The distinction between what is an element of the application architecture, data architecture, and IT architecture can be blurred. As application-specific features become necessary for other applications, they can be migrated into the IT architecture. Applications are typically integrated using the IT infrastructure. It is common in enterprise development, both in one-off systems and in commercial systems, that elements of the data architecture and IT architecture are incorporated into the application architecture. Sometimes this is for reasons of development efficiency, but it can have an impact on how easily a customer can deploy, integrate, and manage the system.

A software application is a computer program or set of programs that uses existing technologies to solve some end-user problem such as the automation of an existing business process. Enterprise business applications are largely information processing applications (as opposed to a video game, which performs a lot of real-time simulation but is not a heavy information processor). Some applications are created for a perceived need that has not been proven. This is called *greenfield development*, and the purpose is typically to tap into new markets and often requires some technical innovation as well as creation of new approaches to solving business problems. What makes this challenging is that the new approach may not have been feasible without technology. For example, applications that perform analytics on customer profile data would not have been economically feasible as a manual business process.

Application architecting is more than the specification of the internal physical structure of the software. It involves creating models of the problem in order to simplify and understand the problem and creating implementation-independent models of the solution that address those problems, for example, creating business process workflows and reviewing these with the end users. It also involves user interface and interaction design. The way the system works should map to how users perceive the system's architecture. Users do not need to know the internal structure; they just need to understand how certain elements work together so that they can reasonably predict the application's behavior.

Summary

In this chapter I presented a brief history of software development, in particular the evolution of software engineering and how a craft of software architecture has emerged as an important aspect of software development. There are several observations we can make about software architecture:

- Systems have architectures, but architectures are not systems.
- Architectural descriptions are not architectures; they describe the architecture of a system.
- Architectural descriptions are composed of multiple views.
- Software architecture design subsumes and integrates many software design methodologies.

In Chapter 2, I present the software product life cycle in more detail and show how various views of the life cycle, including the software architecture view, fit together.

CHAPTER

2

The Software Product
Life Cycle

In this chapter, we categorize the various ways in which stakeholders perceive the software development process and product life cycle using the Rational Unified Process (RUP) as a foundation. We use views, which are ways of categorizing or labeling these different perspectives. The views may appear to be processes from the point of view of individual stakeholders. However, these views are really just different perspectives on the life cycle of a software product and on the software development process. The views presented are:

- Management
- Software engineering
- Engineering design
- Architectural design

When synthesized, they form a coherent view of the entire software life cycle. A software architect will need to understand these views in order to work within them and communicate activities and progress within these views. Managers who do not understand what software architecture is do not know how to view it as part of the product life cycle. It is often mistakenly thought to be the design phase of a project. I find that I often have to defend the architectural specifications and models (artifacts) I am producing by explaining how they fit into the development life cycle and why they are important. The problem stems, in part, from the fact that most software development life cycles do not bring architecture to the forefront as they do requirements, design, implementation, and testing.

The management view is presented first in this chapter. This is based on the RUP life-cycle phases. The software engineering view follows. This view captures how software engineers view the development life cycle. The engineering design view represents a detailed design process view, which can be thought of as zooming into the design aspect of the software engineering view. The architectural view represents the software development life cycle from the perspective of architecting concerns, activities, and artifacts. This chapter ends with a discussion of how the views are related.

Each view of the development process is comprised of phases, activities, tasks, and steps. Intuitively the term *phase* implies some interval of time and is externally distinguishable from another phase. Phases may be serial, each executing one at a time in a strict order. Phases may overlap, in which case a phase begins before a previous phase ends. An example of a phase is the product planning phase. The term *activity* is more abstract than phase. In the context of this discussion, it means a particular type of work performed by an individual or a group. For example object-oriented analysis is an activity. It may be performed within a single phase or across multiple phases.

A *task* refers to a specific schedulable item. A task can appear in a project plan and be assigned resources. An example of a task is to design and implement a specific business object. A sequence of steps comprises a task or an activity. A step cannot be scheduled or tracked in a project plan very easily but refers to a fundamental action performed by a designer or programmer. An example step of the analysis activity is to identify all candidate domain objects that appear directly or indirectly in the customer requirements.

Management View

Managers want to see the progress toward achieving some goal (such as a milestone or deliverable). They typically look for high-level, simplified indicators, such as percentage of work completed. In waterfall-based methods, each milestone and the completion of a development phase is marked by the completion of some set of deliverables such as requirements documents and design specifications.

In modern software methodologies, deliverables are rarely completed before work begins on the next deliverable. For example, requirements are never fully articulated and understood prior to beginning implementation. Sometimes it requires diving into the details of the system's design and implementation to uncover tacit requirements and contradictions in requirements. The architecture of a system, as represented by an architectural description, is not necessarily completed before implementation begins either. As with requirements, it may take some detailed design and implementation effort to further understand the system in order to revise the architectural design. Modern methodologies attempt to account for this by building into the process feedback loops from implementation and testing all the way back to requirements analysis.

This feedback loop is what makes completing certain documents and specifications difficult. Methodologies like RUP do not associate milestones with the completion of specific documents and specifications but rather with achieving some quasi-measurable goal such as the identification of approximately 80 percent of the use cases or the establishment of an architectural baseline of code. These milestones are not so easy to quantify but represent a more realistic and intuitive approach to development. Management is concerned with cost and schedules and the overall quality of the product—or the product life-cycle view. Managers view a software life cycle as a set of milestones and a series of phases, one completing before the other starts. The RUP defines four fundamental life-cycle phases:

- Inception
- Elaboration
- Construction
- Transition

Each phase (shown in Figure 2.1) has a set of exit criteria, or predicates, about the state of some set of artifacts that must be true before that phase is complete and the next phase begins. The life cycle of a product starts with the product's inception and continues sometimes through multiple revisions and ends when the product is retired.

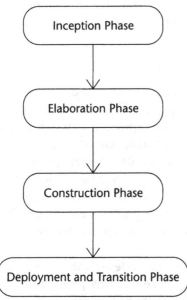

Figure 2.1   Management (product life cycle) view.

The four development phases constitute a development cycle. A product may undergo multiple development cycles during its entire life cycle. The subsequent cycles are called *evolution cycles*. An evolution cycle may begin while the previous development cycle is still in transition and maintenance. It is quite common for commercial software vendors to continue fixing bugs and releasing minor enhancements while the next generation is under development.

Other models of the software product life cycle are possible. The model presented in this chapter captures the essence of a product's life cycle as seen outside of engineering. It is the management or executive view of the product life cycle. You may be inclined to equate this model of software construction with the waterfall method, which is a traditional software development process that has proved to be ineffective for most software development. However the RUP model is not the same as the waterfall model; rather it represents a high-level view of the life cycle as visualized by many product stakeholders and is characterized by specific milestones.

Inception Phase

The inception phase (sometimes called the vision phase) is the first phase of any product development project. It begins when one or more persons identify a real or perceived need (the problem) and envision a system that can satisfy the need.

The exit criteria for the inception phase are a product vision and a business case for the product. In the RUP this is called the Lifecycle Objective Milestone (LCO). The stakeholders who desire the system are called the *acquirers*. They may not be the eventual users of the system. The users may be employees of the acquirers or the acquirers may be the organization that also builds the system to sell to customers (and their end users). The software engineering organization that implements the system is sometimes referred to as the *builder*.

Elaboration Phase

The elaboration phase—the evolution of the system concept and development planning—begins once the acquirers approve the project. This involves requirements engineering (also referred to as gathering or capturing requirements). Sometimes this phase is referred to as the planning and specification phase.

The exit criteria for the elaboration phase are a specification of requirements and an architectural concept. The architectural concept describes a high-level design approach that addresses the requirements. The builders must sign off on the architectural approach before the elaboration phase is complete. The acquirers at this point can make a build/no-build decision based on the feasibility and initial cost and schedule estimates.

In the RUP, the end of this phase is called the Lifecycle Architecture Milestone (LCA). The architecture is by no means frozen at this point, but the majority of architecturally significant quality attribute requirements, such as performance and maintainability, must be specified and the architectural approach must be established, as well as the technology to be used.

Construction Phase

The construction phase begins with a specification of requirements, architectural concept, and project plan. It is during construction that the product is implemented, unit tested, and system tested. The architecture, requirements, and development plan are adjusted as necessary, but there should be relatively few surprises at this point. If there are a lot of unexpected surprises, then the quality of the artifacts needed as input to this phase becomes suspect.

The output of the construction phase is a complete version of the product. The Initial Operational Capability Milestone (IOC) marks the end of this phase in the RUP.

Transition Phase

The transition phase is where the product is transitioned to its users. This includes any manufacturing, delivering, training, and supporting. In in-house development, a product is said to be "in production." For commercial software, the product is "shipped." The output is a final version of the product, including software, supporting documentation, and training and support services. In the RUP, the end of this phase is called the Product Release Milestone. The released version of a product, called a *product generation,* may enter into a maintenance and support subphase where bug fixes are made and small enhancements may be introduced.

Software Engineering View

The engineering view of software development is nearly orthogonal (or perpendicular), to the management view. In the RUP, the product development life cycle is viewed as a two-dimensional model of time (phases) and activities. The engineering view (Figure 2.2) represents a software development project as multiple chains of activities running concurrently and overlapping. This classic waterfall method—borrowed from the hardware design discipline—is composed of discrete engineering phases with the creation of a requirements specification to completion, followed by the creation of a design specification to completion, and finally a manufacturing phase.

One of the problems with applying the waterfall process to software development is that changes usually translate directly into delays of the next step in the waterfall. The changes are therefore very costly because they can cause a delay in the project The waterfall method fostered the notion that software development was like a manufacturing process and that the process itself can control the quality of a product. This is the school of thought represented in the works of the Software Engineering Institute and the work of Watts Humphrey, such as the Capability Maturity Model (Humphrey, 1989) and the Personal Software Process (Humphrey, 1994).

The main activities of software engineering are:

- Requirements analysis and specification
- Design
- Implementation and testing
- Deployment and maintenance

The software engineering view can be visualized as a stream of information flowing through each activity (see Figure 2.2). The inputs into the requirement analysis and specification activity are requirements from customers and other sources. A set of requirements is transformed, via requirements analysis, into functional specifications of system behavior and nonfunctional specifications. This information flows into the design phase and is transformed into a system design. The design information is input to the implementation and testing activity, which transforms the design into a binary system. Deployment transforms the binary system into a production system. Maintenenance involves further iterations of requirements analysis, design, implementation, and testing. It transforms an existing production system into a new variation of the system.

Another way to visualize this process is to think of the input of each activity as a "what" and the output as a "how". The "how" of one activity becomes the "what" of the next activity in the chain. A customer requirement is a "what," and a functional specification of that requirement is a "how." A functional specification becomes the "what" of the design activity and the design description becomes the "how."

In the RUP, the engineering view is concerned with the coordination of requirements analysis, design, implementation, and testing activities—unlike the waterfall process. The engineering activities do not have to run in serial, one completing before the next. It is possible for them to execute in parallel. Each activity is activated in a sense when there is new input to process. In an iterative development model like RUP, each activity may be activated several times. In addition to executing in parallel, each activity may have a feedback loop to prior "upstream" activities, as in the discovery of an ambiguous requirement during design, or the discovery of a design flaw during implementation. In the RUP, these activities run in parallel, some starting earlier in the development cycle, and some ending earlier than others. The emphasis and effort involved in each activity vary over time.

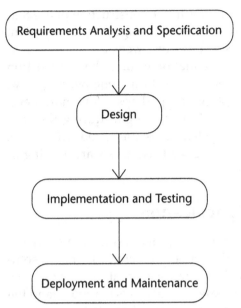

Figure 2.2   Engineering view of product development.

Each software engineering activity maps to many phases of the management view. During the inception phase there is requirements gathering and analysis and relatively little or no design, implementation, or testing. During elaboration there is an increased focus on requirements gathering, analysis, and architectural design. There may also be some prototyping development efforts as part of the design activity and this involves some testing as well. During the construction phase the requirements gathering, analysis, and architectural design activities begin to taper off. The design, implementation, and testing phases are at their peak effort with design eventually tapering off and implementation and testing staying steady partway through the transition phase. Although testing has been performed during construction, more effort is placed into testing during transition.

Toward the end of the construction phase, requirements gathering and modeling cease and design tapers off. Eventually the cycle is down to implementation and testing with the testing activity increasing in proportion to the implementation effort. The final implementation is reduced to fixing bugs found during testing.

The iterative model of development occurs during the construction phase. This is where controlled efforts of analysis, design, implementation, and testing occur in relatively small periods of time. The iterative model can be applied in the elaboration phase as well but it is in the construction phase that it is primarily used. The iterations are short bursts of design, implementation, and testing. A single iteration may be as short as 1 or 2 weeks.

Once the system passes verification and validation testing, the construction phase is complete and the transition phase begins. In the engineering view, deployment involves some additional testing and perhaps a few more iterations of bug fixing. The documentation, which was begun during the construction phase, is finished up and the system goes into production or is shipped. Then the defect reports and enhancement requests start pouring in from customers.

Requirements Analysis and Specification

Requirements analysis is the activity of gathering, identifying, and formalizing requirements in order to understand the actual problems for which a solution is sought. It begins in the inception phase and may continue through the construction phase. The purpose of requirements analysis is to understand the purpose and scope of the system and to document this knowledge as a functional specification, nonfunctional specification, and perhaps a high-level user interface design.

The functional and nonfunctional specifications model the requirements, using natural language prose, semiformal models like use cases and object-oriented analysis, or formal (verifiable) models using something like the Z notation. The purpose of the functional and nonfunctional specifications is to capture enough information and knowledge to create an architectural description of a solution that satisfies the purpose of the application or system. The initial list of requirements from customers, marketing departments, and other stakeholders describes what the problem is. The functional specification describes the behavior of a system that solves the problem. The nonfunctional specification describes the qualities of the system that will also address the problem.

Typically, software requirements are provided by customers or from an internal organization, such as product marketing or product management. Quite often engineers are dissatisfied with the level of detail or rigor of the requirements. It is common in many software development shops and in-house development efforts for high-level requirements to be handed directly to engineers. However, the software architect or architecture team should be the recipient of requirements since requirements drive requirements analysis and architectural design.

Not all requirements specify the problem in purely abstract terms. There are times when it is appropriate to specify some constraints on the system or application. For example, a Web-based application may be part of the problem, not the solution. For example, the problem may be to allow the sales organization to have Web access to an existing data warehouse in order to run some basic reports. The organization may already have an Information Technology (IT) architecture based on Microsoft XML Web Services platform (.NET) technology, Java 2 Enterprise Edition (J2EE) technology, or Common Object Request Broker Architecture (CORBA) middleware. Utilizing the existing IT architecture becomes part of the context in which requirements are interpreted.

Other requirements may narrow the technical solution without specifying exactly what technology is used. For example, a requirement may call for a minimum of installed components on the client machines (for example, "zero code on the client") to reduce the maintenance effort of upgrading and troubleshooting installations. In this case the requirement is really to reduce maintenance and upgrade effort. The solution may be a browser-based user interface or it may be a fairly heavyweight client that has built-in functionality for communicating with another server that manages client application releases to ensure that each remote workstation can be upgraded easily and with minimum user interaction.

Design

Design is the activity of transforming requirements specifications into a technically feasible solution. It is here that design methods such as first principles and design patterns are used. The purpose of design is to map the various requirements to technology and to reason about the correctness of the approach before implementing the solution. Requirements may be specified using several views such as behavioral (use cases), informational (object models), and "nonfunctional" (ad hoc and other methods). The design maps these various inputs to software entities such as objects. The design activity encompasses classic object-oriented design as well as higher-level architectural design methods.

The result of design is a specification of how to build the application or system and the technical constraints on the implementation. For example, a single performance requirement may map to several performance constraints on several related components, which when executed together must satisfy the performance requirement.

Design solutions may be specified informally or by using notations such as those in the Unified Modeling Language (UML). The level of detail of a design specification varies. It is a commonly held belief among software developers that the amount of effort expended on design is never sufficient.

Implementation and Testing

Implementation is where design is transformed into the source code that describes an executable system. Implementation also involves building and testing the system in part and in whole. Some development cycle models separate unit testing, which is the testing of an individual or discrete subsystem, from integration testing, which is the testing of the operation of the entire application or system involving the available subsystems.

As we have postulated, writing source code for a system is a form of design itself. The distinction, then, between implementation and design is in the granularity or focus of the design. The design activity within the engineering view typically involves some higher-level modeling language that may not be directly transformed into source code. Some modeling tools that support UML may have rudimentary code-generation capabilities but don't support *round tripping,* the ability to move between source code and UML views of a system's implementation. Many UML tools do support this capability and thus tend to further blur the distinction between implementation and design.

Deployment and Maintenance

The completed executable system must eventually be delivered to the acquirers and deployed so that end users may use it. An in-house or custom system is deployed into production use and commercial software is shipped to customers. Most business software developed in-house and commercially follows a spiral life-cycle pattern, where new versions with additional features and enhancements are released incrementally.

When an application or system goes into maintenance, it is considered to be complete with respect to the initial vision of the product. The maintenance engineering team is responsible for fixing defects in the system and adding minor function enhancements. In the spiral life-cycle approach, a development cycle is followed by another evolutionary development cycle instead of a strict maintenance phase. It is common to have a "maintenance branch" of a system so that the current and prior releases can both be supported during the evolutionary development cycle. But the earlier versions are typically not maintained for very long. Once the next major or minor version of a product is shipped, some earlier versions are no longer supported and customers must upgrade in order to continue getting support. A product may reach a point in its life cycle where it can no longer evolve and enters a true maintenance phase in the classic sense.

Engineering Design View

The engineering design view is a little different from the software engineering view in that it is a model for pure engineering design. The engineering design view subsumes some aspects of the engineering requirements specification, design, and implementation activities. The engineering design view that I present is adapted for software design from a mechanical engineering design process described by Pahl and Beitz (Pahl, 1996). In this model, the design process is subdivided into four phases: product planning, conceptual design, embodiment design, and detailed design. These phases are sequential, but the activities within each can overlap. As with the activities in the software engineering view, information flows from phase to phase but the phases are not strictly serial (see Figure 2.3):

- Product planning
- Conceptual design
- Embodiment design
- Detail design

"Problems become concrete tasks after the clarification and definition of the problems which engineers have to solve to create new technical products (artifacts)," according to Pahl (1996). In the established engineering fields such as mechanical engineering, *design engineers* create the design of a product and the physical realization of the product is the responsibility of *manufacturing engineers*. Software development has a similar division of labor. The specification of an application is the responsibility of *systems analysts* and the realization of an application is the responsibility of *software programmers*.

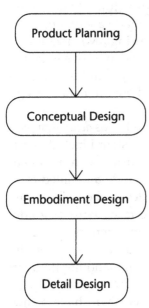

Figure 2.3   Engineering design phases.

The analogy of engineering to software development carries with it the notion that the realization or implementation of a software system is a manufacturing problem and that the input for the implementation of a system is a design specification of the system. A more accurate comparison is programmers as design engineers and language compilers as manufacturing engineers.

Each of these phases focuses on a different level of abstraction and a different set of design objectives. The design phases do not proceed in a pure serialized fashion; rather, they are driven by various inputs such as quality attributes and by the exchange of information among them and in their distinct objectives (such as what types of risks each phase attempts to mitigate). There is a logical flow of information between the phases with respect to time. The product development cycle begins with product planning activities. The output of product planning feeds the conceptual design activities. Conceptual design investigates details; if the details are inaccurate or incomplete, another cycle of product planning may be necessary. The output of conceptual design, or working principles, feeds the embodiment design phase. The term *working principle* refers to a candidate design approach such as a design pattern, architectural pattern, or algorithm that addresses some subset of requirements.

While conceptual design focuses on the search for a working principle or a set of working principles, the embodiment design activities focus on elaboration of a subset of the working principles or just a single working principle if the other candidates can be eliminated. It is possible that during embodiment design there are flaws discovered in the working principles that require another iteration of conceptual design. An assumption made about a particular working principle during conceptual design such as using XML documents to transfer data between a client application and a server may prove to be too slow or too difficult to maintain during embodiment design. In this case, the working principle must be changed or disqualified if there are better design candidates.

The output of embodiment design is sometimes referred to as *detail design* in some software development communities, but to be consistent I include writing source code in the definition of detail design. The output of embodiment design feeds detail design. Embodiment design may include a detailed class hierarchy design, Interface Definition Language (IDL) files, and possibly some source code such as C++ headers for classes, or Java interfaces to use as guidelines or as a framework for programmers to use when implementing the application or system. Issues discovered during detailed design may require another iteration of embodiment design (which may require another iteration of conceptual design or even product planning).

During the product development life cycle, each phase will have a time when it is the dominant activity. In the early stages of development, product planning is the dominant activity and may involve a couple of iterations of product planning and conceptual design and no embodiment or detail design.

During architectural design the emphasis is on conceptual and embodiment design. Toward the end of the development life cycle (the construction phase), detail design will be the dominant activity, although there may be some iteration of embodiment design as well. Product planning and conceptual design should be fairly complete at this point. If it isn't, and coding begins, then planning and conceptual design problems may be uncovered when they are more costly to fix in terms of schedule and effort.

The architectural description is developed and revised during all engineering design phases. Each phase emphasizes a subset of the architectural models. Models that capture the problems, the application domain, and the intended behavior and other quality attributes of the system are created during the latter half of product planning and during conceptual design. Also during conceptual design, high-level representations of the internal form or structure of the system are created such as structural models and models that represent how technologies may be utilized.

During embodiment, design representations of lower-level software structures and technology utilization are created. Finally, during detail design, the actual source-level artifacts are created, which feed the tools that produce the executable system. There is definitely some overlap in the models that are created and revised and the design phases. For example, technology models are created as early as the conceptual design phase, yet continue to be refined through the detail design phase.

Product Planning: Specification of Information

Product planning begins with a vision of a product or the identification of a need and takes into account the market, the company, and the economy. Product planning occurs during the inception phase but they are not the same. Product planning includes the activities conducted during product inception. Once the product development life cycle goes into the elaboration phase and beyond, the product planning activities should be complete or revisited infrequently.

During product planning, the problem is defined (the task is clarified) and a requirements list is created. In engineering design, the product of this phase is called the *specification of information*. In software development, these are the *functional and nonfunctional specifications*. The requirements do not necessarily identify all of the required quality attributes or functionality but rather establish the core capabilities of the application or system.

Conceptual Design: Specification of Principle

During the conceptual design, the domain problem is analyzed and structured and a set of working principles or solution concepts is created or revised. The output of conceptual design is a candidate architecture or concept also called the *specification of principle*. A typical practice in the conceptual design phase is to produce multiple solution variants from which further architectural analysis and evaluation can be performed. The models developed in this phase are the conceptual models, but that doesn't mean that they are purely logical models devoid of any technology decisions. The term *conceptual* in this context should not be confused with the notion of a user's *conceptual model* of how a system works, which we will refer to as *virtuality* or *cognitive model*.

A conceptual model for our digital library example system may identify the use of XML for content representation during editing and authoring and the use of Extensible Stylesheet Language Transformations (XSLT) for generating the presentation or published content. The exact XML application (vocabulary or Document Type Definition [DTD]) and the details of the XSLT are not necessarily mentioned because the purpose is to establish a working principle.

Embodiment Design: Specification of Layout

In established engineering fields, embodiment design refers to *specification of layout*. Other terms such as *main design, scheme design*, and *draft design* also capture what is meant by embodiment design. In software design the selected architectural design concepts identified during conceptual design are fleshed out. It is common to carry forward a subset of solution concepts found during conceptual design and to perform architectural and engineering evaluations on those designs.

During this phase the project development plans are firmed up as the architecture solidifies and cost, resource, and time estimates are made. It is during this phase that the architectural activities are wrapped up and software engineering design is emphasized. Some coding may begin on prototypes or early prototypes created during the conceptual design phase. It is common for an architecture team to build a basic skeleton of the application or system to serve as both a prototype and/or proof-of-concept and to serve as the basis for further development during the detail design (implementation) phase.

Detail Design: Specification of Production

This is the implementation phase in software engineering. Recall that the production and manufacturing process in software development is trivial. Many authors compare the execution of a compiler as the equivalent of a production or manufacturing process. The process also consists of packaging software and distributing it. (Many companies are now using the Internet as a software delivery vehicle so that the distribution process is relegated to uploading the software to a server that customers or potential customers can download to their personal computers.)

In established engineering fields, this phase is where the physical arrangement, dimensions, and other material properties are specified and captured in schematics or other drawings. The output of this phase is called the *specification of production* and is detailed enough to begin the production and manufacture of a product. There are no product design decisions made beyond this point. In building architecture the specification of production is the *blueprint* along with requisite *engineering drawings* that a construction company uses to guide the actual construction of the building. In software it is the *source code* and other *machine-readable artifacts* that result in the construction of the final executable system. Source code is a specification of an abstract machine, and a compiler realizes that machine in platform-specific machine instructions (including byte codes) and data formats.

Architectural View

The architectural view provides a different but complementary perspective to the management, software, and engineering design views. The traditional architect's role is to help the acquirer understand his or her needs more fully and accurately and to create an architectural concept of a system that is feasible to build, given available technology, resources, and time. The architect also oversees construction. The architectural view of a software development cycle is centered on the design of the application or system and how the design drives the development. This is referred to as *architecture-driven software construction* (Sewell, 2002). The four phases of architecting are as follows:

- Predesign phase
- Domain analysis phase
- Schematic design phase
- Design development phase

These phases are sequentially related (see Figure 2.4) but, like the software engineering and engineering design phases, they do not necessarily occur in a single sequential pass. The four phases above when combined with the following build phases form an architecture-driven software construction method:

- Project documents phase
- Staffing or contracting phase
- Construction phase
- Postconstruction phase

These phases are sequential and milestone-driven, similar to the management view.

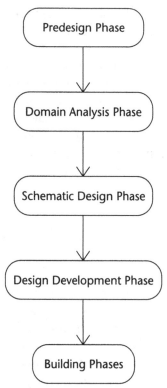

Figure 2.4   Architecting phases.

Predesign Phase

Traditionally, the architect is involved fairly early in a project. In software development, the software architect may be part of the product planning team as well as the engineering team. The architect may have relevant domain expertise and contribute to the vision of the product. This is more often the case for commercial software development and in-house development. In contracted development, the architect may be part of the contractor's organization, not the acquirer's organization, and therefore not necessarily involved in product planning. Regardless, the software architect may need to participate in product planning and the analysis and formulation of requirements as well as the creation of broad budget and schedule objectives by establishing the scope and scale of the project. The architect must listen to the acquirer and study the entire enterprise context in which the application will be a part. The architect must let the acquirer make value judgments such as what features are and are not important in the application.

The architect must study the enterprise in which the application or system is a part. Recall from Chapter 1 the four types of architecture that form an enterprise architecture. The architecture of a business application may need to take into account the information architecture of the organization, not just the information model of the application itself, since often the enterprise application addresses a limited aspect of the entire organization's enterprise problem. In addition, the application architecture may need to take into account the underlying IT architecture itself. If an application server, Web server, database vendor, operating system, or middleware product is chosen before application architecture begins, then it must be considered part of the underlying IT architecture.

The existing technology platform or *technology stack* becomes part of the context in which requirements are formulated, and not part of the solution. An enterprise software vendor must also consider these other architecture types because they become part of a customer's requirements. Often a customer has an investment in technologies such as application servers and database servers. If an enterprise software vendor does not use Original Equipment Manufacturer (OEM)-platform technology, a customer may resist purchasing platform technologies from another vendor when they already have comparable technologies.

Domain Analysis Phase

During domain analysis the software architect strives to understand as completely and accurately as possible the needs of the acquirers and users and the application domain and to document this knowledge. Sources of domain knowledge include domain experts, domain-related literature, and existing requirements specifications from earlier or similar systems. This phase corresponds closely to the requirements analysis and specification software engineering activities. With respect to the management view, the bulk of domain analysis would occur during the elaboration phase and continue through the construction phase.

Domain analysis is one of the most important activities of software architecting. It is, in my experience, the single most ignored activity in software development, especially in commercial enterprise software product planning. I believe that well-crafted domain analysis models contribute significantly to the success of enterprise application development. Software engineers tend to focus on the computer science domain. It is up to the architect to ensure that the engineers understand the application domain models because it is those models that represent the semantics of the problem domain. Solving the wrong problem can cause entire projects to be scrapped, wasting time and money.

Schematic Design Phase

During schematic design, the software architect prepares the architectural-level design, which is specified in an architectural description. This design is depicted in high-level models that represent the behavior of the system, the information captured in and processed by the system, the user interface and user interaction design, the modular structure of the solution, and the technology needed to implement the application or system along with the rationales for the various design and technology decisions.

This phase involves a lot of communication between the architect and various stakeholders and reviews and evaluations of the design variations represented in the architectural description. With respect to the engineering design view, this phase emphasizes conceptual design development.

Design Development Phase

The design development phase focuses on refining the architectural description and selecting among alternative designs. The architectural description is evolved to the point where accurate schedules can be created. The schematic design and design development phases are often iterated and the boundary between them tends to blur as the architecture converges to a final design that is detailed enough to assess risks and to make a decision to proceed with development. With respect to the engineering design view, this phase emphasizes embodiment design.

Building Phases

The building phases described by Marc and Laura Sewell (Sewell, 2002) depart from the analysis and design focus and compare closely with the management view. In their book they consider the design development phase to be a building phase. I have included it in the above sections to emphasize it with the other architecting (design) phases, because this book focuses on those phases and not on the other building phases.

In the project documents phase the architect focuses on development concerns such as how the system should be constructed and in what sequence the components should be developed. A description may be prepared of how the system should be constructed. This would include a construction plan, a user interface style guide, and a test guide.

During the staffing and contracting phase the architect may help the acquirer identify a development contractor or help with the creation of a development team using internal resources. In building construction, the building architect would assist with the details of contracts and cost assessments. This phase may not even occur in most software development efforts, especially if the acquirer is also the builder or if the builder is a commercial software vendor.

The construction phase mirrors the phase of the same name in the management view. From the architecture perspective, the architect oversees construction ensuring that what is built is valid with respect to the architectural description. The architect is involved in design reviews and in the analysis of design problems uncovered as well as the handling of change requests. Even though the bulk of architectural design is complete, there is still need for the architect to make changes to the design and to assess the impact of those changes on the architecture itself and on the cost and effort of development.

The post-construction phase corresponds to the transition phase in the management view. The architect may assist in the deployment of the system and in training users. The architect may also remain involved with maintenance efforts.

Synthesizing the Views

Each of the views of software development involves some set of phases or activities. In the management view, the inception phase is an interval of time followed by the elaboration phase, which is a distinct interval of time. In the context of a single project or incremental release, once the inception phase is complete you never go back to it; it is a milestone that cannot be unreached.

These phases don't overlap by definition, but within these phases there are overlapping and repeated activities such as requirements gathering, requirements analysis and specification, design, implementation, and testing. Each of these activities also occurs in time but they are not phases in the sense that once one is complete you move on to the next, never to revisit it or only to revisit it in some predetermined scheduled time (as a task). These activities are reentrant and may be performed within the context of some development cycle iteration. A phase in the sense of a project life cycle isn't iterative; otherwise, there would be no sense in having the concept of a phase to judge the progress of a product. In a spiral and/or evolutionary life-cycle model, there may be several development cycles, but these are not the same as iterations, which occur within a development cycle.

An activity may be part of a larger task and may involve many steps. The tasks are specific to the problem we are solving. In this case, the tasks help us accomplish the goal of engineering software and are defined by the goal. The specific activities and artifacts produced are defined by a methodology.

Let's use an executing program as an analogy for the software engineering life cycle. An executing application has phases. It has a load phase where it is initially loaded into memory, assigned resources, and started. It has an execution phase where work is performed. Finally, it has an exit phase where the resources are returned to the operating system and the program is unloaded from memory and nontransient data persisted. Within the execution phase, the program performs many tasks based on how the user uses the application. A single task (such as creating a document) may involve several activities such as accepting input from a keyboard, formatting runtime object data into a storage format, and writing that data to a file or database.

Each activity is intended to accomplish the goal of the task itself and the type of activity may be incidental. It may not be necessary to format the data prior to persisting it, depending on the target of persistence. The formatting activity is incidental to the task. An activity is made up of individual nondecomposable steps, which are the programming language statements that comprise the activity such as the various operating system calls to create a file and write bytes to the file. The implementation of the activity is the objective of the programmer, and each individual programmer may utilize a different style or algorithm to accomplish the activity. The software architect chooses the activities that compose a task based on factors such as requirements and prior experience. Each architect may compose a task using a different set of activities yet still accomplish the same goal.

Similar to our program design analogy, the tasks of software engineering can be accomplished in a variety of ways using the activities that are appropriate given the design of the engineering organization and its processes. The task of engineering software may be accomplished using activities such as structured analysis and design or object-oriented analysis and design. Different organizations will use different activities based on their collective experience and skills to accomplish the same goal. What all this means is that there is no one right way to design and construct software. You should choose the activities that make the most sense given the project at hand, including finding a balance between risk and development speed.

We can also view a development cycle as data flows, where each piece of data belongs to some engineering document such as requirements or design. A document can be thought of as a data store; every time it is modified, its changes flow to another document. In between each flow is a process that transforms the data. A process in between a requirements document and a design document is a transformation process that transforms a set of requirements into a set of design elements. From this view, there are no explicit phases. The transformation processes are the activities and the types of documents we are storing, and they constrain the types of activities that can be used. These documents are also referred to as *models,* and this view can be thought of as a model-driven approach.

As you can see, no one view captures the essence of the development cycle. When we look at the development cycle as a data flow involving model transformations, we are ignoring the management aspect and the engineering iterative aspect, because neither of those concepts can be effectively captured in this particular view. Likewise, when we view the development cycle from the management view, we ignore the model transformations and only see specific milestones, which might be the completion of some particular models.

We can see by analogy that the description of the architecture of a software system has a similar characteristic to the description of a software development life cycle: It must involve multiple views. There are also similar dualistic views of software architecture. On the agile side of software design is the anti-model and/or focus on source code architecting. On the heavily planned side is the idea that every document must be up-to-date and maintained just as thoroughly as source code and that every aspect and design decision of the system must be represented in documentation.

Although it is tempting to see these two views as opposites, they can also be viewed as points on a two-dimensional view with one axis being technical expertise and the other being customer satisfaction. More accurately, the various individual practices within each methodology can be placed on such a plane.

Summary

In this chapter, we looked at the various ways in which the development process can be modeled and visualized. Each represents a different perspective or stakeholder point of view. We looked at these perspectives in order to better understand how architecture fits into the development process. Typically, management does not understand how software architecture fits into the development life cycle. The software architect or architecture team will have to educate management about how it does fit.

The four points of view presented were management, software engineering, engineering design, and architecture. These are not mutually exclusive views. Each contains some overlapping concepts and ways of visualizing the process. However, the details of each are different and require some understanding.

In the next chapter, we look at the concepts and principles of the software architecting process in detail.

CHAPTER

3

The Architecture Design Process

The architecture design process is an extension of the general engineering design process described in Chapter 2. Architecture design focuses on the decomposition of a system into components and the interactions between those components to satisfy functional and nonfunctional requirements. A software system can be viewed as a hierarchy of design decisions (also called *design rules* or *contracts*). Each level of the hierarchy has a set of design rules that somehow binds or connects the components at that level. In a simple client/server architecture, the design rules could be the specification of the interface between the client and the server. The next level of the design hierarchy would describe the client as a set of interacting components and the server as a set of interacting components. Each branch of this hierarchy has its own design rules that are not visible to other branches. Thus, the decomposition of the client is hidden from the server and vice versa. In this chapter I focus on the process of architecture design. The primary output of the architecture design process is an architectural description.

Recall that the architectural view of software development is composed of a predesign phase, a domain analysis phase, a schematic design phase, and a design development phase. The focus of each phase is on a different, but possibly overlapping, set of problems. In the predesign phase, the architect is concerned mostly with forming and understanding the enterprise context in which an application will exist. This is represented by a model that depicts the system as an entity within a community of other entities, such as other software systems and human users. During the domain analysis phase, the application requirements are analyzed and structured. In particular, the requirements are those around the problem domain but not specific to the domain of software itself, such as user interface or HCI-related requirements. During the schematic design phase, the architect begins to develop the solution models such as identifying the modules of the system and the design rules that establish the boundaries between modules. Modules are discrete units of design work that rely on shared information and also have hidden information. Finally, during the design development phase, the architecture is refined and possibly multiple variations are created in order to explore the best fit.

The basic architecture design activities presented here can be practiced during any phase of the development process; however, to derive the most benefit to the project, they should be done as early as possible. These activities can be viewed as a linear set of steps that are often repeated as hidden assumptions or missing information is identified during later phases. Each of these phases is comprised of finer-grained design steps. I am omitting requirements gathering and analysis steps from this list and only concentrating on the steps that focus on producing the architectural description of the system. The basic architecture design process is composed of these steps:

1. Understand the problem.
2. Identify design elements and their relationships.
3. Evaluate the architecture design.
4. Transform the architecture design.

The first step is arguably the most crucial because it affects the quality of the design that follows. Without a clear understanding of the problem, it is not possible to create an effective solution.

In the second step, we identify design elements and their interdependencies. In the early phases of the design project, we perform a naïve functional decomposition of the application, which establishes a baseline for future design tasks and design transformation. An example of this method can be seen in Jan Bosch's *Design and Use of Software Architectures*, which focuses on product-line architectures for real-time and embedded software systems. In Bosch's model, this step is called *functionality-based architectural design* (Bosch, 2000).

The third step involves assessing the architecture for conformance to architectural quality attribute requirements. The functional behavior of the application cannot be ideally tested from an architectural decomposition. However, many other quality attributes can be assessed by inspecting the design or by implementing prototypes of the architecturally significant component interactions.

The fourth step involves the application of design operations to transform the architecture design into a new design that addresses the quality attribute requirements better than the previous design. The phase may be repeated multiple times and even performed recursively.

Understanding the Problem

Many software projects and products are considered failures because they did not actually solve a valid business problem or have a recognizable return on investment (ROI). Why spend money building a system to automate a business process if the total cost of ownership is greater than it would have been had no system been built at all? Software engineers who are not given clear direction of the problem to solve may end up focusing their efforts on solving technical problems that ultimately do not address the original problem. I call this the *implementation trap*. To avoid the implementation trap, you should be able to ask yourself what problem the design decision solves. If the answer is a technical or implementation problem, then ask the question again of this problem. Asking this question repeatedly should eventually lead to the original business problem. If you do not reach the original business problem or if the original design decision to address the business problem is unsatisfactory, then this is a good indicator that this particular design decision path has led to the implementation trap.

In one project that I joined rather late in the effort I encountered several examples of the implementation trap. The system was an XML-based content management and publishing system. There was a component that generated unique numbers for content authors to use in naming their XML files. This component was a command line utility that would print a list of sequential numbers to the console. Users would specify how many numbers they wanted to reserve and would save the output, usually storing it in a file on their workstation. The unique number generator, together with a style guide for how to name a file, assured that filenames were unique so that when an author checked a file into the repository it would not conflict with existing files. The naming was based on a string of integers, but the numbers were not entirely random. The next assignable number was stored as a number in a database record. Every request for a block of numbers would advance this number to the next available number.

This solution was based on an incomplete understanding of the problem the system was addressing. The solution led to numerous other downstream problems such as usability and reliability. These problems began to dominate the development effort as programmers tried to increase the system speed and add more features in an attempt to make it easier to use.

The solution was intended to address the fact that the XML repository they used required all files to have unique names. The second problem they were addressing was related to usability. By reserving blocks of sequential numbers, it was argued, the authors would be able to remember their files' names for later retrieval and for easier communication with an editor regarding specific files. An earlier proposal to use globally unique identifiers was rejected. The group encountered some reliability problems as the database server was frequently down or being modified and for some unknown reason the next available number would get corrupted or lost. The solution as built was confusing to use, and the team developed more features on top of this to solve the unique filename problem. Eventually the original problem was forgotten.

By thinking about the original business problem and also about usability and reliability, an alternative solution emerges. With respect to usability, the system could simply inform the user that a file with the same name already exists and it could suggest an alternative name (perhaps by adding a number to the end of the name that resulted in a unique filename). The user could accept the default name or try typing another name. This is a solution that is commonly used in any system where users are creating accounts and specifying usernames. If the requested username is taken, the system may suggest another name constructed from the original name and a number. This makes the system easier to use, is more reliable because it relies on fewer components, and is no more difficult to implement. It is certainly easier to maintain.

The original business problem being solved was to efficiently and effectively manage large volumes of intellectual assets. Instead of relying on content authors to creatively name their files to suggest the contents of the file and to make them easier to find, a meta-data layer can be used. The meta data can be used to categorize the files as well as attach attributes to make file identification and retrieval easier. The meta data can be updated without changing the file. This addresses the real problem of finding files.

Somewhere during the development process, a decision had been made and from that decision more decisions were made until the original problem had been forgotten and a lot of development effort was being spent on maintaining the problems introduced by the rather complex solution. You can probably find some examples of the implementation trap in projects that you have been involved with in the past.

Identifying Design Elements and Their Relationships

In this step, we establish a baseline decomposition that initially splits the system based on functional requirements. The decomposition can be modeled using a design structure matrix (DSM), which represents the dependencies between design elements without prescribing the granularity of the elements. A first draft of this model could be created during the predesign phase, and then revised during subsequent steps.

The architecture of a software application is often represented as a set of interconnected modules or subsystems, often called *components.* These modules are organizational constructs that structure source code, but often are not directly visible in the source code. Source code is an abstraction of machine instructions and data patterns structured in terms of a programming language's grammar. Two programs written in different programming languages but compiled for the same hardware platform result in binary programs that use the same machine instructions.

The Java and C programming languages provide very different language concepts. C provides weakly typed user-defined data structures (the struct), and Java provides a strongly typed class mechanism for user-defined data structures (the class). However, it is possible to conceive of a Java program and a C program that, when compiled, result in the same machine code and data patterns. Java is compiled to a byte code and interpreted by a Java Virtual Machine (JVM) that is itself compiled for a specific hardware platform. It is theoretically possible to write a C program that is identical to a Java program together with the JVM.

In terms of hierarchies of components, both the Java and C programs can be thought of as structures that are composed of lower-level components. Programming languages define a set of components in terms of programming language statements and keywords. Java and C language statements, such as the declaration of an integer and the assignment of a value to it, can be thought of as a component that is comprised of a set of lower-level components that are machine instructions and data patterns. This is similar to the way a computer chip can be composed of components called *gates,* which in turn are composed of lower-level components, such as circuits. Thus, a computer chip and a software program are hierarchies of components.

This physical view of a software application can be viewed from an even higher-level set of components called *software modules.* Today's programming languages do not provide a consistent set of constructs that can be considered architectural components. Therefore, the physical architectural view of a software application is typically a logical representation that cannot be compiled. Researchers are studying Architectural Description Languages (ADLs) in an attempt to define such languages. There is also work under way on executable Unified Modeling Language (UML) that would allow an architectural description to be compiled and tested (as a simulation). Thus, in the future, if ADLs do succeed and become part of the standard toolkit for application developers, then our hierarchy of components view of software would be extended one level higher, as seen in Figure 3.1.

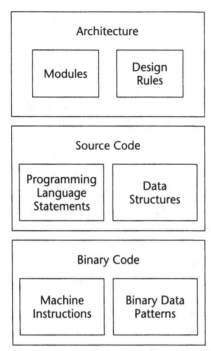

Figure 3.1   Software as a hierarchy of components.

By representing the architecture in terms of design elements (and their corresponding design tasks), this model helps us to find the interdependencies that couple modules and to establish design rules that define the interfaces between modules. The design structure matrix (DSM) is equivalent to a task structure matrix (TSM), in which each design element is represented as a design task and the dependencies between the design elements become dependencies between design tasks. These dependencies identify design decisions that must be made in order for two or more interdependent design tasks to be completed. The dependencies also represent the paths through the design that are affected by design decisions.

The functional decomposition can also be modeled using blocks and arrows, but since we are striving for some level of systematic design, we usually depart from such models fairly quickly in the process. UML package diagrams with dependency associations can be used (see Figure 3.2). As the number of design elements increases, the diagram becomes difficult to interpret. A matrix is more effective for larger amounts of information. Figure 3.3 depicts the same design structure as a matrix. Both models represent the same information.

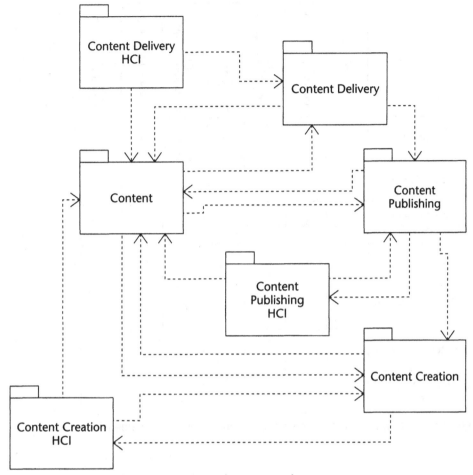

Figure 3.2   Design elements represented as UML packages.

The DSM is interpreted as follows. The dependencies of a given element are represented as an x in a cell along the row of that element. The os along the diagonal are just a helpful visual marker; it is meaningless to state that an element is dependent upon itself. In this example, the design element Content is dependent on Content Creation, Content Publishing, and Content Delivery. Every element is dependent on the Content element. Therefore design decisions affecting the Content element affect design decisions in every other element.

This initial functional decomposition will undergo many transformations. The design elements do not necessarily correspond to physical modules as the UML diagram in Figure 3.2 suggests. The modules will be discovered in time, as the model is refined in subsequent steps. We'll look at DSMs and TSMs in more detail in later chapters.

	Content	Content Creation	Content Creation HCI	Content Publishing	Content Publishing HCI	Content Delivery	Content Delivery HCI
Content	O	X		X		X	
Content Creation	X	O	X				
Content Creation HCI	X	X	O				
Content Publishing	X	X		O	X		
Content Publishing HCI	X			X	O		
Content Delivery	X			X		O	X
Content Delivery HCI	X					X	O

Figure 3.3 Design elements represented as a matrix of interdependencies.

The identification of design elements and their relationships can be further subdivided into the following steps:

1. Define the system context.

2. Identify the modules.

3. Describe the components and connectors.

The first two steps utilize the abstraction design technique (not to be confused with the design operator of the same name, which we'll discuss later). Abstraction is a design technique that allows you to focus on a particular level of detail without having to focus on all aspects or details of the system. An abstract model represents only the essentials that are necessary for reasoning about the system at a particular level of abstraction. The second step involves the application of design operations (discussed in detail in Chapter 9) to split the system into module types.

The last step involves creating descriptions of instances of module types in typical runtime configurations. The difference between identifying module types and instantiations of different system configurations depends on how configurable the system is as well as how different the runtime view of the system differs from its static module view. In a simple system where there is a one-to-one relation between module types and instances, there is no need to perform both steps. In a product line or product family architecture, the distinction between these steps is important because there may be several possible physical arrangements of a system that are sufficiently different to warrant independent description and evaluation.

Defining System Context

The system context helps describe the application from an external perspective, that is, that of the users and operators of the application or system. The system context is useful in describing the purpose of the system as well as for identifying the external interfaces to the system. The input to defining the system context is the initial requirements list.

The external behavior of the system is mapped to the interfaces of the system. Each interface represents some coherent subset of system functions. External entities may be at a higher level, lower level, or at the same level as the system itself. Bosch uses the term *entities* to refer to components in the context view (Bosch, 2000). Higher-level elements compose the system being described with other elements to form a larger system. Lower-level entities are utilized by the system being described (that is, they are the components that compose the system). Entities at the same level are standalone components that are not depended upon but may interact with the system being described in the context of a higher-level element.

Defining the system context is related to understanding the problem domain that the system addresses. An initial model of the enterprise context of the system can be created by diagramming the existing business processes, artifacts, people, and existing systems. The new application or system should fit within this context. A use case diagram is a common way to depict the system context. The diagram can be augmented to include business-level objects (documents, records, reports) that are a visible part of the existing way of doing things. For example, in an insurance application, an insurance claim can be shown as an object that is associated with a set of use cases. A reusable model of an application of problem domain is called a *domain model*.

The model of the system context should be fairly intuitive and understood by even the least technical of stakeholders. This model communicates the purpose and scope of the system. In commercial enterprise software development, it is not always possible to produce a single-system context model, but rather may require several exemplar contexts.

Identifying Modules

Modules are discrete units of software (binary and source). Binary modules are instantiated at run time and these instantiations are commonly called *components* and *connectors*. A given module may contain the specifications for several component types and connector types. The component (instances) may be of a fixed number in some situations. For example, a Web server executable, when launched, results in a single Web server component instance. The *Web server module* is the binary code that exists as a set of program files. The *Web server component* is a running instance of the Web server.

I have seen some confusion over the use of the terms *module, component*, and *connector*. A *module* is a discrete unit of design that is composed of a hidden set of elements and a set of shared elements. Modules have high internal cohesion and low external coupling. Modules may represent the physical packaging of the application's binary code, which can be described further by component types and connector types. Components and connectors describe the physical instantiation of a system. The term *component* is often used to mean a component type or module. A *module* refers to a unit of software that can be designed, implemented, and compiled into a deliverable executable system or subsystem; it is a unit of execution. A *component* is a runtime entity, the definition of which exists in a module. A classic modular architecture is a client-server system. The client and the server are two modules. The server exports some elements such as a set of publicly visible relational database tables and views. The client knows about this publicly visible schema. The client and server are unaware of the internal composition of the other.

A module may contain several component definitions. The client module may contain many class definitions for various user interface components (objects). These components don't exist until run time. Thus components in this example are the objects in the client. A component can be composed of other components (objects) that are not visible to other objects in the client. A component could also be a distributed object.

A modular architecture is an application or system that is composed of two or more modules, each of which can be modified internally without affecting the other. Modules can exist in the source code and in the binary form of the system. In the source code, a module represents some set of source code files that exhibit high internal cohesion and low external coupling. The term *coupling* refers to the interaction or connection between two modules. The term *cohesion* refers to the interaction or connection between the elements within a single module. To achieve low external coupling, the interface between two modules must be fairly stable and static. During the design process, these interfaces are the result of establishing design rules (Baldwin, 2000). A design rule may be:

- A common data format, which may be the specification of a particular set of business entities represented as XML using an XML Document Type Definition (DTD). If the connector between two modules is the common data format, then both modules can change internally without affecting the other. Only changes to the DTD force all of the dependent modules to change.

- A procedural interface such as a set of Java classes, which can also act as a connector between modules. For example, the specification of the public classes and methods in the `Java.lang` package. The package may exhibit high internal cohesion, meaning that changing protected method signatures may require extensive changes to other implementation classes but has no effect on the external or exported interface of the package. Likewise, the module that imports the package has no effect on the package. Therefore, these two source modules can evolve independently from one another as long as the public interface of the package doesn't change.

- A wire-level protocol, which can also act as a connector between modules. For example, HyperText Transfer Protocol (HTTP) and HyperText Markup Language (HTML) are common connectors for Web-based client applications with Web servers. The client and server implementations can change without affecting the implementation of the other since they only agree on the HTTP and HTML specifications.

A source-level module may not represent a binary module. For example, a C++ application may be compiled together with a set of third-party classes that have an established interface. If the implementation of the library changes, the application must be recompiled and redeployed but the application source doesn't need to be modified. In this case we have achieved the benefits of modularity but only at the source-code level. Binary-level modules remove the need to recompile modules when the implementation of another module changes. In the C++ world, there are several technologies that aim at solving the recompilation issue (that is, solving the problem of binary compatibility). Component Object Model (COM), for example, is Microsoft's common object model that allows applications to be composed of modules that can be internally modified without requiring the application to be recompiled. Common Object Request Broker Architecture (CORBA) can also be used to achieve this level of modularity.

Note that both of these technologies have the benefit of removing programming language dependencies; two components can be written in different programming languages, yet still be connected. In C applications you can achieve binary compatibility by compiling procedures into shared libraries. Applications do not need to be recompiled if the implementation of the procedure changes, as long as the signature remains the same. Another term for this decoupling of modules is *late binding*. C++, unfortunately, was not designed with binary compatibility in mind but can be used with COM or CORBA. Java, since it uses late binding on every method call, achieves full modularity, and changing implementations of modules in a Java application does not require recompiling the application. The Java Virtual Machine itself is an example of a module that can be replaced without recompiling Java classes.

Some texts refer to design rules as *contracts* (as in *design by contract*). We'll learn more about design rules in the context of design and task structure matrices in Chapter 5. I will use the term *module* to refer to both the source code and the binary forms interchangeably.

Bosch (Bosch 2000) defines archetypes as the core functional abstractions that compose the system within a context. The archetypes help represent the nature of the system and are primarily used in communicating the system architecture concept and in the identification of actual components. It is considered desirable to have a small set of highly abstract archetypes that can be combined or synthesized in a variety of ways to produce the required quality attributes for at least a major portion of the system, if not the whole system. Too many archetypes complicate the system design and approach an implementation level view of the architecture. Metamodels are examples of archetypes.

For example, consider a repository-based architecture, which has two basic archetypes: the repository and its clients. The clients may eventually be stand-alone applications that are very different from one another, each with its own architecture; but from an archetype perspective they are essentially the same because they all interact with the repository via a single interface. The repository provides the same services regardless of the specific client design or implementation. We will see that some design and architecture patterns can be helpful in identifying archetypes.

Archetypes can be used to describe external entities as well as the logical components that compose the system or application. The relationship between archetypes is defined usually in terms of control flow and data flow. Archetypes are not necessarily found in the application domain, so they may not be represented in the requirements analysis models (such as actors in a use case model or objects in an analysis model). However, archetypes may be represented in the implementation (for example, the archetype may be an implementation object). The archetypes represent recurring functional patterns within the solution, for example, databases, directories, and human/computer interaction (HCI) elements. Archetypes help communicate the architectural concept to all stakeholders and form a basis for identifying concrete components.

Describing Components and Connectors

Components typically refer to the runtime instance of some unit of software. For example, in an executing system there may be two HCI components (a collection of Java Server Pages, Servlets, or Active Server Pages), two Web server instances, and a single database component even though there are only three *modules*:

- The HCI package
- The Web server executable
- The relational database executable

Connectors, like components, can refer to a unit of software or some communication mechanism (like UNIX pipes), and it can also refer to a runtime instance of a communication mechanism or a specific instance of a pipe between two filter processes. HTTP is a general connector *type* while a specific physical HTTP connection is a connector (an instance of a connector type). I will use the terms *component* and *connector* to refer to the runtime instances of design elements. This is similar to classes and methods in object-oriented programming. A class is a specification of an object and exists in a binary unit such as a library or executable. An object only exists during run time. Sometimes a class is also an object. Likewise, methods are specifications of routines and are part of a module and a specific invocation of the method (as identified by a particular execution stack) is a runtime instance of that method. Often when we speak about the objects of the system, or the object model, we are referring to the prototypical objects. This language seems more natural than to talk about the *classes* of the system.

The identification of modules and components is the central activity of software architecture design. Many of the quality attributes are embodied in the components and their connectors. For example, specific modifiability quality attributes are affected by the functional dependencies between components and subsequently between modules. As we will see, some quality attributes will be reified as design tasks, and the dependencies between these new tasks and existing design tasks can be analyzed to identify those design parameters that should become design rules.

Components and connectors are discussed in greater detail in Chapter 7.

Evaluating the Architecture

The third step involves evaluating the architectural design to determine if it satisfies the architectural requirements. The design is evaluated in order to gather qualitative measures or quantitative data, both of which are *metrics*. Each metric is then compared to the quality attribute requirements (see Chapter 8). If the measured or observed quality attribute does not meet its requirements, then a new design must be created.

Architectural designs can be evaluated in a variety of ways. However, the less formal the architectural design model, the less specific are the results. In order to evaluate an architecture design, you must have clearly articulated the quality attribute requirements that are affected by the architecture. It is not enough to say "the system must be fast" or "the system must be easy to modify or adapt to customer needs." These statements may be acceptable in an initial requirements list (or marketing requirements document), but they are not specific enough to evaluate the design against. Such requirements must first be articulated as specific quality attributes and their acceptable values. Most quality attributes are not quantitative in nature so their values may not be numeric. A performance quality attribute will usually be stated as some numeric range or set of ideal numbers. A modifiability requirement may be reified as a scenario called a *change case*. The change case describes what exactly is being changed and how it is being changed. The acceptable value for this attribute might be that such a change is possible without requiring rework of more than one module. See Chapter 14 for more details on architecture evaluation.

Transforming the Architecture

This step is performed after an evaluation or informal assessment of the architectural design. If the architectural design does not fully satisfy its quality attribute requirements, then it must be changed until it does satisfy them. However, instead of starting from scratch, we can take the existing design and apply design operators to it in order to transform it. The new version of the design is then assessed and the process continues until a satisfactory design is achieved. Sometimes you may need to reverse (undo) operations that were already applied and go down a different design path. You may also be creating several candidate designs at the same time. Starting with an initial root design (perhaps a single monolithic module), you may create a directed graph of designs. Each node represents a design decision path. Some paths may merge, in which case the application of design operations are commutative. In this case, you may transform some of the designs and eliminate ones that are obviously not going to transform well based on the requirements.

A design is transformed by applying design operators, styles, or patterns. There are two types of design operators: those that affect the modular architecture and those that affect the component architecture. There are six modular operators (Baldwin, 2000):

- *Splitting* a design into two or more modules
- *Substituting* one design module for another
- *Augmenting* the system by adding a new module
- *Excluding* a module from the system
- *Inverting* a module to create new interfaces (design rules)
- *Porting* a module to another system

Similar to the modular operators are design operators. The basic design operators identified by Bass (Bass, 1998) are:

■ *Decomposition* of a system into components.

■ *Replication* of components to improve reliability.

■ *Compression* of two or more components into a single component to improve performance.

■ *Abstraction* of a component to improve modifiability and adaptability.

■ *Resource sharing*, or the sharing of a single component instance with other components to improve *integrability* (the ability to integrate applications and systems), portability, and modifiability.

Modular and design operators are very similar. The modular operators are concerned with the module view of the system: those units of individual design and development that primarily affect the nonoperational qualities. The design operators are concerned with the runtime component view of the system, which are those units of execution that primarily affect the operational qualities.

Summary

In this chapter, we discussed the fundamentals of a software architecture design process, which can be thought of as a framework for architecture design. This framework is not a methodology; rather, it is a basis for most design methodologies. The framework is composed of four key activities: understand the problem, identify design elements and their relationships, evaluate the architecture design, and transform the architecture design.

In the next chapter, I explore fundamental concepts of methods of the software design process. Design methods are the rules, principles, and heuristics that help an architect to identify design elements and to transform one element into another. Identifying design elements, like identifying objects in object-oriented analysis and design, is easier said than done. The methods in the next chapter will help the architect discover, evaluate, and transform design elements.

CHAPTER 4

Introduction to Software Design

Higher-quality design, not just higher-quality development processes, is necessary in order to achieve a high-quality product. But what characterizes a higher-quality design, and how do we achieve it? And, more fundamentally, what characterizes an activity as design, and what is the product of design? This chapter presents the fundamental methods of the software design process and establishes the scope of the architectural level of design. The same fundamental design principles and methods apply whether a software architect is analyzing the problem domain, specifying the function of an application to address the problem domain, or designing the structure or form of the software. They also apply when a software engineer is creating a detailed design (including coding) or testing an implementation or designing a development environment in which to create the code. A generalized method of design is presented. The main topics in this chapter are:

Problems in software architectural design. This section addresses why design is so difficult and sets the context for the remainder of the chapter.

Function, form, and fabrication (the Vitruvian triad). This section introduces the three aspects of software architecture, which can also be described as purpose, structure, and quality. These aspects of architecture help form a conceptual framework for architectural design.

The scope of design.   This section defines what activities are considered to be design activities.

The psychology and philosophy of design.   This section presents some concepts around the subject of how people design things and what characterizes the mental activity of designing.

General methodology of design.   The last section presents fundamental design methods that apply to software architectural design and other aspects of software design.

Problems in Software Architectural Design

Experience shows us that as the size and complexity of applications and their development teams grow, so does the need for more control of the design of the application. An ad hoc approach to application design and implementation does not scale with respect to the size of the application in terms of functions and other quality attributes. This is often manifested in what is called the *software crisis.* We need better control of the design process in order to improve the quality of the product and make more accurate predictions of the amount of effort required to develop a system.

The obstacles to achieving high-quality architectural design in software development are:

- A lack of awareness of the *importance of architectural design* to software development
- A lack of understanding of the *role of the software architect*
- A widespread view that designing is an *art form,* not a *technical activity*
- A lack of understanding of the *design process*
- A lack of *design experience* in a development organization
- Insufficient *software architecture design methods and tools*
- A lack of understanding of how to *evaluate designs*
- *Poor communication* among stakeholders

Most of these obstacles stem from ignorance around what software architecture and design are and why they are critical to the success of an application or other system development project. This ignorance results in an inability to effectively communicate what problems an application is really addressing and how a technical solution solves those problems.

The solution to the problem of inadequate design must address the obstacles to achieving adequate design. The solution involves the following:

- Evangelizing the importance of software architecture
- Improving software architecture education
- Using architecture methods and tools

There are many authors evangelizing software architecture today; for example, Sewell and Sewell make a case for software architecture as a separate profession from software engineering (Sewell, 2002). There is a strong need for more education in the field of software architecture. Some authors believe that it is a discipline of its own, separate from (though related to) software engineering and requiring its own colleges. At the core of the solution is the need for architecture methods and tools. By tools I mean the methods, techniques, principles, heuristics, and catalogues of reusable design elements (for example, design patterns).

The solution to the communication obstacle is not just to create more communication channels, but to improve the quality of the information being communicated. Weekly design review meetings may improve the transfer of information, but they won't improve the transfer of knowledge. Information may (and will) be interpreted differently, and so we need to make what we communicate more meaningful and rely less on individual interpretation. Standardized (or at least mutually agreed-upon) architectural terminology, design processes, and description languages are extremely important to effective communication among a project's stakeholders.

At the core of design is the notion of problems, obstacles, and solutions (interestingly, this corresponds with the design of this and other chapters). A solution to the problem of software design, in a nutshell, is the careful planning and systematic execution of a design process and the production of design artifacts (models and specifications). Fundamental to understanding design is the understanding of what design *is* and what differentiates the act of designing from other activities. In the next section, we look at design in a broad architectural context.

Function, Form, and Fabrication: The Vitruvian Triad

Vitruvius wrote in his *Ten Books on Architecture* that an artifact (the result of architecting) should exhibit the principles of *firmitas*, *utilitas*, and *venustas*. These three principles are known as the *Vitruvian triad*. The principle of firmitas, or *soundness*, "will be observed if, whatever the building materials may be, they have been chosen with care but not with excessive frugality." The principle of utilitas, or *utility*, "will be observed if the design allows faultless, unimpeded use through the disposition of the spaces and the allocation of each type of space is properly oriented, appropriate, and comfortable." The principle of venustas, or *attractiveness*, "will be upheld when the appearance of the work is pleasing and elegant, and the proportions of its elements have properly developed principles of symmetry." A translation of Vitruvius can be found in Rowland (Rowland, 2001).

The Vitruvian triad is a useful anecdotal device for thinking about software architectures and the process of architecting. Utilitas includes the analysis of the purpose and need of the application (function). Venustas includes the application of design methods to balance many competing forces to produce a useful system that serves some application (form). Firmitas includes the principles of engineering and construction (fabrication). A sound artifact requires sound engineering. Thus we can think of the Vitruvian triad as the principles of *function, form,* and *fabrication.*

An application or software system is constructed based on the specification of its form, which satisfies a function. The form includes the specification of distinct quality attributes that, through a realization of components in a system, satisfies the function. Architectural design is what brings function and form together. In software architecture, the terms function and form may be confused with functionality (for example, functional requirements or features) and internal code structure (for example, architecture). Function in the architectural sense really means the *need, purpose, utility,* or *intended use* of the system or application. One may ask "What is the function of this application?" or "What is it used for?" or "What purpose does it serve?" In other words, what *problems* does the application or system *solve*? Architecting begins with a specification of an application or system in terms of the functions, capabilities, and other qualities that it must possess.

Function and Product Planning

Part of the product-planning phase, as we will see later in this chapter, involves the analysis of the problem domain. The product of this analysis is a formulation of the requirements that an application or system must satisfy. The requirements establish the function of the application or system, not to be confused with the functional specification of the system (that is, part of the form).

For the architectural metaphor to make sense, an application's architecture must address end-user needs. The architecture of a building, for example, is (partially) perceivable to the inhabitants of the building (it's something they see in the exterior and interior of the building and something they experience when they go about their daily activities inside and in the proximity of the building). The architecture of an application likewise must be (partially) perceivable to the users (inhabitants) of the application (which is different from the user being exposed to the internals of the application). This cyber-reality or *virtuality* of the application architecture goes beyond human computer interaction or human factors or even user interface design. The functional architecture may not be obvious from the structural architecture and vice versa, but sometimes one does follow the other.

Form and Interaction Design

Alan Cooper draws a distinction between design that directly affects the ultimate end user (*interaction design*) of the application and all other design (*program design*). Poor interaction design contributes to what Cooper calls *cognitive friction*. Cognitive friction is "the resistance encountered by a human intellect when it engages with a complex system of rules that change as the problem permutes" (Cooper, 1999).

The interaction with software applications is high in cognitive friction because of the large number of states and modes that an application can have. Mechanical systems are low in cognitive friction because they tend to have relatively few states and relatively few modes. In software applications, the mode the application is in affects the behavior of a given function or operation. Selecting a menu item or clicking on a button may have different effects, depending on the mode of the application. Cognitive friction is not necessarily bad, just as having a large number of states and modes in an application is not inherently bad. What we judge as good or bad is how we manage this complexity in the interaction design of an application.

Terry Winograd (Winograd, 1996) refers to interaction design as simply *software design*. "Software design is the act of determining the user's experience with a piece of software. It has nothing to do with how the code works inside, or how big or small the code is." The product of interaction design is the *user's conceptual model* or *virtuality*. The user's conceptual model is based on his or her experience with the software. Other terms that convey the same idea are *cognitive model, interface metaphor*, and *ontology*. Cognitive friction occurs when a virtuality is poorly designed, that is, designed without the user in mind. Cooper says, "Almost all interaction design refers to the selection of behavior, function, and information and their presentation to users." This is an aspect of the field of research called human/computer interaction (HCI). HCI is composed of four threads of research (Carroll, 2002):

- Software engineering methodologies of prototyping and iterative development
- Software psychology and human factors of computing systems
- Computer graphics and software user interfaces
- Models, theories, and frameworks of cognitive science

I extend the definition of end users with respect to virtuality to include programmers. If you are architecting an enterprise application platform or framework that doesn't have an application interface (other than required administration and installation interfaces), you still need to consider the virtuality of the system in terms of its application program interface (API). An API is a type of language; it has words (the functions, methods, classes, and other data structures) and grammars (the constraints on how objects are created and combined, the order in which methods are called). A well-crafted API is easy to learn and apply, unless, of course, the implementation is defective. For example, many Java 2 Enterprise Edition (J2EE) APIs are well designed; they solve very specific problems, the class designs are logical and intuitive, and their constraints are fairly simple. Different APIs can be combined or *synthesized* to solve larger problems. An API that is a kitchen sink of functionality that does not have a well-designed conceptual model is difficult to learn.

A related concept is the *application domain*. The application domain is the part of the world in which an application's effects will be felt, evaluated, and approved by users (Jackson, 1995). This is a different connotation than the idea of a generic domain or class of applications. The term *environment* is sometimes used to mean the same thing. The correct identification of the application domain is necessary in order to focus on requirements. The virtuality of a software application must be congruent with the application domain. The problem being solved is shaped by the definition of the application domain. Use cases are an example of an application domain modeling technique. The Reference Model for Open Distributed Processing (RM-ODP) enterprise viewpoint language also addresses the definition of the application domain (the enterprise in which various systems interact to achieve some objective).

You can see already that there are at least two views or aspects of an application's architecture: the *function* and the *form*. In this book we are concerned with both aspects of an application's architecture.

Cognitive Friction and Architectural Design

Let's consider an example in a different design domain. Donald Norman in *The Design of Everyday Things* (Norman, 2002) gives an example of a consumer refrigerator's control panel for adjusting the temperature of the freezer and the fresh food compartment. There are two controls, one marked with letters A through E for adjusting the freezer and another marked with numbers 1 through 9 for adjusting the fresh food compartment. But the instructions for modifying the temperature of one compartment or the other require adjusting both the freezer and fresh food controls. The initial settings are C and 5. To make the fresh food colder, the numeric control must be moved up to a higher number and the lettered control must be moved to a prior letter, for example, the settings B and 8. To make only the freezer colder requires a setting such as D and 8. Getting the temperature right in both compartments requires experimenting with the two controls.

The controls are nonintuitive, and the instructions provide no hint as to how to effectively change the control settings, requiring the user to guess and wait for the temperatures to change and settle to see if they reach the intended values (usually a 24-hour period). The problem is that the controls were directly affecting internal structures: the numeric control adjusting the cooling unit and the lettered control adjusting the proportion of cold air being directed toward the refrigeration compartment or the freezer compartment.

What this illustrates is that the user interface didn't map naturally to a user's conceptual (mental) model of how the refrigerator should be adjusted, such as one control for adjusting the temperature of each compartment individually. In other words, the virtuality of the refrigerator as embodied in the controls did not abstract away the internal structure (not to mention that the written instructions made its use even more confusing). A good user interface can hide local complexities in an application, but if the overall functional metaphor is unnecessarily complicated, then the application itself will appear incongruent and hard to use and will frustrate users.

Another example is found in Bass and Coutaz's *Developing Software for the User Interface* (Bass, 1991). They describe an interactive system for operating a mobile robot. The purpose of the system was to allow an operator to specify a mission for a mobile robot within a physical environment. The mission specification would direct the robot through an environment that included obstacles. There were two approaches they could have taken with respect to the interaction design of the system. The first approach would be to require the user to specify the mission in a way that is comprehensible to the physical robot, since this low-level specification was necessary to motivate the robot. The preferred approach, however, was to hide this complex implementation from the operator and instead allow the authors to define a mission in terms of higher-level descriptions that could be transformed into a low-level mission specification.

The behavioral and information models of the system commonly represent the virtuality of a system. The requirements of a system can map to many behavioral and information models; therefore, creating a good virtuality requires attention to these fundamental models. The internal structure of the refrigerator was based on engineering design. It was an optimal solution for the cooling of two individual compartments using a single refrigeration coil. The user would not be aware of this internal optimization and would rather work with more natural concepts. Likewise, the mobile robot mission specification was also based on engineering design. It was an optimal solution for motivating a physical robot through a physical environment. The user would not be exposed to this structural detail but rather to a more qualitative environment for specifying the robot's mission in terms of obstacles to avoid and routes to take, allowing the computer to generate a physical quantitative path.

Fabrication

Vitruvius's *firmitas* is the principle of quality (soundness, durability). The product of architecture and construction must be a high-quality system. The quality of a system is based not only on the design of the system but also on the selection of technologies used in the implementation of the system. I chose the term *fabrication* to connote both the product of construction as well as the construction itself (but certainly not to mean a *falsehood*, which is one connotation of the term).

An architecture must be realizable; it must be possible to build the system as described by the architectural description. That may sound obvious, but it is often not even considered as an architectural attribute. It must be possible to apply current software engineering practices and technologies toward the implementation of the application or system that is described and to satisfy the specified quality attributes. It must be possible to build the system given the available resources such as time, staff, budget, existing (legacy) systems, and components. If existing technologies are insufficient for the problem at hand, will the team be able to invent what is necessary?

For example, several years ago there were no standard commodity application servers so many in-house development projects and commercial enterprise vendors had to build application servers into their products or original equipment manufacturer (OEM)-specific vendor application servers. The architect had to take this into account: Were the staff skills, project budget, and schedule sufficient to build the application server? Today, systems that require application servers tend to be easier to build because there is no need to invent an application server. Commercial application servers are ubiquitous and relatively inexpensive. A good architecture identifies those factors of the solution domain that can be satisfied using commercial off-the-shelf (COTS) components, taking into consideration the cost of licensing the technology versus the cost of building it.

Application Architecture

Interaction design that addresses concerns other than structural design is key to understanding the difference between application architecture (see Chapter 1) and more general software architecture (such as the architecture of a compiler). Although the design principles in software development are universally applicable to high-level and detail-level design as well as different software domains (compilers or enterprise applications), it is important to distinguish between the types of objectives that drive the design activities. Interaction design is usually not a quality of compiler architecture. A compiler does have a virtuality: Its problem domain is that of textual information conforming to formal grammars and having some target language to which it can be compiled.

Example

Traditionally, part of the architecture role was assumed by *systems analysts*, who analyzed the problem and specified a functional model of the system that would address the problems. For example, consider a system where a customer order entry is written by hand and later keyed into a system. This is a time-consuming and error-prone process. An organization may realize that this system cannot scale and therefore brings in a team of Information Technology (IT) specialists to analyze the problem and propose a solution. The analysts determine that the following problem statements capture the essence of the existing system:

- Writing an order by hand is slow (reduces the number of customers a given sales associate may service and may negatively affect sales figures).

- A lot of the form data may already exist in some fashion if the customer has placed an order before (for example, delivery address, payment information).

- Writing an order by hand is error prone (the wrong customer information may be written, such as account numbers or product codes).

- Keying information into a software application later in the process is another opportunity to introduce errors in the data.

In addition to the requirements, the systems analysts may discover some additional features that were not envisioned by the acquirers but which support the overall objective of the system. Some examples of these suggested features are:

- When an existing customer profile is accessed, the sales associate may also have access to previous orders for that customer. This information may help the sales associate to make suggestions to the customer or even simplify the order creation process if the customer is reordering. This can potentially speed up the order entry process and possibly increase the amount of the individual sale.

- The system can keep track of the products previously ordered by the customer and provide a list of suggestions for other products. The sales associate can use this suggested product list to make suggestions to the customer, potentially increasing the amount of the individual sale.

These statements make up the problem and define the function (utilitas) of the application. After understanding the crux of the problem, the analysts or application designers begin identifying the functional requirements (features and capabilities) and other quality attributes that make up part of the architecture of the application. Suppose our team proposes the following requirements:

- A PC-based order entry system at each sales associate's desk.

- A graphical forms-based order entry system that is linked to a customer database and products database.

- Auto-completion of some form fields to make entry faster: for example, the user begins typing in customer's last name and a list of possible customers to choose from appears on the screen. The user may stop typing the name and then scroll or use a mouse cursor to select the customer; continuing to type will reduce the field of potential customers.

- Selecting the customer from the auto-completion view causes the form to be partially completed, including everything from the customer database that is relevant, for example, full name, billing address and information, shipping address and instructions.

- The auto-completion view will provide enough information on screen to allow the sales associate to determine that it is the correct customer before selecting it (for example, there may be a lot of Smith, Steve entries).

- If the user accidentally selects the wrong entry, it must be easy to undo the action and clear the form quickly (such as pressing a single key on the keyboard or clicking on a single button on the screen).

Some of these requirements have already begun to suggest the form of the internal structure of the solution: We can see that there is a customer database and product database that all workstations can access, and there is an order entry program or application accessible from the workstation. Other than these three functional components, there is not much that has been revealed about the internal structure of the system.

Each of the functional requirements above addresses the problems in some combination. For example, the auto-completion feature is intended to address the slow order entry problem. Typing into a form on a screen may not be significantly faster than handwriting fields on a paper form, especially if the user is not a proficient typist. However, automatically filling in several fields can significantly improve the speed with which a user can complete a form by reducing how much he or she must type. The other requirements related to the auto-completion of the form support the main capability and are intended to ensure that the feature is indeed useful in speeding up form entry and reducing errors. The analysts didn't have to specify these features and could have instead relied on the designers and engineers to come up with features that support the objective of speeding up form entry. We can assume that our analysts have some knowledge of solution patterns such as these and therefore have included them in the specification. They could annotate these requirements as preferences, knowing that they will satisfy the objective, but allow the engineering team to present other solutions that also address the same objective.

In addition to the intended function of the system, the designers must consider business-related quality attributes. Some examples that may affect the architecture are:

- Cost of implementation
- Cost of deployment, administration, and technical support
- Cost of training
- Time to deliver

The return on investment (ROI) should be the overriding concern of the system designers because the *utilitas* of the system is not to make order entry faster and less error prone, rather it is to increase revenue. A system that increases productivity by a factor of 4 but which costs more to implement than the company will realize in several years can probably be considered a failure. The cost of implementation includes development staff salaries and development tools such as workstations and software. Deployment and implementation costs include not only staff salaries for installation and administration but also the cost of purchasing workstations for sales associates, the time and cost of training, and the time lost mastering the necessary skills to use the system. Will the new system actually be faster than handwriting orders or will it prove to be a hindrance to its users? Will it be usable?

The Scope of Design

At this point you should have an idea of what the scope of architecture is with respect to software development and with respect to software engineering. In this section we look at the scope of design in general with respect to application development.

Tasks and Activities of Design

Any design activity can be seen from many points of view:

- Psychological
- Systematic
- Organizational

From the *psychological* view, design is a creative process that requires knowledge in the appropriate disciplines such as software engineering, computer science, logic, cognitive science, linguistics, programming languages, and software design methodologies as well as application domain-specific knowledge. HCI approaches software development and use from the psychological aspect.

From the *systematic* view, design is seen as an architecting or engineering activity that involves finding optimized solutions to a set of objectives or problems while balancing competing obstacles or forces.

The *organizational* view considers essential elements of the application or system life cycle. Application development begins with a market need or new product idea. Application design (or, more generally, product design) starts with planning and ends when the product reaches its end of life (in software this means executing an end-of-life strategy and implies that a product is no longer maintained or supported). There may be some recycling of software elements to be reused in other products.

Design tasks may be classified by a variety of characteristics. The following characteristics are based partly on Pahl and Beitz (Pahl, 1996):

- Origin of the task
- Organization
- Novelty
- Production
- Technology
- Horizontal domain
- Quality attributes

Origin of the Task

There are many possible origins for a design task such as:

- Product planning (especially for commercial software)
- In-house software (custom systems)
- Systems integration
- Production and field testing

The genesis of a software application may involve a group responsible for product planning, also known as product management. The product-planning group identifies a real or perceived need and establishes the requirements of an application or system. The need for the system may be internally generated to solve some in-house business problem, or it may be market driven with the intention of selling the software. Sometimes systems that are originally designed for internal use are commercialized and sold externally, after executives discover their potential resale value.

Some software vendors do not create and sell complete applications, but rather domain-specific application frameworks. This is common with enterprise software vendors. The vendor cannot anticipate every potential customer need so instead focuses on building a platform or framework that provides general application domain-level services along with a software development kit (SDK) for building applications on the platform. The assumption is that it is ultimately more cost effective for the customer to license the platform and build on it than to build the system from scratch. A customer may make a special order for a system, which is handled by the vendor's own consulting organization (sometimes called *professional services*). A company may start the process by hiring an outside software architecture consultant to assess its needs and make recommendations and proposals. Sometimes an enterprise vendor sells a partial solution to the executives of a company without input from a software architecture team or the engineering organization (much to the dismay of the engineers).

In-house software may be built by a company's own IT or engineering organization or may be contracted out to an outside software development firm. This type of design usually starts with some internal organization identifying a business need for an application or system.

Some tasks start out as specific systems integration problems in which case the requirements are much more rigid, and there is more need to interact with other engineering or design groups. Systems integration may involve third party to third party integration, third party to internally developed system integration, and even integration between internally developed systems such as is common when integrating different departments of the same organization. This last form of integration is commonly the result of a merger or acquisition or even an integration effort between two different enterprises (Business to Business Integration [B2BI]).

In the context of engineering machines or devices that must be manufactured, there are design tasks related to the creation of production machines, jigs and fixtures, and inspection equipment. Likewise, in software development the production-level work requires development and testing environments, configuration and release management mechanisms, and bug-tracking systems. Unless you are using a completely integrated off-the-shelf system for developing software, you will most likely have to assemble a system from various vendors, open source projects, and internally developed tools. The creation of a development (environment) system is a design task much like the development of an application, but is often not treated in such a manner.

Organization

The design and development process is commonly organized around the structure of a given company or development organization. Some common organizations are product-oriented; some are problem-oriented.

In *product-oriented* companies, product development and production responsibilities are divided among different divisions based on product type.

For example, it is common in enterprise software companies to have a platform division and one or more application divisions based on general application domains. Sometimes the application divisions are the only users of the platform, and sometimes the platform is sold as a product (such as a relational database or an application server).

Problem-oriented companies organize work according to a division of labor along domain boundaries such as database administration and user interface design. An organization based on design phases divides specific design phases among divisions. For example, product planning, architectural design, and implementation (detail design) phases may be assigned to individual organizations. I have seen examples in industry of each of these approaches as well as hybrids of them. Each organization type affects the choice of design activities and how they are performed as well as affecting the role architects and engineers assume.

Novelty

Some design tasks require much more invention and creative problem solving than others do. The novelty of the problem can be characterized as follows:

- Original design
- Adaptive design
- Variant design

Original design starts with a clean slate. The designers start with a set of problems and objectives to which no known solution principles exist. Original designs may be created through the synthesis of known solution principles and existing technology or it may require inventing new technology. For example, several years ago I worked on a project where one of the primary problems to solve was to create a generalized mechanism for transforming structured (hierarchical) data to other hierarchical form. At the time the XML 1.0 specification had just been published and technologies like Extensible Stylesheet Language Transformations (XSLT) were not available. The problem was novel at the time and required inventing a technology for tree transformations because such a technology did not exist.

Adaptive design starts with known or established solution principles and adapts the principles to fit the current problems or requirements. Adaptive design may involve some original design as new components are added to meet the new requirements. In a software development system or application, modifications made during the maintenance cycle may involve adaptive design unless the modifications are so localized and isolated in the source code as to not require any conceptual or embodiment design work.

Variant design starts with an existing design that must be changed only with respect to some nonfunctional quality attributes. For example, a system may need to be reworked to handle greater user loads or to perform certain operations faster. Some variant design may not be possible at the detailed design (implementation) level and may require new embodiment or even conceptual design, which is no longer variant design but may be adaptive or original design.

Production

Software may be created for either a one-off custom system or for resale (either as shrink-wrapped applications or enterprise platforms). One-off software system production is similar to one-off or small batch production in established engineering fields. The design activities for one-off system development should emphasize risk reduction. Development of throwaway prototypes is not always economically feasible. Functionality, maintainability, performance, and reliability and/or availability are commonly the paramount qualities.

Commercial enterprise software production is similar to large-batch or mass production where the product is used by customers solving similar problems but with different requirements. Functionality, performance, extensibility, adaptability, and usability are commonly the paramount qualities. Functionality in commercial enterprise software tends to be more general than in specific in-house systems.

Technology

Different technologies require different design methods. The working principles of user interfaces are different from business logic involving distributed transactions and require different design activities. Some technology areas that affect design methods are:

- Information representation
- Data storage
- Data transformation
- Business logic
- User interface design
- Vendor platforms

The above list is by no means exhaustive of the types of software technologies available today, but does demonstrate the varieties that exist. User interface design methods include those proposed by Bass and Coutaz (Bass, 1991). Information representation design methods include object-oriented analysis and entity relationship modeling. Some vendors have suggested design methods for building applications using their proprietary technology.

Horizontal Domain

Systems can be characterized by their relative complexity. A plant (typically highly complex) is composed of machines and instrumentation, which in turn are composed of machine assemblies and components (typically less complex). In software application development we have similar complexities that affect the design tasks. I call these *horizontal domains*.

Each horizontal domain is a layer that incorporates the components of the lower layer. In this model each layer is not necessarily more complex than the lower layer (except in the sense that the higher layers inherit the complexity of the lower layers). An enterprise application may be less complex to design than an operating system, but it is more complex in the sense that it is composed of the operating system and other underlying technologies. The following list is an example of horizontal domains. The domains can be further subdivided; for example, the enterprise applications can be divided into high-level components and objects. The demarcation of a horizontal domain is based on the types of concerns addressed by design and the types of patterns, methods, and tools specific to a domain:

- Integrated enterprises (B2B)
- Enterprise integration: systems of applications (integrated applications)
- Enterprise applications (point or vertical solutions)
- Software libraries, databases, application servers, operating systems (platforms)

Quality Attributes

One of the largest factors that affect the design task is the set of required quality attributes of the system or application. Most design methods focus on functionality. Functional models such as use cases typically drive object-oriented projects. Attributes such as modifiability are not easily expressed in purely object-oriented terms and need supplemental textual descriptions to represent the design. Each attribute must be considered during design and usually requires the architect to make multiple passes at a design. A class design may start by addressing functionality only. Then another pass is made to incorporate the modifiability requirements while making sure that the functionality is not affected (in terms of the functional requirements, not necessarily in the actual interaction design of the application, which may change). Likewise, many passes are taken at a design to incorporate the various requirements and to evaluate the design and design tradeoffs.

There are many competing quality attributes, and the architect must find a suitable design that strikes a balance among them. For example, modifiability and performance are commonly competing requirements because modifiability design techniques usually incorporate extra levels of indirection (interfaces) and stricter encapsulation of data and services to make modifications more local and less pervasive.

Performance design techniques, however, usually incorporate fewer levels of indirection and optimizations to data structures in order to improve operation execution times. Cost is usually competing with everything else, and it is common that usability is sacrificed first.

Some common quality attribute characterizations are:

- Functionality
- Buildability
- Cost and time to market
- Performance
- Usability
- Security
- Availability and reliability
- Modifiability

Architecture versus Engineering Design

Many design tasks in software development may be considered either strictly architectural or strictly engineering. Sometimes the distinction is fuzzy. Production-based design issues (the design of a software development environment for a particular organization or project) is considered an engineering activity (but is commonly not even regarded as a design activity because it is not a product design-related activity).

One way to characterize the difference between software architecture design and software engineering design is in scope and complexity. While engineering design concentrates on implementing specific quality attributes using technologies, architectural design concentrates on formulating the quality attributes and system characteristics and selecting the working principles that balance many competing quality attributes. One may extend the definition of software engineering to include what I described as architectural design, but the distinction between the two types of design is important (even if the boundary is fuzzy) because it establishes two separate disciplines with different objectives and which use different tools and methods.

The Psychology and Philosophy of Design

Software design is rooted in the fundamentals of language, logic, and knowledge. In this section, we take a look at the psychology of design and the application of logical reasoning as the basic means of problem solving.

Design is a creative problem-solving activity that involves intuitive and discursive thought. The *intuitive thinking* process is mostly subconscious and is characterized by flashes of insight and inspiration commonly triggered by some association of ideas. The *discursive thinking* process is conscious and deliberate where facts and relationships are analyzed and combined in a variety of ways, evaluated, and then disposed of. The products of discursive thinking are knowledge structures, also known as *semantic networks*.

Problems, Obstacles, and Solutions

All design methodologies consider design as an activity of finding or creating solutions to problems given a set of obstacles to overcome (see Figure 4.1). Among the types of obstacles that exist between a problem and its solution is a lack of understanding of the problem. Fundamental to good design is a grasp of the problem being solved; without this understanding it is hard to create a good design because it cannot be assessed based on its effectiveness in satisfying the problem. This is not to say that designs created without a complete understanding of the problem are inherently bad, but the likelihood of having stumbled onto the best solution is diminished. Design without context is unpredictable, and in today's compressed software development schedules and increased demand for application capabilities, unpredictability is the enemy.

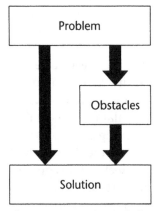

Figure 4.1   Design solution represented as a function of problems and obstacles.

Since design is predominantly creative, it cannot be fully measured and understood. Experience has proved that adopting systematic approaches to design can bring a degree of predictability in terms of the amount of time required to design, as well as the quality of the design. Systematic approaches shouldn't hinder creativity, but rather serve as a catalyst for creative thought.

There is no singular design method that is superior; rather, there are good or poor choices for which method to employ given a unique set of circumstances. The software architect should exercise judgment when using a particular design method for a particular aspect of a project in order to avoid the pitfall of adopting a comprehensive methodology wholesale only later to discover that it wasn't entirely appropriate. Object-oriented analysis and design are popular methodologies but not always the best choice, especially with architectural design, which may not be at the level of objects and classes.

Recall that specifying the function (*utilitas*) of an application is commonly referred to as *analysis* and that specifying the form (*venustas*) is commonly referred to as *design*. Analysis is commonly understood to be the phase or activity where the problem is articulated or structured in order to clarify the problem and to facilitate the application of design methods in order to derive or discover a solution. Software development is characterized as an activity of creating problem-solution pairs. This is why design patterns are so popular, because they capture many known problem-solution pairs. The pattern's context defines some types of obstacles of the problem.

Aristotelian Reasoning

Software design shares some things in common with the philosophical investigations of a subject matter. Whereas logic and philosophy intend to investigate some subject fully, software design stops at practical limits within the context of solving a practical problem. In the article *An Aristotelian Understanding of Object-Oriented Programming*, Rayside and Campbell take the position that achieving conceptual integrity (Brooks, 1975) requires the ability to reason with order, with ease, and without error.

Aristotle's work on logic (the *Organon*) establishes reason as the tool of tools. In the language of software we can consider reason as a meta-tool. Reason can be used as a tool for *understanding* and as a tool for *discoursing*, which is the formation of new truths about something. Thomas Aquinas divided the Organon based on three rational operations used in the formation of knowledge: definition, predication, and inference. Definition and predication are tools of understanding, and inference is a tool of discoursing.

> **Definition.**   By applying reason, we can apprehend (literally "reach out and grasp") something. The art of definition is in the grasping of the unity in things, which we express in words. Once we have found the

unity of things, we must find what differentiates it from other things. There are two kinds of distinction: accidental and essential. *Essential* distinctions tell us *the kind* of thing it is. *Accidental* distinctions tell us something about the thing other than what it is. In software modeling techniques, it is common to search for the objects or components that comprise the system view and to organize them into classes or types. After these types have been identified, we look for essential distinctions, such as the specific attributes that characterize things in the type, for example, specifying the data members of a class or the set of operations (the interface) of a component type.

The activity of defining things characterizes analysis (such as object-oriented analysis). Therefore, the goal of analysis is the apprehension of some problem or application domain. Accidental distinctions are not represented in modeling or programming languages. However accidental distinctions are made, sometimes subconsciously, about the classes in a model. For example, statements like "components of type A must not have knowledge of the structure of data in components of type B" are accidental distinctions. Components of type A are not specified or coded with the accidental distinction (there is no way to represent it), but it may be specified in an architectural model using natural language descriptions.

Predication.   Predication, the second operation of reason, is also a tool for understanding. This is the operation of creating statements about a subject in which a predicate is either affirmed or denied. A statement either *composes* a predicate with a subject or *divides* a predicate from a subject, and therefore a statement is either true or false. For example, in object-oriented designs the statement "class A is-a class B" is a statement that is either true or false. The predicate (also called a *predicable relation*) is the phrase "is-a class B" and denotes a subclass relationship in this case. The subject class A may be composed with this predicate as above or it may be divided such as in the statement "class A is-not-a class B." In this example, I modified the predicate in the context of the statement to be grammatically correct. However, to be a little more mathematical, I could have said "*not* class A is-a class B," where *not* is an operator that negates the predicate, thus dividing it from the subject class A. Whereas definition helps us find universal things, predication helps us discover the relationships between those things. If we don't do a very good job at defining our concepts, predication can be difficult.

Inference.   The purpose of the third operation of reason is the discovery of new truths about subjects. This operation involves the ordering of statements with the purpose of drawing a conclusion. This ordered set of statements and conclusion is called an *argument*. An argument is either *valid* or *invalid*. The conclusion of an argument is also a statement and is therefore either true or false. In Aristotelian logic, this argument is called a *syllogism*. In architecture, one type of inference operation is the assessment of an architectural design (addressed in Chapter 14).

Designers usually apply these operations in an iterative fashion and at varying levels of abstraction, although they probably are not consciously aware of which operation they are applying. Definition and predication are the basis of abstract thinking. The notion of design as a problem-solving activity is an application of the rational operators.

Recall that one of the most common obstacles to good design is lack of understanding of the problem. By applying the rational operations of definition and predication, the designer is better able to apprehend or grasp the true nature of the problem. However, there is no design operation that can be easily applied, so we rely on our existing body of knowledge contained in our own memories and in design catalogues. Even if we understand the problem, it may not be represented in a way that facilitates the discovery of existing solutions. So we divide and conquer in order to refine our understanding of the problem, looking for more common subproblems (abstractions) that, when synthesized, describe the original problem. Again, we search for solutions to our new set of problems.

For experienced designers, this process may be intuitive and proceed in the subconscious. Less experienced designers may need to apply these steps consciously and systematically until it becomes second nature. In order to master the art of software architecture, the architect needs to practice these techniques until they are part of his or her subconscious.

General Methodology of Design

In this section, we look at the general elements of a design method based on Pahl and Beitz (Pahl, 1996). Not all design methods include all of these elements, but these elements are present in all design methods:

- Purposeful thinking
- Analysis
- Abstraction
- Synthesis
- General heuristics

Purposeful Thinking

Design requires systematic thinking, which separates design from routine tasks. Systematic, or *discursive*, techniques are not the opposite of creative techniques nor are they the opposite of subconscious, or *intuitive*, thought. Relying on intuition alone, however, is not a good design practice so we need to be more deliberate in our approach to design. A purely intuitive approach to design has several disadvantages: The right solution rarely comes at the right time, the results depend on the architect's skills and talents, and the solutions may be negatively influenced by preconceived ideas (also called *fixation*). Intuition can lead to good solutions but requires conscious and deliberate involvement with the problem. Discursive thought can stimulate intuitive thinking. Programmers experience this frequently. A programmer may spend hours or days struggling with some problem only to have the solution come to her while she is away from the computer, not even consciously thinking about the problem.

Design should be primarily discursive; that is, it should proceed deliberately in a stepwise fashion. Unconscious procedures can be transformed into deliberate and systematic methods through systematic rules, clear task formulation, and structured design procedures.

Errors are unavoidable so our processes must allow for this. Therefore the architect should analyze the design for errors or weak points in the early stages of development. Clearly defined requirements and problem statements help reduce the risk of design errors by minimizing the amount of guesswork that goes into the design process as well as minimizing the amount of rework that would otherwise be necessary. A discursive design approach helps reduce errors by enforcing systematic testing of design ideas and assumptions early in the development process. Fixed design ideas (assumptions) should be avoided and existing methods and tools should be adapted as necessary (don't let a given methodology artificially constrain you). The deliberate use of specific methods for failure or error identification should be used.

Creativity is inhibited or encouraged by different influences. Some techniques for encouraging creativity are:

- Interrupt the activity to create incubation periods (but be careful; too many interruptions can be disruptive).
- Apply different solution-finding methods.
- Move from abstract to concrete ideas.
- Find and collect information from design catalogues (such as design patterns).
- Divide work among architecture team members.
- Make realistic plans: Realistic planning is found to encourage motivation and creativity, while unrealistic planning is inhibiting.

Analysis

Analysis is the decomposition of complex systems into elements and their interrelationships, identifying essential distinctions, and discarding accidental distinctions. The activities of analysis include identification, definition, and structuring with the purpose of acquiring information about a subject that can be transformed into knowledge. Analytic methods are useful in all stages of software design, from requirements gathering to evaluating designs and technologies to implementation.

Formulating problems clearly and unambiguously, via analysis of an application domain, helps avoid many expensive design and implementation errors. Careful analysis and formulation of problems are two of the most important and effective tools a software architect has. All design methodologies have some analysis aspect. However, I find that many modern design methodologies tend to blur the distinction between analysis and design. Many object-oriented methodologies promote a seamless development concept where the problem or application domain is continuously transformed into a solution, for example, Object Modeling Technique (OMT). In practice, the analysis is rarely done or is not done adequately.

Structured analyses in software, such as the techniques of Gane and Sarson, Yourdon, DeMarco, Ward and Mellor, and the Structured Systems Analysis and Design Methodology (SSADM), are methods for formulating and structuring the problem. Structured analysis is a process where the problem is formulated in terms of data flows, as represented in data flow diagrams (DFDs) and in system state transitions as represented in state transition diagrams. These models emphasize a hierarchical structuring of the functions of a system.

Similarly, object-oriented analysis, such as the techniques of Jacobson, Booch, Rumbaugh (OMT), and Yourdon and Coad, are techniques for structuring the problem domain in terms of objects, their interrelationships, and their class hierarchies. Whereas structured analysis emphasizes a functional hierarchy, object orientation emphasizes a data hierarchy.

All systems have weak areas. In established engineering disciplines, weak-spot analysis is performed to discover weak spots in a design. Similarly, in software architecture we can perform weak-spot analysis on a design by evaluating a design against known metamodels. For example, an application user interface design may be evaluated against the arch/slinky metamodel to determine its weaknesses (see Chapter 11). After gaining knowledge about the weakness of a particular design, the architect may make revisions to the design. Weaknesses that are discovered may not be relevant to a given application or system, especially if the weakness doesn't negatively affect the known quality attribute requirements.

Analysis aids in the search for solutions by decomposing a problem into individual, more manageable subproblems. When a problem seems difficult, sometimes a new formulation of the problem may prove to be a better place to start. Most software design problems are the result of a lack of understanding of the problem being solved.

Analysis is the technique whereby we create definitions and identify predicable relations between defined things. A problem domain model will typically consist of definitions or classes (universals) of objects or functions and their relations.

Abstraction

Through abstraction, we can infer more general and comprehensive relationships among the elements of our problem. Abstraction reduces the complexity of a problem while emphasizing the essential characteristics of it and aids in the discovery of solutions. Abstractions are not always invented; sometimes they are discovered by using existing abstraction models and attempting to fit the problem into them.

This is an example of predication: A statement is created about the problem abstraction and an existing model such as "problem A (new) is a form of problem B (existing)." An otherwise seemingly novel problem may turn out to be a variation of an existing problem to which some known solutions already exist. By formulating problem A in terms of problem B, the architect then only needs to find suitable abstractions for the remaining part of problem A. A problem can have many abstractions, and, using a discursive approach, the architect can discover several suitable abstractions and apply many existing problem models. Metamodels or reference models are examples of such reusable abstractions.

Analysis aids in the discovery and evaluation of abstractions. Not all analysis results in abstractions, but most abstractions are discovered via analysis.

Synthesis

Synthesis is the combining of individual elements or parts to produce a new effect. It is the integration of solutions to subproblems and the evaluation of the resulting system. When we decompose a problem via analysis into subproblems and discover solutions to those subproblems, there is still the risk that synthesizing those solutions will not solve the larger problem entirely or, worse, the solutions will be incompatible. Existing abstraction models may also be synthesized to form larger, more specialized abstractions. Synthesis is not only applied to the models of software architecture, it is also applied to the design methods.

General Heuristics

In this section, we look at some heuristic design methods. Heuristics are techniques that are characterized as the searching for suitable solutions. These methods apply to many design tasks: ·

- Persistent questions
- Negation
- Forward steps
- Backward steps
- Factorization
- Systematic variation
- Division of labor and collaboration

The Method of Persistent Questions

This method is useful when applying any systematic procedure such as requirements engineering (systems analysis), architectural design, and architectural evaluation. Requirements are almost never complete or at the right level of abstraction and the architect must help the acquirer to discover the essential requirements of the application they are envisioning during the analysis of the requirements. Persistent questioning stimulates ideas and intuition and helps to eliminate assumptions and preconceived notions. The method of persistent questions is a tool that the architect may use when analyzing the problem to discover useful abstractions, as well as a tool for evaluating solutions. An architect or architecture team may even keep a database of standard sets of questions for various purposes. Such a database of questions helps extend the memory of the architect and transfer useful design methods and knowledge to others. Asking questions is considered one of the most important methodological tools, and the technique is found in many existing product development methodologies.

This method is fundamental to the discursive method, and it seems so obvious that we may not even realize we're using it. This makes it easy to overlook, even though it is the cornerstone of any analytic method.

The Method of Negation

The method of negation is also known as the *method of deliberate negation* and *systematic doubting*. The method starts with a known solution that is divided into statements (truthful predicable relations) about its individual parts. These statements are then negated. For example, the statement "class A is a class B" is negated. This deliberate inversion of the solution, that class A is not a class B, may lead to new solution possibilities. Consider another example of a system that uses a two-phase commit for transactions. By negating this statement and assuming that the system won't use a two-phase commit approach, we are forced to consider the consequences or some alternatives.

An alternative may be the use of asynchronous message passing and the use of compensating transactions. A variation of this method is the deliberate omission of elements, such as removing the notion of class A altogether and seeing what other solution possibilities arise. This may lead to nothing, but the potential of discovering a different solution is improved.

The Method of Forward Steps

The method of forward steps is also known as *the method of divergent thought*. It starts with a first solution attempt and proceeds to follow as many solution paths as possible, yielding other solutions. The method of forward steps is not necessarily systematic and usually starts with an unsystematic divergence of ideas. For example, the first solution attempt at an application problem may be to apply a client/server architectural style. By applying forward steps, the architect follows several paths such as browser-based client, Web client with browser plug-ins, fat client with embedded browser, or fat client that speaks HTTP with the server.

This method can be applied to any model at any level of abstraction and is typically followed recursively as far down a path as possible. For example, starting with the fat client that speaks HTTP solution, additional application of the method of forward steps could yield solutions like fat client with local storage, fat client with server-side storage only, and fat client with heterogeneous local and server-side storage. The process can follow any path. This is a good way to brainstorm over an object model of the application domain as well as the choice of technologies in the solution domain. This method is similar to the method of systematic variation.

The Method of Backward Steps

The method of backward steps is also known as the method of convergent thought. In this approach, the architect starts with a goal in mind rather than the initial problem. This technique is most useful for setting up an engineering design process for a product and a product development plan after the architecture has been determined. Starting with the final objective of the development effort, all (or a reasonable subset of) possible paths that could have led up to the objective are retraced. This method is useful not only in preparing an engineering process but also for organizing an engineering department around the architecture of a product (known as Conway's law).

The Method of Factorization

This method is the basis of the refactoring technique, popular among software engineers when reworking existing source code to make it more readable, manageable, maintainable, and reusable. The method involves breaking a complex system into less complex elements or *factors*. Factorization is a type of analysis method. In architecting, this technique is used to find the essential problems being solved (for example, factoring the objectives into subobjectives). Just as in mathematics, the factorization may not be obvious and requires some insight, skill, and lots of practice. In algebra, you may factor an equation by introducing zero as a factor. Similarly, finding that one of the factors of a publishing system is a file-versioning repository may not be obvious (although the experienced architect may see the factorization immediately). Another example is taking what may appear to be an indivisible component and finding a way to divide it into two components and an interface.

The Method of Systematic Variation

The method of systematic variation of solutions may have originated with Leonardo DaVinci. DaVinci kept meticulous notes on his ideas and inventions and applied this technique to derive multiple variations of ideas, each varying only by a single characteristic from the former. The method starts with a generalized classification structure, such as a class hierarchy, that represents the various problem characteristics and possible solutions. By systematically varying a single characteristic, the architect may discover more optimized solutions. The approach yields a *solution field*. Evaluation techniques can be applied to each solution to determine its suitability.

Division of Labor and Collaboration

The study of human factors has found that implementing large and complex tasks requires a division of labor. The more specialized the task the more important the division of labor. Software development tasks are commonly based not only on functional areas of the system but also on the technology used. We typically have user interface designers, user interface engineers, middle-tier engineers, back-end or database engineers, test engineers, configuration management engineers, and so on. A complex application or system also benefits from a division of labor with respect to the architecture. For example, it seems natural to separate the tasks of requirements engineering, functional specification, interaction design, and structural design, all of which are in the scope of architecture. However, whenever there is a division of labor there is an information exchange problem. Systematic methods and the creation of models can help overcome this problem.

Summary

Design is a creative problem-solving activity that involves finding or creating solutions to problems given a set of obstacles. Architecting typically starts by formulating the problems that need to be solved. The three Aristotelian operations of reason can be used in formulating problems and rationalizing about their solutions. The operations of definition and predication are used to gain understanding of the problem. Definition is the creation of universals and predication is the creation of Boolean statements about the universals. The last operation of reason, inference, is used to discover new truths about universals and their relationships. Inferences are arguments, which are ordered statements and a conclusion. The conclusion is also a Boolean statement.

There are three principles of architecture: *utilitas* (function), *firmitas* (fabrication, quality), and *venustas* (form). These principles form an interdependent triad. The function of an application is a different, though related, concept than the functional specification of an application. The intended function of the application is expressed as problems and, through the application of analysis, is divided into more manageable, less complex subproblems. Analysis involves the rational operations of definition and predication. The first phase of design, product planning, is to transform these subproblems into a functional specification. The functional specification or behavioral model of an application is one aspect of the architectural design that is created in order to better understand the intended function or need of the application. During conceptual design the functional design and structural design are elaborated. Functional design corresponds to the externally facing design or interaction design of an application or system. This is the aspect of the architecture that is perceived by users. Interaction design focuses on the creation of a virtuality that reduces cognitive friction. Structural design is concerned with the internal physical design of the software itself as embodied in source code and other electronic artifacts that are compiled into an executable system. Heuristic design methods, such as the method of forward steps and the method of systematic variation, are applied to produce a solution field consisting of several candidate structural architectural designs called solution principles, or concepts. Conceptual design artifacts are not purely logical models; they also specify working principles, which may include the identification of technologies or design patterns that can be used to solve the problem. The methods applied during conceptual design involve the application of inference to discover new solutions and to evaluate existing solutions.

The architecture design or design candidates are evaluated, disposed of, or further refined during embodiment design. The same rational operations and design methods are applied but now the focus is more on elaboration of the solution and less on formulation of the problem. Detail design involves the specification of layout and in software is the activity of implementation and testing.

In many software development methodologies, a distinction between the conceptual phase and the embodiment phase is not explicit and is usually referred to simply as design, as in analysis and design. Many methodologies, such as OMT, promote a seamless development model where the models of analysis and design are combined into one evolving model that starts as a formulation of the problem and evolves into a solution model.

In Chapter 5, we take a detailed look at the concept of complexity and modularity and how it affects the architect's understanding of the problem and solution. The modular operators are presented, which are design operations that can be applied, together with the design methods. In Chapters 6 and 7, we see how design decisions are represented as models and architectural views of a system.

CHAPTER 5

Complexity and Modularity

Complexity is one of the primary problems that we attempt to address with software development tools and methods. Complexity, if not managed, can cause a product to be low quality or delivered late, over budget, or the project could be cancelled completely. There are no easy solutions to removing complexity and improving productivity and quality. The best we can do is reduce or manage complexity. Modularity is a fundamental principle for achieving simplicity of design and development effort and thus reducing and managing complexity.

The first section of this chapter discusses complexity: what it is and how it affects the development effort, the maintainability of a system, and other aspects of the software and development process. I introduce a tool called the design structure matrix (DSM), which is a way of representing elements (such as software components or design tasks) and their relationships (the dependencies between components and design tasks). A DSM allows us to visualize the inner structure of a system in a way that is much different from the usual box and arrow diagrams such as Unified Modeling Language (UML) package diagrams. The following section discusses modularity and how it helps manage complexity. In this section, we learn that the DSM not only helps the software architect understand the complexity of a system but serves as a tool to help decompose the system. By visualizing the system as a matrix of dependencies, the software architect can hunt for hidden complexities, factor the system where there are natural loose couplings between elements, and introduce new elements (for example, interfaces) to reduce dependencies in order to better decompose or modularize a system.

Complexity in designs and processes can be measured by the interconnectedness of things. In order for a system or process to exhibit complexity, it must be composed of multiple parts that are interconnected. We refer to these connections as dependencies. If some task or design element B is dependent upon A, then performing task A (or modifying design A) must occur before performing task B (or modifying design B). In the design context, if we have already created design elements A and B and we change A, then we must change B. If A and B are interdependent, then changing A and B forms a loop and making a change in one requires making a change in the other.

Complex systems can be represented as a graph where the nodes correspond to design elements or tasks and the directed edges correspond to dependencies. An example of such a graph is depicted in Figure 5.1, where elements A and B are interdependent.

An arrow from A to B indicates that B is dependent upon A or B *follows* A (that is, design information flows from A to B). A given system graph of N nodes can have at most N squared minus N arrows (we don't count arrows that originate and terminate on the same node such as one may find in a state diagram). As N increases, the number of potential dependencies increases exponentially. In a simple system—say, three nodes—there are at most 6 possible dependencies (3 squared minus 3). In a system of four nodes, there are potentially 12 possible dependencies.

Graphs appear in most of our modeling diagrams. A class hierarchy is a type of graph with dependencies defined as generalization/specialization relations. A classification scheme is one way to manage complexity because you cannot have a circular dependency in terms of generalization relations. Given N classes, you will have a potential maximum number of inheritance relations of N minus 1. For example, with three classes you will have a maximum of two relations and with four classes you will have three relations.

Introducing other types of relations between classes (such as *uses* or *aggregation*) potentially increases the number of dependencies. If there are multiple types of relations possible simultaneously, say, three types of nonmutually exclusive relations, then we have potentially three N nodes in our dependency graph (or N nodes where each node is a vector of three elements).

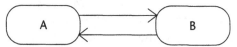

Figure 5.1 Interdependency between tasks A and B.

The directed graph (digraph) is a convenient diagram, as long as the number of nodes doesn't exceed our ability to view the diagram and analyze it visually. In the UML we might show the module view of the system using package icons and dependency relations between the packages. If the model involves several packages and many dependencies, the diagram becomes difficult to analyze visually.

Another way to represent a digraph is by using an N by N matrix where the same elements appear as rows and columns in the same order. In this model the diagonal of the matrix is ignored. It represents the same information as a graph, but in a more compact and machine-readable format. This matrix is called a *structure matrix* or a *dependency structure matrix*. Figure 5.2 contains four simple examples of structure matrices. There are two applications of the structure matrix used in this book: the *design structure matrix* (DSM) and the *task structure matrix* (TSM).

The DSM is a powerful tool because you can model the internal structure of many kinds of systems. You can use DSMs to model software architectures, organizations, and business processes. We will use DSMs throughout the book to represent the modular view of an application's software architecture and its corresponding design tasks (process). In Figure 5.2 (a), Element B is dependent upon Element A. In Figure 5.2(b), Element A is dependent upon Element B. In Figure 5.2(c), there are no dependencies between A or B. In Figure 5.2 (d), both Element A and Element B are dependent upon each other; that is, they are interdependent. Figure 5.1 and Figure 5.2(d) represent the same system.

The general rule for reading DSMs is that the element corresponding to a given row is dependent upon (or consumes information from) the elements in the columns for which an X or any other marker appears in the corresponding cell. You can also read it downward, as the element corresponding to a given column provides for the elements in the rows for which an X or any other marker appears in the corresponding cell. The order of elements in the rows must correspond identically to the order of the same elements in the columns. Other than that restriction, the actual position or order of elements is arbitrary. By reordering the columns (and the corresponding rows), the software architect can visualize the architecture in different ways to possibly learn about better ways to organize the system.

An important property of structure matrices is that a design structure matrix (the architecture) is equivalent to a process or task structure matrix that represents the order in which elements are designed in detail (and implemented). We saw this in Figure 5.2 with design elements A and B and their associated tasks. The relationship between the architecture of a system and the process in which it is implemented form a feedback loop so that changing one requires potentially changing the other to restore the balance. Such a system is called a *complex adaptive system*.

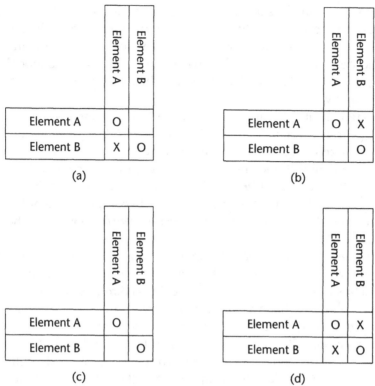

Figure 5.2 Interpreting DSMs.

A system's architecture is usually associated with the modules of the system. The boundaries between modules are the design rules. These design rules establish which dependencies are factored into a separate set of design decisions that are made before any other design decision is made. If two groups of design elements have a single interdependency—such as the format of a data file—then this data format design task can be made earlier in the design process rather than later. Eventually the design rule (or a set of design rules) that separates two modules can become fixed and future development can occur in parallel. An interface is therefore a first line of defense that an architect has in preserving the technical integrity of the system. This fixed set of design rules is called an *interface*, and they may be standardized. Thus, future modifications can be made to modules without affecting other modules. It also becomes possible to replace modules with different implementations or even to reuse modules in different contexts where the interface is the same.

Complexity

In this section, we will define complexity, then look at how complexity affects the system and its models, as well as how to identify and measure it. We will learn that complexity depends on the context of a description. From one view a system may appear simple and from another it may appear complex. This will help you recognize when a design is more complex than another or where the inherent complexity lies within a given design so that we may organize our designs better.

Complexity arises in many aspects of software design, including:

- Requirements
- User interface
- "High-level" design
- "Low-level" design
- Source code

Understanding Complexity

We typically consider a software design *complex* if it requires a long description. This does not necessarily mean a textual description, but rather a more abstract concept such as describing the relationships between the structural elements within the system. The greater the number of dependencies between elements, the longer the description. It is common to add extra layers of objects in a system design in order to achieve certain quality attributes. In order to improve modifiability, we need to isolate changes to as few modules as possible, ideally one. To improve adaptability, we introduce abstractions that allow modules to be substituted for other modules such as deployment time. Introducing more elements can increase the number of dependencies between elements. However, with careful design and use of principles such as abstraction (see Chapter 4), more elements can be added to a design while simultaneously reducing the ratio of dependencies to elements. I say ratio because the overall number of dependencies may increase, but each individual element tends to become less coupled with the next.

As the complexity of the architecture increases, the complexity of the individual modules can decrease. Hierarchically decomposing a system allows us to distribute complexity across multiple components by dividing the labor of design and freeing the designers of individual modules to make more design decisions with fewer interdependencies.

We can also reduce the apparent complexity of a system design by our choice of design language, which can be words, pictures, or a combination of both. If we can reduce the length of a description without changing the meaning of the thing we are describing, then we have reduced the apparent complexity of the system. In natural language we reduce the complexity of concepts by introducing standard terminology. Whole disciplines revolve around the creation of terms that express concepts and the relationships between concepts. A single word or name can contain a great deal of information. The same is true for design patterns. A design pattern is a compact description of a common design problem-context-solution triple. Using patterns in describing designs helps reduce the apparent complexity of the design because it shortens the description of the design. This relies upon the assumption that all readers of the design know the patterns. However, over time the industry learns the new language and any two developers can say the word "singleton" and understand what is being communicated. The reduction of apparent complexity is also called improving the comprehensibility of a system. While the internal structure of the system may still be complex in terms of interactions, it is easier for a human to comprehend the system.

Abstraction is the technique by which we introduce new concepts or names. A name is an abstraction that can be used to describe many instances of the concept to which it is associated. In programming languages, names allow us to attach complex structures or classes to a simple character string (the identifier). It is such a natural part of programming today that we take it for granted. Well-chosen abstractions improve the comprehensibility of a system.

Granularity and Context

Murray Gell-Mann says, "When defining complexity it is always necessary to specify a level of detail up to which the system is described, with finer details being ignored. Physicists call that 'course graining.'" (Gell-Mann, 1994) Dr. Gell-Mann uses the analogy of a grainy photograph that must be enlarged in order to see some details. At some point the observer can see the individual photographic grains. At this level only a few dots can be seen from which an image is to be conveyed. At this level of detail, or *granularity*, it is difficult for the observer to understand what the picture is.

This also applies to UML diagrams, since, like any model, they necessarily leave out some details of the design being described. A component diagram leaves out details of individual objects and their attributes, methods, and interactions with other objects. A sequence diagram models object interaction but leaves out details of object attributes and some methods. Only the methods necessary to convey the interaction are shown. This expresses how a set of objects communicates but it does not show relationships with other objects that are unrelated to the given scenario. Trying to understand the architecture of a system by looking at low-level design models and source code is like looking at the photographic grains and trying to determine what the picture is.

Let's see how context can change the apparent complexity of a system. Figure 5.3(a) through (e) shows a series of DSMs. First look at each of the five matrices and put them in order from least complex to most complex.

The answer to the previous question depends on the context of the question. In other words, what are we describing? If we are just describing the matrices themselves without interpreting the elements, then the least complex matrices are Figure 5.3(a) and 5.3(e) because they are the simplest to describe. Figure 5.3(a) is fully connected and Figure 5.3(e) is fully disconnected. I don't have to say any more to describe them. If I rearrange the rows and columns, the matrices still appear visually the same.

Figure 5.3(b) requires a longer description. In its current form I can describe it as fully connected underneath the diagonal. But this description relies on the order of the rows (and columns). If I were to reorder A and B, then the X would appear above the diagonal so my generic description is incorrect. I must describe the system in terms of its individual elements and their relationships, and this description will be longer than the description for the systems depicted in Figure 5.3(a) and (e).

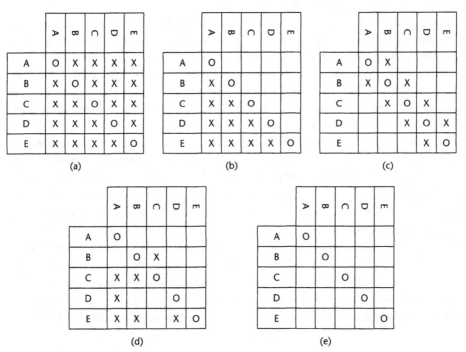

Figure 5.3   Varying degrees of complexity.

I could shorten the description to describe the system as a layered architecture. I would assign each layer an ordinal and specify that it is a particular variation of layers in which a higher-level layer depends on every lower-level layer but lower-level layers do not depend on higher-level layers. The description is more complex than the simplest descriptions, but is simpler than our first description that required describing all 20 relationships.

Figure 5.3(c) contains only eight relationships, so its description is shorter than Figure 5.3(b). However, if we take the same approach to describing the system in terms of patterns, we can reduce the overall complexity of the description (improve the comprehensibility of the description) by describing the system as a layered architecture. In a classic layered architecture, only adjacent layers share a dependency. Thus, elements A through E can be called layers 0 through 4, respectively, and that is sufficient to describe their interactions.

Basically, this new way of describing the system design is about the same complexity as the description for the design represented in Figure 5.3(b). Figure 5.3(d) contains seven relationships, so it should require a shorter description than Figure 5.3(b) and 5.3(c) without using patterns. However, there is no obvious pattern to Figure 5.3(d) because the relationships are somewhat random, so we cannot substitute a portion of the description for a pattern. Therefore, Figure 5.3(d) requires the longest description when using patterns to describe Figure 5.3(b) and 5.3(c).

Without patterns, we would have had to describe each system in terms of each relationship. Figure 5.3, having the most relationships, would require the longest description. The context of the last discussion was in describing the system and its relationships. If we change the context, the complexity of each system changes. If we view each system in terms of the design effort to create it, we see that the more connections there are between elements, the more design dependencies there are, and hence the more complex the design process.

The complexity of the design effort is confounded by interdependencies. In Figure 5.3(a), every element is interdependent. Making a single design change in one element ripples throughout every other element, which potentially causes a feedback loop as changes to the other elements trigger yet more changes. The system in Figure 5.3(e) is the simplest to design because there are no dependencies whatsoever.

We still have not taken into account information about specific relationship types. The prior discussion assumed that the relationships were homogeneous. We were describing the interconnectedness of things but not the specifics of the connections. Another discussion can take place in the context of the types of relationships. If each relationship represents a different interface between design elements, then the more numerous the relationship types, the more complex the system and hence the longer the description. Again, patterns are useful because they can help reduce the description.

We can change the context of our description based on the granularity of the information. If we zoom out from the matrix, there may be additional elements that influence the visible elements. Let's assume that the system depicted in Figure 5.3(e) represents the development of five completely unrelated operating systems by five noncooperating vendors. The design decisions of one vendor do not affect those of another. But there is a hidden element. Each of these vendors is dependent upon a certain vendor's hardware architecture. Let's assume that our five vendors are producing operating systems (OSs) for the same hardware platform. Then each OS vendor is dependent upon design decisions made by the hardware designers. This relationship is depicted in Figure 5.4.

What would happen if one OS vendor were working closely with the hardware designer? Suppose the vendor of OS A partners with the vendor of Hardware X so that design decisions made for OS A may influence Hardware X. A design decision for OS A could cause a design change to Hardware X, which in turn may cause design changes to all the other dependent OS designs, as depicted in Figure 5.5.

	Hardware X	OS A	OS B	OS C	OS D	OS E
Hardware X	O					
OS A	X	O				
OS B	X		O			
OS C	X			O		
OS D	X				O	
OS E	X					O

Figure 5.4 Operating systems and hardware DSM.

	Hardware X	OS A	OS B	OS C	OS D	OS E
Hardware X	O←X					
OS A	X	O				
OS B	X		O			
OS C	X			O		
OS D	X				O	
OS E	X					O

Figure 5.5   Operating systems and hardware DSM with added dependency.

We can also change the context of what we are describing by zooming in to see more details. Figure 5.6(a) represents a system in which elements B, C, D, and E all depend on element A. If we expand element A in Figure 5.6(b) to see its internal organization, we see that it is composed of four elements that have a fairly complex relationship. We also gain more information about exactly what elements B through E are dependent upon. B and C depend on the same element, but D and E depend on separate elements. Thus, our description of the system is a little more complex than in Figure 5.6(a), in which B through E are simply shown as being dependent on A. Figure 5.6(b) reveals that not all design decisions made for A affect the other elements.

As we have seen, the meaning of the complexity of a system can vary, depending on the context in which we are viewing the system as well as what we are describing about the system. In order to really understand our system, we have to represent it at a meaningful granularity. Too granular of a view may make the system appear overly simple. Too fine-grained of a view and we have too much information. Part of managing the complexity is in our ability to improve the comprehensibility of a system. While this doesn't actually reduce the system's complexity, it improves our ability to understand and reason about the system.

(a)

	A	B	C	D	E
A	O				
B	X	O			
C	X		O		
D	X			O	
E	X				O

(b)

	A.1	A.2	A.3	A.4	B	C	D	E
A.1	O	X						
A.2	X	O	X					
A.3	X		O					
A.4			X	O				
B		X			O			
C		X				O		
D			X				O	
E				X				O

Figure 5.6 Changing the granularity of the model.

Modularity

In the previous section, I hinted at how modularity can help us manage complexity. We cannot eliminate complexity in a given design, but we can manage it by isolating highly interdependent elements of a design and working around them. It may be possible to transform a design into a simpler design. Modularity is the primary principle by which we manage complexity of designs and design tasks by identifying and isolating those connections or relationships that are the most complex.

Modules can be thought of as being composed of private hidden information and publicly or *exported* visible information. Modules *import* other module's exported information. The concepts of coupling and cohesion are important to understanding how to create a modular architecture and to understand the complexities of systems. Modules can be thought of as being composed of design elements. A design element is both a set of design decisions within a system (as represented by a DSM) and a corresponding set of design tasks (as represented by an equivalent TSM). Design rules are publicly visible design elements. A system's decomposition can be represented as a hierarchy of design rules and hidden design elements. The modular operators are operations that are applied to a design to transform it into another design. The application of modular operators can either introduce new design rules or remove them. These operators can help us achieve a simpler design.

Architecture and Modules

There are two related design aspects or views of a system. The first is the static design-level view of the system's hierarchical structure in terms of modules. A module is usually associated with a packaging of source code or its binary representation. The other view is the runtime component view of the application. A component, in the context of this book, is a runtime entity, such as an object or an assembly of objects. A module is a discrete package of software, for example, a Java library or a relational database, and executable and associated runtime libraries. A component is a runtime entity like an executing database server or a Web server. There may be multiple instances of the same type of component, for example, two database servers (one performing the role of replication server) or a cluster of Web servers, all of which are identical copies of the software that are compiled into a single module. A component is not necessarily an instance of a module in the same way that an object is an instance of a class. A component is potentially a hierarchy of components, where each subcomponent may exist in separate modules. A module may contain the software for one or more components. The term component is often used in other literature to refer to a module. In order to keep the discussion clear in this book I will typically use the term *component* to refer to a runtime entity and *module* to refer to a design time entity.

Importing and Exporting

A module has *exports* and *imports*. A module can only import what another module exports. These imports and exports can be thought of as abstract interfaces, but not interfaces in the procedural sense. The interface to a module can be anything such as a data format (for example, an XML DTD), a procedural interface (for example, a set of public Java classes and interfaces in a single package), or a middleware-dependent interface (for example, a message queue and a standard message format). Whatever a module exports becomes visible to all outside modules.

In Java, a module can be written as a package and the exports are all publicly visible elements such as public classes and their public members, interfaces, and public static classes and members. Another module written in Java imports the publicly visible elements (the interface to) another Java module by using the import keyword. One Java module does not have to import everything from another Java module; it can selectively import a subset of the publicly visible elements of a given package.

I use the term *interface* in the abstract sense, to mean something that is imported or exported and not to mean a specific interface such as a Java interface definition. Thus, the interface of a module written in Java includes all of the public interfaces in the package that make up the module.

Coupling and Cohesion

Coupling refers to the connection between two modules. *Loose coupling* refers to two modules that have relatively few interdependencies, where the internal implementation of a module doesn't affect its interface. We achieve loose coupling by encapsulation, that is, by hiding as many design elements as possible and only exporting the essential elements. In Figure 5.7, we see an example of loose coupling between modules A and B (the heavy squares). A.1 is the export of A in this example and B imports this element.

Cohesion refers to the density of dependencies within a module. In Figure 5.7, we see that within the modules A and B are many dependencies and interdependencies. However B is unaware of the internal complexity of module A. The elements A.2, A.3, and A.4 can change without affecting module B. If the elements within a module were relatively or entirely independent, we would say that the module exhibits low internal cohesion and may not really be a good fit for a module. In this case we may split the elements into distinct modules.

	A.1	A.2	A.3	A.4	B1	B2	B3	B4
A.1	O							
A.2	X	O	X					
A.3	X	X	O					
A.4			X	O				
B1	X				O		X	X
B2					X	O	X	
B3	X					X	O	
B4					X		X	O

(b)

Figure 5.7 Coupling and cohesion.

Design Elements and Design Rules

Typically, we take a first pass at decomposing or *splitting* our system into several subsystems. First we perform a functional decomposition of the system. A *horizontal* split separates the system into logical blocks of functions or use cases. Any given application use case is associated with a single subsystem.

For example, the login use case is a function of an authentication subsystem. A *vertical* split separates application use cases from lower-level common use cases or functions that are shared among application-level use cases. Data access is a common shared component. This first pass at identifying subsystems helps us begin our search for the modules of the system. Each block itself should be further decomposed to some set of finer-grained design elements, so that the dependencies between these design elements can be analyzed. We use a DSM to model this decomposition. Eventually, we have a DSM that contains atomic design elements.

An example of an atomic design element is the schema for some entity; for example, a database schema for an entity or an XML DTD for some XML representation of an entity. A dependency, as depicted in the DSM, means that changing the design of one element will require a change in the design of the dependent element. Any element that relies on data that conforms to the entity schema, for example, must be modified if the schema changes. We are all familiar with these kinds of dependencies. However, we can group changes into roughly two categories: those changes that affect the semantics of the design element and those that affect the implementation only.

By identifying these types of changes, we can start to produce a design that becomes more resistant to implementation-only changes. In database design, we commonly use views and stored procedures to hide the implementation details of the entity tables. This allows the table definitions to physically change without requiring the exported parts of the view or stored procedure to change; hence, any design element depending on the view or stored procedure does not need to change. Of course, this assumes that the table definition change doesn't change the semantics of the entity. If the semantics change (data fields are removed and new ones are added, for example), you may need to change to the exported parts of views and stored procedures.

This rough identification of change types doesn't tell the whole story. It is possible to augment the semantics of a design element without affecting dependent elements (this is the hallmark of object-orientation and interfaces). It is even possible to restrict the semantics and still not need to change dependent elements. It is also possible that a mere implementation change, which doesn't change semantics, still requires changes to the exported information and hence dependent elements.

Our initial view of a system is of a single monolithic system with many interdependent design tasks. When we start to modularize our design, we select some place to divide the system. We group one set of design elements into one potential module and the other set of design elements into the other potential module.

This grouping doesn't make our system modular. In order to do that, we need to select those design elements that form the strongest dependencies between our potential modules and establish their design first. These elements become the interface between the two modules. These design elements are called *design rules* (Baldwin, 2000). We can visually group these elements into their own module in the DSM. In Figure 5.8(a), we see our initial view of the system. The two potential modules are outlined in the gray squares in the upper left and lower right, with a third overlapping square identifying the interdependencies.

Analysis revealed a need for two independent modules to satisfy some set of functional and nonfunctional requirements (perhaps we want the block of functionality E, G, and H to be pluggable to support modifiability). For example, the upper block may represent the user interface portion of the system and the lower right block may be the application business logic portion. By making B, C, and F into design rules we have the structure represented in Figure 5.8(b).

Notice, however, that the design rules are still dependent on D. In order to have a true set of design rules, there should be no X marks in any of the white cells. In order to solve this problem we split D into two design elements, based on the dependency. These new elements are D1 and D2. D1 is moved into the design rules and D2 remains with A. This new system decomposition is depicted in Figure 5.8(c). This is our canonical architecture form. The gray band down the left is our design rules, which are those interfaces or module connections that are established as the architecture, and the remaining independent blocks, which go down the diagonal of the matrix, are our modules.

In Figure 5.9 we see a possible interpretation of the same DSM. The design rules (the architecture) include things like the shared data representation (the format of business object data) and the interaction style (whether application logic functions are synchronous or asynchronous). Our original design element D could have been the data format. The separation of D into D1 and D2 could have been the establishment of a common shared data format between the User Interface (UI) and Application Logic (D1) and the data representation that the UI rendering element needs (D2). By splitting them apart, the needs of the data-rendering code in the UI do not affect the application logic.

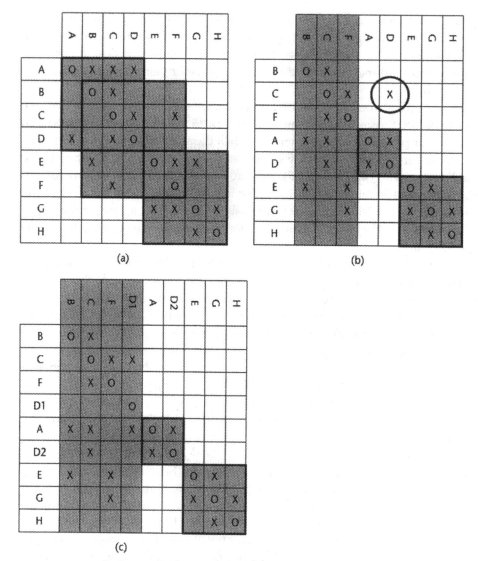

Figure 5.8 Analyzing a DSM for system modules.

Another way to view this model is through a UML package diagram (Figure 5.10[a]). The whole system is represented as a top-level package called the Global Design Rules with two independent modules:

- User Interface
- Application Logic

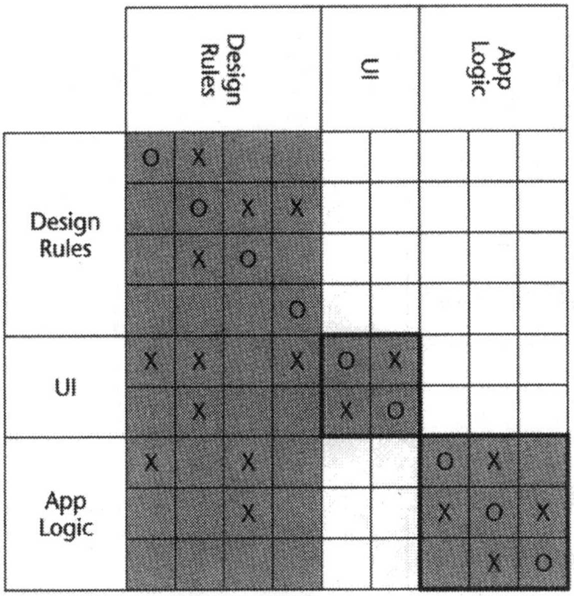

		Design Rules				UI		App Logic		
Design Rules		O	X							
			O	X	X					
			X	O						
					O					
UI		X	X		X	O	X			
			X			X	O			
App Logic		X		X				O	X	
				X				X	O	X
									X	O

Figure 5.9 A modular system.

The Global Design Rules package may not represent a physical module. For example, if the Global Design Rules are a set of data formats such as for a set of XML documents passed between the UI and Application Logic, then this package may exist as a set of DTDs, or it may exist only as a textual description or specification of the XML documents. The Global Design Rules may include physical artifacts like Java interfaces (for example, the Java Data Base Connectivity (JDBC) application program interface (API).

In Figure 5.10(b), we see the usual depiction of an architecture where the User Interface component is connected to the Application Logic component. Recall that the modular view is the design time view and that the component view is the runtime view. In the runtime view of Figure 5.10(b), the Global Design Rules are not instantiated as a component. Only the User Interface and Application Logic components are instantiated. The connecting element between them is not depicted as a separate component, although this is stated implicitly in the arrow icon. The connecting element depends on how the two components are physically linked. The connecting element may be the set of procedure calls (object methods) used to interact with the Application Logic component. It may also represent an XML file that is shared between two processes (in this case the User Interface is a client of some sort and the Application Logic is an application server that works asynchronously).

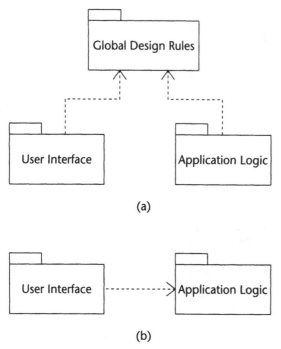

(a)

(b)

Figure 5.10 Depicting hierarchical structure.

In the latter example, the dependency arrow in Figure 5.10(b) may not be an accurate representation of this file-based client-server interaction. Another package may be needed to represent the shared data file or a combination of a file system and the shared data file. The file system and its API are an implicit third module that the other two modules depend on.

The interfaces between modules are the design rules. These design rules establish which dependencies are factored into a separate set of design decisions that are made before any other design decision is made. A dependency between two groups of elements indicates the order in which the design tasks must be done. All design decisions are subject to change so making the critical ones earlier reduces a lot of the risk associated with productivity and scheduling. Eventually the design rules that separate multiple modules can become fixed and future development can occur in parallel.

This fixed set of design rules may become a standardized interface, especially if the design rules are shared across vendors. Thus, future modifications can be made to modules without affecting other modules. It also becomes possible to replace modules with different implementations or even to reuse modules in different contexts where the interface is the same.

Task Structure Matrix

The design structure matrix maps to a task structure matrix. Once the DSM is stable, you can see the interdependencies between design tasks and therefore schedule the order in which design tasks are executed. In the simplest designs, the dependencies are simple and obvious, making a TSM unnecessary. In a relatively complex system the interdependencies between design tasks can be subtle. If you were to commence the design and implementation effort without creating a DSM and without analyzing it to establish the design rules, many seemingly parallel design tasks would affect design tasks that were thought to be complete.

In addition to identifying the interdependencies between design tasks, the TSM provides tracing information that is useful in analyzing changes in requirements. In Figure 5.11 we see a simplified TSM for a business application that contains two business objects. The hierarchical structure can be misleading. Although design (and implementation) changes to the UI elements do not affect the business objects and search object, it is possible that a design flaw or missing requirement could be discovered while designing a UI element that requires changes to the business objects.

In a system in which the requirements are not well understood, there may be hidden interdependencies. It is common that the product planners change the application requirements after seeing the user interface. Models of the system semantics such as use cases and object models may be too abstract for many people responsible for creating a list of requirements. The user interface is a good way to validate assumptions about requirements because people can see a tangible example of the system's behavior and information model. As we'll see later in the design process, this helps to reduce the risk of requirements changes by emphasizing the identification and structuring of the problem early in the development effort. A change in the requirements for business object 1 (element A) would potentially require redesigning elements C, D, E, and G. A change in the requirements for object 2 would affect fewer tasks. Thus business object 1 is a relatively high-risk design element and the design process should emphasize the evaluation of the requirements and design for this area.

Analyzing the design task structure helps us make judgments about which areas of the application to model, using intermediate models such as detailed object models and wire frame UI or even UI prototypes. The more complex the DSM, the more risk there is associated with requirements changes and design defects.

	A	B	C	D	E	F	G
A. Business Object 1	O						
B. Business Object 2		O					
C. Bus. Obj. Search	X	X	O				
D. UI Screen 1	X			O			
E. UI Screen 2	X		X		O		
F. UI Screen 3		X				O	
G. Email Notifier	X						O

Figure 5.11   A TSM for a business application.

Modular Operators

Modularity strictly enforces the invariance of the interfaces between software modules. The DSM helps us discover the modules and determine which design elements must be converted into design rules in order to produce stable interfaces. The six modular operators are:

- *Splitting* a design into two or more modules
- *Substituting* one design module for another
- *Augmenting* the system by adding a new module
- *Excluding* a module from the system
- *Inverting* a module to create new interfaces (design rules)
- *Porting* a module to another system

The modular operators are very similar to the design operators in Chapter 9. The modular operators affect the architecture from the point of view of static design elements, which I refer to as the *modular view*. The design operators are applied to the runtime view of the architecture, which I refer to as the *deployment view* (from the UML deployment diagram).

In some literature, the term *component view* is used to mean both the static and runtime views of the system. Sometimes the terms *component* and *component instance* are used. In this book we distinguish between the two views because they emphasize different, though overlapping, quality attributes. The two views provide a more complete view of the architecture than any one view by itself. Modifying one view potentially requires modifying the other. A simple decomposition of a business application into a client and a server may look the same in the modular and component views. In Figure 5.12 we see a UML component diagram that represents the relationship (a dependency) between a client module and a server module. In Figure 5.13 we see a UML deployment diagram that represents the relationship between multiple client component instances and a single server component instance.

Suppose that we apply the design operator called *replication* to the server component instance in order to improve the reliability of the system. We would then have a deployment diagram as shown in Figure 5.14. However, our modular view would need to change as well. We wouldn't introduce a second server module, since both server component instances are identical copies (although they may have different states). We would have to change the modular design to show a new module that implemented the replication design element as in Figure 5.15. The dependency between the client and server modules hasn't changed. The server module has a new dependency, which is the replication mechanism module.

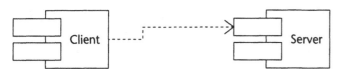

Figure 5.12   Client and server modules and their physical dependency.

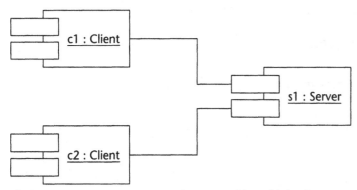

Figure 5.13   Server component instance with multiple client component instances.

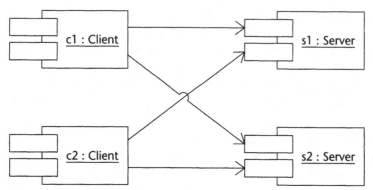

Figure 5.14   Multiple client and multiple server component instances.

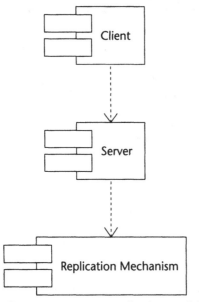

Figure 5.15   Server replication module.

Splitting

Splitting is the operation of separating a set of design tasks as represented in a DSM into multiple groups. These groups should exhibit high internal cohesion and low external coupling to begin with. The more interdependencies between two arbitrary modules, the more complex the design rules and hence the architecture. A DSM may need to be reorganized in order to discover the possible module candidates.

Consider the example in Figure 5.16, which is a shuffled version of Figure 5.8(a). Initially, this DSM does not visually suggest a module structure. We can manually rearrange the structure until some modules become more apparent. Sometimes the logical groupings of application functions help with this discovery, but for a complex application there may be many potential modules that are not obvious from the specification of the functions. We will see in Chapter 11 that using metamodels can also help us discover possible modules via standard functional decompositions.

Baldwin and Clark suggest that designers follow these four steps with respect to splitting (Baldwin, 2000):

1. Accumulate and organize knowledge about specific design task inter-dependencies.

2. Perceive that "the time is right" to make the design modular.

3. Formulate design rules specifying architecture, interfaces, and tests.

4. Enforce design rules for the duration of the design process.

Once a design has been split into two modules, the design becomes a hierarchy of modules. The design rules are the top-level design module and the two modules created from the split become independent modules.

	E	A	B	D	F	G	H	C
E	O	X				X	X	
A		O						
B		X	O					X
D				O				X
F	X				O	X		
G		X			X	O		
H	X					X	O	
C		X	X					O

Figure 5.16   A reorganized DSM hides the modular structure of the system.

There are also some algorithms that can be used to find those design tasks that exhibit higher interdependencies. These are especially useful when visual inspection is difficult due to the size of the DSM. The Massachusetts Institute of Technology (MIT) posts some DSM tools on their Web site (http://web.mit .edu/dsm/) including spreadsheets that make it easy to construct a DSM. These tools have built-in DSM partitioning algorithms to help rearrange the matrix into modules. Thus, we have the structure in Figure 5.8(c), which is also depicted graphically in Figure 5.10(a).

A module itself may split independently from other modules. This is how a hierarchical design is formed. The subhierarchy of each module is hidden from other modules at the same or higher levels. This means that the design of hierarchical modules can change as long as the design rules for that module do not change. The higher-level modules depend on those design rules. A hierarchical architecture takes a lot of the complexity out of understanding the design of a system and allows for modules to be designed by different teams. This is how we can achieve the division of labor and/or collaboration design method described in Chapter 4. An example of a design hierarchy is shown in Figure 5.17.

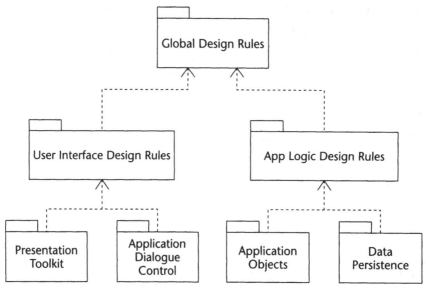

Figure 5.17   Hierarchy of modules.

Substituting

If two different designs serve the same function but with different quality attributes, then it is possible that one can be substituted for another. Substitution allows one module to be replaced by another module that adheres to the same design rules but which may be designed very differently internally. When the design rules are based on industry standards (such as JDBC and Structured Query Language [SQL]), substitution allows an organization to use one of potentially many commercially available modules (sometimes referred to as *commercial components*).

Substitution also allows an organization to create multiple competing designs for a given component to find the best design. For example, we may use the methods found in Chapter 4 to create multiple variations of a design. Without establishing design rules for a given module, such variation at the module level would not be feasible.

Splitting and substitution are complementary operations. Without splitting, it is not possible to substitute modules. An architecture team can explore many design operations by recursively splitting and substituting. However, if some design path turns out to be a dead end and the splitting at one level is negated, then any design efforts below that level are also negated. Splitting and substitution do not necessarily occur within a given project effort; they can be applied over many evolutions of a system's design and across vendors. We certainly see it in the evolution of standard APIs (those controlled by an industry standards body and those that are proprietary by "open"). If the API designers change the design rules, then they must either produce design rules that are backward compatible or else require everyone to modify their modules that are based on the previous design rules.

Augmenting and Excluding

Augmenting and *excluding* are complementary operations, as they both apply only to systems that have already been modularized. Augmenting means adding a module to a design, and excluding means leaving a module out of a design. Exclusion is common in product families where customers may choose which modules they want and which they don't. This operation is applied to systems with quality attribute requirements—such as adaptability and extensibility—or systems that need to exhibit a high degree of configurability. A *configurable* system is one in which an initial system can be deployed using a subset of available modules. A *reconfigurable* system is a configurable system that can later be changed by augmenting or excluding modules.

By designing a modular system, the company can initially exclude a set of modules and build a minimal though useful application. If the product sells, then the company can invest in the development of additional modules to augment the existing system. If the design rules for such a system are published openly, then there is room for competitive module designers to develop modules that are substitutions.

Augmentation does not always follow an initial architecture or product plan. When looking at the computer industry, we see that augmentation has led to many great innovations and applications of computers. The same happens with software as well. A database for a specific application is an example of augmentation applied to relational database technologies. Of course, relational databases and application servers are designed with the intention that they will be augmented. Commercial software vendors can also build open systems with augmentation in mind, relying on the inventiveness of other software developers to apply their technology in new application areas.

In one company that I worked for, this operation was applied to the Open Data Base Connectivity (ODBC) API. We developed an application that would effectively make any type of data source appear to be a relational database using the ODBC API as the access mechanism. For example, an XML source could appear as a set of relational tables accessed from any system that could use ODBC. Thus, we augmented just about any existing technology that already utilized ODBC, such as many Web tagging technologies that allowed data from an ODBC source to be embedded into HTML.

Inversion

Inversion is the operation of breaking encapsulation. A module has hidden information and a hidden implementation that allows it to change without affecting other modules in the architecture. Inversion takes this hidden information and makes it visible as new design rules. Inversion can occur when we are refactoring code, for example, to find reusable elements. A good module design will eventually lead to inversion as reusable generic mechanisms are discovered.

Inversion does not necessarily expose all implementation details. Inverting a Java module (for example, a package) may involve taking previously protected classes or methods and making them public or even creating new public interfaces as abstractions to these newly discovered reusable elements. The creation of interfaces not only introduces new design rules but also creates the potential for substitution.

Porting

Porting a module is the operation of using the module in a different system. This is a more general definition of the term, which typically means taking source code that compiles for one hardware platform and compiling it for a different hardware platform, sometimes requiring a change to the source code. Java boasts a "write one run anywhere" philosophy, which allows for a single-source system. Those of you who have spent much time writing in C and C++ can appreciate the ability of Java to run on just about any hardware platform.

The term in this context is more general. It simply means to use a module in a different system than the one it was originally designed for. In other words, the module is applied in a different system. Part of application product development is the discovery of such portable modules.

Summary

Complexity is probably the most influential force in the development of design methods and tools. It can overwhelm an application development effort, reducing the quality of the system and making it very expensive to develop. Modular design is one of the most effective ways to manage complexity. Using the design methods outlined in Chapter 4, you can design an application that exhibits less complexity and contains modules to manage existing complexity.

The design structure matrix (DSM) is a powerful representation model for learning about the complexities of a design (and even a problem space). The DSM allows the interdependencies between design elements to be analyzed. A DSM is isomorphic to a task structure matrix (TSM). A development organization can use the TSM to discover design tasks that may pose a higher risk to the development effort. The TSM serves as the basis for creating a development schedule or task chart. A TSM effectively is a work breakdown structure.

Our architectural design is transformed by the application of operators. The modular operators start with a DSM of design elements, but the quality of the resulting modular design depends partly on how the design elements themselves are selected. The creation of a design for a complex application requires several iterations and possibly many permutations. The design methods of Chapter 4 are precisely intended to help discover these design elements by allowing the architect to create several design variations. You may traverse down several paths, applying operators in different orders to different versions of a DSM before finding the best design. Our systematic design methods help manage this task of design discovery. The design principles in Chapter 9 are also used to find the right decomposition of a system into design elements as well as to assist in discovering the best places to split the design.

CHAPTER 6

Models and Knowledge Representation

Modeling is a fundamental activity of software architecting, and of software design in general. Models are abstractions that facilitate the design process by allowing us to focus on subsets of a problem and are one of the primary artifacts for capturing knowledge about a business problem and a technical solution. The model is the language of the architect and is a means of communication between all system stakeholders and the architect. Models assist in reasoning about the system's qualities and provide implementation guidelines for system developers. Models help us manage complexity by capturing details about aspects or views of a system while ignoring nonessential details. Models help people communicate effectively, and they can help bridge the gap between technical people (such as software architects) and nontechnical people (such as project sponsors).

In the previous chapter, we discussed concepts and principles of software design in general. In this chapter, I address what models are and how they are used in software design, the roles of models and the types of models, and how they interrelate. Models are used to represent knowledge in both the problem domain and the solution domain. Models compose views of a system. Views are aspects of a system that address a specific set of concerns of stakeholders. In the next chapter, I address the specification of models using modeling notations to produce architectural descriptions. The concepts in this chapter form a foundation for the rest of the book, as they will be explored in greater depth in the following chapters.

What Are Models?

A model of a software system is an abstract representation of knowledge about a system. A model is an approximation or idealization of selected aspects of a system such as its structure, behavior, operation, or other characteristics (IEEE, 1990). Models are realized as diagrams, formulae, textual descriptions, or combinations of these. Models may be grouped into views of the system, where each view represents some aspect (or dimension) of a system, such as its behavior, information, or performance. Views are composed of models that together represent some particular aspect of the system and address a specific set of concerns. For example, the information view of a system may include object models, entity-relationship models, data flow diagrams, and Unified Modeling Language (UML) activity diagrams. An architectural description is composed of views (see Chapter 12). A model focuses on a part of the system while excluding other knowledge. An object model of real world entities cannot contain every piece of knowledge of that entity. For example, a knowledge management system can contain limited representations of people's knowledge as objects or entities, but may not capture tacit or experiential knowledge. This is depicted in Figure 6.1. There are many possible representations of a system, some embedded in others, but all interrelated and interdependent and specified at some level of abstraction. I will use the term model in the context of this chapter to refer to representation models, unless otherwise noted.

The architect uses models to specify a particular aspect of a system. This allows the architect to focus on problem-solving activities on a particular set of qualities of the system, within a given set of concerns, at a particular level of abstraction, and within a given design phase.

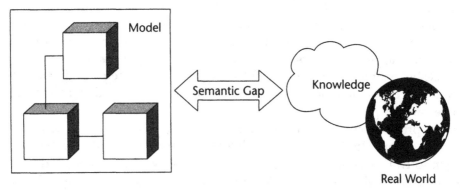

Figure 6.1   Models are representations of knowledge.

The term *semantic gap* refers to the discontinuity between a thing being modeled and the model's own representation of that thing. Semantic gaps occur in all parts of the architectural model and system implementation. For example, there is a semantic gap between the customer's list of requirements and a binary system built to satisfy those requirements. Consider an example such as improving the efficiency of publishing content in a content system so that there is a recognizable return on investment over the current manual process. The semantic gap is the distance of a mental leap between this abstract customer requirement and some implementation. It is not obvious that the object model, modular structure, or external behavior of a system satisfies this requirement. As systems become more complex, the form of the system is no longer identifiable from its function, or vice versa (that is, the semantic gap widens). The semantic gap can also refer to the discontinuity between the way the system works and the user's perception of how the system works. The semantic gap appears in mapping high-level programming language constructs to simple processor instruction sets. In this chapter, I refer to the former connotation, unless otherwise noted.

The larger the semantic gap between a model and reality, the harder it is to judge the correctness of the model. The greater the semantic distance between two models, the more difficult it is to trace concepts between them. This can hinder the design process. One way we can address the problem of the semantic gap is by using more models to help reduce the gap. Instead of writing code directly from a list of customer requirements (a huge semantic gap), we produce intermediate specifications that contain models such as system behavior and information processing. We can introduce even more models between these. You can think of the customer's or sponsor's requirements as one cliff and the binary system as another, and the dividing chasm is the semantic gap. Each set of models or specifications are pillars upon which we can span a bridge of understanding. The more pillars there are, the shorter each segment of bridge; hence, less effort is required to make the mental bridge between one side and the next.

The Language of Models

Models are specified in modeling languages or notations and textual descriptions. Modeling languages can range from expressive to informal. Expressive modeling languages have a more complex syntax and well-defined modeling constructs. For example, UML class models provide a rich language for expressing classes and their interrelationships. UML package diagrams, on the other hand, have a simple notation and a loose interpretation.

Natural language is needed where modeling notations don't exist or are limited in the concepts that they express. Natural language is also used to augment, extend, or clarify a model when the modeling language itself is not expressive enough or the model is too complex to absorb just by studying the model diagrams. UML diagrams are commonly extended via notes, constraints, and other non-UML conventions such as boxes drawn around groups of objects or classes to identify some relationship. (See Figure 10.12 in Chapter 10 for an example.)

There are three parts to interpreting system representation models:

- Syntax
- Semantics
- Pragmatics

Syntax tells us how to use the elements of the modeling notation and in what ways these elements may be organized, connected, or related. *Semantics* is the meaning that a particular model has. *Pragmatics* is the broader context in which a model is related and the constraints and assumptions affecting the model. Each element provides a necessary context for the next. A model serves no pragmatic purpose if it is meaningless. Semantics cannot exist without syntax.

A model is specified in a modeling notation, which has syntax. For example, the UML specifies several modeling or diagramming languages such as a grammar for representing class relationships. The syntax of class diagrams specifies how class elements and association elements—such as generalization and bidirectional associates—can be related or connected. A class, for example, may have a generalization association to another class, but not to itself. Nor can a class have a bidirectional association with nothing.

The modeling elements within the syntax have meaning. A diagram containing a class element connected to another class element via a generalization association is interpreted as an inheritance relationship in the object-oriented sense. A diagram composed of two classes connected via a bidirectional association element is interpreted as a "uses" relationship between the two classes. Developers know how to interpret these models and can respond to them with programming language implementations such as Java or C++ classes.

Pragmatics comes into play when we consider what the diagram means in the context of a system architecture and life cycle. This is a higher-level interpretation of the model. A diagram may be depicting the relationship between two conceptual entities captured during requirements analysis, it may be depicting the actual implementation of two classes within a particular programming language, or it may be modeling something in between such as the logical relationship between two information objects that are eventually implemented in a relational database. A given modeling language can therefore be used to create models with different interpretations.

Models and Human Comprehension

Models are meant to simplify tasks of reasoning about system properties. "By relieving the brain of all unnecessary work, a good notation sets it free to concentrate on more advanced problems, and in effect increases the mental power of the race" (Whitehead, 1948).

Models are abstractions that facilitate the design process by allowing us to focus on subsets of a problem. Abstractions, when used during development, allow us to work in parallel and isolate developers from design decisions of other developers. By decomposing a problem into layers of abstraction, the architect can focus on key solution structures while ignoring other design concerns. An experienced architect knows what to focus on and what to ignore at any level of abstraction.

What Are Models Used For?

In this section, we see that models can be used to represent systems knowledge. Models in general are used both to simulate existing systems as well as to guide systems analysis and design. Models for simulation are primarily used to discover new behaviors of a system that is being studied, such as a naturally occurring system. Systems analysis models help people understand the characteristics of a system or problem to solve. Design models assist architects in making design decisions before the actual system is constructed, when such decisions are more cost-effective.

Some models may transcend a given system implementation. If you use the appropriate modeling techniques, you should be able to reuse many design models. A model can become:

- A standard object model for a particular problem space
- An implementation-independent model for guiding future versions of the system to take advantage of new technologies
- An architecture or design pattern

The products of specification and design are much like the semantic structures that make up our own memory. They are networks of ideas: facts and their relationships. A useful model for discussing knowledge about a system is George Klir's hierarchy of systems knowledge (Klir, as cited in Zeigler, 2000). There are many such models, and this one is used because it is satisfactory for our purposes of discussing software design. The hierarchy of systems knowledge defines four levels of knowledge: the types or nature of knowledge that may be possessed about a system and whether it is real or artificial. System design is a type of system problem, along with systems analysis and systems inference.

There are four levels of system knowledge in Klir's framework:

Source.   The variables we know about and wish to measure or observe in order to gather data about the system.

Data.   The data that we have collected from the source system.

Generative.   A model or means for generating the data of the previous level.

Structure.   An assemblage of components that implement the generative model.

The lowest level, or *source level*, of systems knowledge is the knowledge of what system variables we want to measure and how they are to be measured in order to gather data about the system (for example, experimental data). The next level, the *data level*, is the actual data that we have collected from measuring a system or the nonquantitative facts that we have learned by observing a system. The *generative level* is where we have created a model that can generate the measured data or produce observed behavior. The highest level, the *structure level*, is where we have an implementation of the generative model composed of physical or software components. In systems simulation theory, it is the arrangement of components in a simulation that gives us the generative behavior.

There are three fundamental systems problems: systems analysis, systems inference, and systems design. These problems correspond to transitions up and down the hierarchy of systems knowledge. In *systems analysis*, the system may or may not exist. We are trying to understand the system's behavioral characteristics given its real or intended structure. This involves moving from higher levels to lower levels, for example, using a generative model to generate data in order to understand the system.

In *systems inference*, the system exists and we are trying to infer (discover) how the system works based on observing its behavior. This involves moving from the source level to the data level (measuring or observing the system) and then creating or searching for a generative model that can produce the observed results.

In *systems design*, the system does not exist and we are trying to create a good design for it. This involves moving from lower levels to higher levels. For example, we have a means of generating the data or behavior and we want to realize this behavior by assembling components together in such a way as to produce the desired behavior or data.

The most relevant systems problem to this discussion is the systems design problem. The modeling and simulation framework systems design can be viewed as a problem of fitting a structure on behaviors: The system doesn't exist and therefore we cannot gather observational data. However, we know how we want the system to behave so we generate our own data. This is the difference between inference modeling and design modeling.

In software architecting, we are concerned with systems analysis and systems design. This framework is important in discerning whether a given activity is characteristic of analysis or design. In general, analytic techniques can be applied throughout an application's life cycle. It is not a term reserved only for the classic meaning as in *object-oriented analysis*. For example, performing evaluations on design models is an analysis activity. All analysis activities share some general problem-solving techniques, regardless of whether we are analyzing an existing business to determine what the software should do or whether we are analyzing the output of application performance measurements.

Systems Analysis Models

In the context of software architecting, the system under analysis is not our target system but rather the system that we are trying to automate, such as a business process. In this case we know the structure of the system, and we are trying to understand its behavior (for example, achieve a generative level of knowledge). Once we have partially specified the behavior, we can then begin systems design. Both analysis and design proceed in an iterative fashion with output from the systems analysis models (the required behavior) feeding the input of the design models.

In this book, I will also refer to systems analysis models as *problem space models*. Both problem space models and solution space models are collectively called *representation models*. Representation models are the kinds of models that we are most interested in with respect to software architecting.

Systems Inference Models

Simulation models are used to make predictions of an existing system's future state or behavior. An example of this is mathematical models (formulae) for determining the position of a moving body with respect to time. These models are not derived at by design, but rather via inference techniques based on collecting experimental data by observing a *source system* and applying numerical techniques for fitting equations to the data. For example, *linear regression* is the fitting of experimental data to linear models.

These models are important because they allow us to apply mathematical reasoning to a problem. This in turn enables us to understand, predict, and control the outcomes in naturally occurring systems. A given system may have several inferred models depending on the observational and numerical techniques applied. Simulation models are judged by their ability to accurately predict the future behavior or state of a system.

There are three classes of simulation models, each based on the kind of mathematics used to generate data. Differential Equation System Specifications

(DESS) model systems have continuous states and continuous times. Discrete Time System Specifications (DTSS) model systems operate on discrete time bases (such as automata) utilizing difference equations. Discrete Event System Specifications (DEVS) model systems are systems in which some or all of the data take on discrete values at arbitrary points in time.

Systems Design Models

Models for system design are basically the opposite of models created from experimental data. In this case there is no source system. Rather there is a *target system*, the behavior of which we know but the form of which we don't, hence the classic design principle *form follows function*. As I've already stated several times, there is a tendency in software development to become overly focused on the form, losing sight of the original function.

In this book, I will also refer to systems design models as *solution space models* or *solution domain models*.

What Roles Do Models Play?

Roles relate models to tasks and responsibilities of the architect and other stakeholders within a system life cycle. Design methodologies define the types of models to create and their roles in the system life cycle. The architect selects the types of models to use based in part on choice of methodology and in part on the needs of the organization. Software development organizations usually do not adopt a methodology in full but rather adapt one by taking from it techniques and models that are essential for the system to be developed and the environment in which it will be designed. Selecting the essential techniques and models requires sound judgment by the architect. Models serve many purposes and roles in software architecting:

- Models are a primary means of communication between all stakeholders.
- Models provide guidelines for software developers to implement the system.
- Models assist in making design decisions and assessing them.
- Models can be reusable artifacts for future development and serve as documentation for system users and future maintainers.

Roles are not mutually exclusive; a given model may serve many purposes. Models are the only medium for communication about the system when the system doesn't yet exist. Clients verify that the system will meet their needs by evaluating functional and behavioral models.

Communication between Stakeholders and the Architect

There are two goals of client communication: determine the client's objectives and constraints and ensure that the system reflects the client's value judgments, since not all objectives may be possible to achieve. The client's value judgments are used when a compromise between several objectives must be made. For example, it may be necessary to remove feature functions in order to meet the client's schedule or the client may change the schedule to accommodate nonnegotiable features. The client must make these decisions based on his or her values; the architect cannot make this decision on the client's behalf.

The key to communication is using an agreed-upon vocabulary. This means that the terms used by the communicating parties have agreed-upon definitions. In my experience, a large percentage of time is spent in software development meetings arguing over trivial things because of miscommunication. I attempt to address this early in a project's life cycle by creating or finding metamodels that provide consistently defined terms. The closer these models are to the client's or user's language, the better.

Models assist in communication by addressing specific concerns. The client is concerned with the system satisfying the required needs. A model that specifies how distributed objects bind at run time will not be of much use to the client in this context and may be confusing and result in wasted time. Models that specifically address system functions would be the most appropriate. Specific modeling languages also promote communication by limiting the modeling elements to a particular, well-defined set of concepts. For example, models that address client concerns of functionality may include concepts like system objectives, actors, resources, and policies constraining actors and resources. We will see in Chapter 13 how viewpoints in architectural descriptions are used to specify models that address specific concerns through the use of viewpoint languages.

Design Decisions and Design Assessment

Models can be used to test assumptions about the system before building it. Models are not the system and therefore the results of testing models must be considered an approximation of how the system will behave. Nevertheless, it is easier and cheaper to assess models as early as possible in the design phase when changes to the design are cheaper to make. Therefore, modeling is a cost-saving activity that helps address the software crisis.

Representation models allow us to reason about a system that does not yet exist. This reasoning includes making decisions about the form or structure of the intended system. Models capture design decisions throughout the design process and allow us to validate assumptions and measure the design without necessarily building a complete working system. By working within the confines of a particular modeling notation, we are able to apply design principles and patterns that would not otherwise be available to us. For example, unless we actually have an object-oriented design model, we would not be able to apply object-oriented metrics to test our design for certain qualities such as extensibility or maintainability.

Guidelines for Detail Design

When discussing logical flow of data in a system, less experienced software developers often get caught up in implementation details of data flow and object interaction and do not first consider the logical interaction and, more specifically, the problem to be solved. The architecture assists in detail design by providing guidelines and models that help the developer make effective detail design decisions. It is difficult or impossible to enforce the architectural integrity of a system without having a means for communicating the architecture to the developers.

At a higher level, the architectural models such as design structure matrix (DSM) and task structure matrix (TSM) assist in work breakdown by specifying modules that can be effectively developed in parallel by individuals or teams.

Reusable Technical Artifacts

Models that are specified as part of an architectural description may be reused for a variety of purposes. System maintainers need specifications in order to determine how new features should be added. Software architects may derive a new system based on a prior system. This is difficult and time-consuming if the architectural specification for the prior system doesn't exist.

Modeling the Problem and Solution Domains

Models can be divided into two groups: those that model the problem domain and those that model the solution domain. Solution domain models can be divided into platform- or technology-independent models and platform- or technology-specific models. Problem domain models can be divided into systems analysis models and requirements analysis models. This is depicted in Figure 6.2.

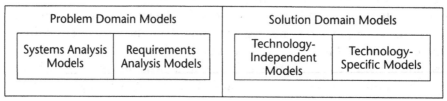

Figure 6.2 Problem and solution domain models.

Problem Domain Models

Commonly, the activity of creating problem domain models is called *analysis*. Methodologies for systems analysis include structured analysis, information modeling, and object-oriented analysis. A goal of problem domain modeling methodologies is to minimize the semantic gap between the real system (for example, an enterprise) and its representation models. Reducing the semantic gap means that the system has a better chance of achieving the quality attributes you are trying to achieve.

Understanding the Problem

Before system requirements can be determined, it may be necessary to understand the characteristics of the system that is to be automated. One common definition of systems analysis is the modeling of a system in order to understand its behavioral characteristics. The needs of an organization can then be understood once the problem is understood.

Analyzing the Requirements

Requirements models are specifications of all known system functions and quality attributes. This is more than a model derived from a typical customer or marketing lists of requirements. It also incorporates the long-term goals of the system (such as the strategic vision of the system, especially if it is released incrementally). The requirements specification is a response to a recognized need.

Solution Domain Models

Commonly, the activity of creating solution domain models is called *design*. Where architecting design ends and engineering design begins is not clear and not completely necessary to distinguish in our discussion. A goal of solution domain modeling methodologies is to reduce the semantic gap between the various models that form a chain of models from the problem domain models to the implementation.

Solution domain models map problem domain model elements to solution domain model elements. There are two categories of solution domain models: platform (technology)-independent models (PIM) and platform (technology)-dependent models. Platform-dependent models describe the system with respect to platform technologies such as CORBA, .NET, or Java 2 Enterprise Edition (J2EE). PIMs are useful for designing the system to avoid platform biases as well as to create a potentially reusable system artifact. PIMs are blueprints for a specific system that can be realized using a variety of platform technologies.

One of the main purposes of solution domain design (as expressed by models) is to serve as a basis for the division of labor for system construction. If you must divide labor among multiple people and coordinate the delivery of those modules, you need a model that expresses this modular decomposition.

Technology-Independent Models

The technology independent models are a response to the requirements specification. These models are specified in a language that generalizes platform services without specifying a particular platform and specifies system structure without using specific programming language constructs.

For example, the RM-ODP engineering viewpoint language is a platform-independent language for describing distributed objects in terms of generalized distributed object services (see Chapter 13). This model may be responded to with a platform dependent model mapping the constructs to CORBA, J2EE, or .NET technologies. These models can be reused in systems implementation. Standardized design metamodels such as the arch/slinky metamodel (see Chapter 11) are examples of technology-independent models.

Technology-Dependent Models

The technology-dependent model is the response to the technology-independent model. This model maps the former to a specific technology platform or programming language, tracing the generalized services to specific technologies and the generalized system structures to programming language constructs. For example, the RM-ODP technology viewpoint language maps engineering models to technology models. In the technology viewpoint models, generalized services are mapped to specific technologies. These types of models serve as development guidelines.

Views

Models may be classified by or organized into views. For example, models can be categorized as either problem domain models or solution domain models as was discussed earlier. *Views* are *aspects* or *dimensions* of an architectural model. For example, three-dimensional geometric objects may be models with several views, each depicting a side of the object. According to the IEEE 1471 (IEEE, 2000), a view is a "representation of a whole system from the perspective of a related set of concerns." A view can contain one or more models. Views are instances of viewpoints, which are generalizations of views. A view is a technical specification and a viewpoint is the language of the view specification. We can identify views as either containing problem domain models or solution domain models. We will learn more about views and viewpoints in Chapters 12 and 13.

Some common architectural views are:

Objectives/purpose.   Describes what is needed.

Behavior/function.   Describes what the system does (to satisfy the objectives).

Information/data.   Describes the information created by and retained in the system.

Form/structure.   Describes the physical structure of the software (for example, modules and components).

Performance.   Describes how effectively the system performs its functions.

The most prevalent views defined in most methodologies are the informational and behavioral views. All business applications process information (that is why they are called information systems). These two views are interdependent. However, we are able to consider one without the other by way of abstraction. Other terms for information are *data* and *state*.

When architecting modern software systems, we need to broaden the set of fundamental system views because our systems are far more interactive and distributed, and are extensions of many off-the-shelf technologies. Information and behavior models are no longer sufficient to represent the system in enough detail to guide its implementation. You also need views of distribution, views of user and external systems interaction, and views that specify how commercial or standard technologies are used. User interaction is not modeled well in older-style behavior models liked data flow diagrams. We extend our behavior models to include user interactions.

Views represent a separation of concerns, although there is linkage or tracing between views. For example, function is different than form but is not independent of it. This linkage may be difficult to spot; an experienced architect can explain these linkages to a layman. This understanding is what separates a modeler from an architect.

The architect must determine which views are most critical to the software system's success. Views provide an integrated picture of the entire system, and the selection should be sufficient to guide its implementation. Extraneous views and models clutter the design process and may negatively affect schedules because they can fuel more communication. As stated earlier, simply having more communication will not solve communication problems, but in fact can contribute to them. Missing views and models can make the semantic gap between existing views large and also have a negative impact on schedules as well as the design. This is a critical step that is often missed or skipped.

Objectives and Purpose Models

Systems are built to serve some useful purpose as defined by the client's needs or wants. One of the roles of the architect is to help the client identify the system's objectives and priorities. Some objectives can be stated and measured precisely; others are abstract and cannot be expressed quantitatively. Functional objectives can be specified with precision, but objectives such as maintainability are harder to define. The architect must prepare models to help the client to clarify abstract objectives. These models may be provisional and exploratory, discarded after the objectives have become more concrete. These models are sometimes referred to as *requirements analysis models*. They serve to facilitate communication and understanding of the problem to be solved.

Refinement of objectives is a key to successful design. A design that is not a response to well-defined objectives tends to address the wrong problems and may lead to unnecessarily complicated implementation. Objectives models should retain the client's and user's language.

Some objectives can be captured in a use case model, though the use case model is also a form of behavioral or functional model (see *Behavioral Functional Models* later in this chapter). In a use case-driven methodology, an initial set of use case models starts out as a model capturing the client language in terms of roles assumed by people and external systems (the environment of the system being designed) and high-level types of interactions or scenarios. These models are not sufficiently expressive to capture other objectives such as nonfunctional requirements, however, and are usually supplemented with additional textual requirements specifications. One goal of the use case approach is to represent required system behavior in a language that is easily understood by the client, yet has a small semantic gap between it and the next level of models, such as the object analysis models.

It is important to realize that a requirements specification represents a family of solutions. There are many possible architectural descriptions that can be created given a single requirements specification. The experienced architect knows which aspects of the requirements are most critical and can potentially narrow the wide range of possible solutions. Likewise, any number of implementations (detail designs) can derive from a given architectural description. This is depicted in Figure 6.3.

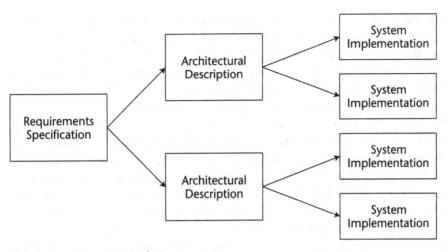

Figure 6.3   A family of solutions.

Every design decision effectively creates a new path down a design decision tree rooted in the requirements specification and terminating at a single system implementation. There can be more than one system implementation that satisfies the client's objectives. The less clear the objectives are, however, the more likely the architect will wander down the wrong architecture path. It is important that the architect strive toward understanding a problem before getting too deeply into design. This principle applies at all design phases and for every model being created. The first architectural response to the objectives will itself introduce new problems, and unless the architect understands and can articulate those problems, the next layer of models will be addressing unnecessary concerns. The good architect knows when to proceed into the design of parts of the system for which the objectives are understood while balancing the activities of refining the remaining ambiguous objectives.

Behavioral/Functional Models

Functional or behavioral models specify what the system does. These models are a response to the functional objectives in the objectives models. The importance of behavioral models increases as systems become more complex and as their behavior becomes less evident from the system's form. In simpler systems, the function and the form of a system are very close, and it is easier to infer one from the other.

The architect must determine the level of detail needed in the behavioral model. Too little detail and the client may not understand the behavior being provided or the developers may implement the wrong functionality. Too much detail and the models may become incomprehensible and difficult to maintain during the design life cycle, which could have the same side effects as too little detail. Either case may also lead to delays in the schedule.

In modern software development, we usually only start with a partially specified behavior model because we usually do not have a complete set of fully defined requirements and objectives before design begins. We address this problem by using methodologies that promote iterative refinement of requirements and system design. We create models of the target system, and we test or measure these models against the desired quality attributes. Because software design involves a trivial manufacturing phase, we can actually deliver partially working systems to the client. The client may verify that the system satisfies the quality attributes correctly as well as validate their original requirements and their value judgments. Each iteration of design allows the users and acquirers to refine their requirements and for the models to be refined, respectively.

It is usually not practical to validate all design models with respect to the quality attributes. Some models are refinements of other models that have already been validated. The refinements are the necessary operations to reduce abstraction in the system design and move toward specificity and eventually the executable system itself.

There are several kinds of behavioral models:

- User interface prototypes
- Scenarios and threads
- State transition diagrams
- Process models

User Interface Prototypes

User interface (UI) mock-ups are a very effective means for conveying to the user how a system will work. User interface mock-ups should be developed early in the process to ensure client acceptance and user satisfaction. Mock-ups may be simple UI specifications with sample screens or they may be semi-functional prototypes (a type of scale model).

Scenarios and Threads

Scenarios and threads are commonly modeled using use cases and sequence diagrams. Use case modeling is an effective technique for capturing behavioral or functional requirements. Use cases are types of scenarios, and the models may be refined with several specific scenario models called *sequence diagrams*. Use cases can also be refined with UML activity (state chart) diagrams. Sequence diagrams capture a single thread or path through a use case. Use cases represent behavior by example and are considered a narrative form of specification. That is, they are specified as a dialogue of interactions between actors and the system itself.

As we have seen, use case diagrams can be used in more than one view. This duality of purpose can be an effective tool for bridging the semantic gap between views but can also be a source of distraction, leading the architect away from the original objectives and not leaving behind a tangible specification of just the objectives models. Finding the appropriate balance is a challenge for the architect.

Sequence diagrams are used to specify a use case in more detail. They represent objects sending messages in time. A sequence represents a single thread or path among many possible paths for a scenario. Branches are not typically modeled using sequence diagrams. There is no one level of abstraction for sequence diagrams. They may be as abstract as representing the highest level of functional decomposition of a use case or as detailed as showing actual programming language objects interacting at methods. Like use case models, sequence diagrams can bridge the behavioral and structural views. Therefore, sequence diagrams can suffer from the same side effects.

There are two types of behavior requirements: the threads that a system *must* produce and the threads that a system *must not* allow. It is common to represent the former but the latter are just as useful, and together the two provide a very expressive behavioral specification.

Behavioral specifications are a very effective means of communicating with the client as well as providing specifications that drive the design phase and test specifications.

State Transition Diagrams

State transition charts or finite state machines represent the behavior of a system as a set of states, transitions between states, and events that trigger transitions. Petri nets are a form of state transition diagrams commonly used to model real-time and embedded systems. UML activity diagrams are a type of state transition diagram that can be used to represent the state of a system, of a component, or of individual programming language objects.

Process Models

The data flow diagram (DFD) is a traditional process model used to identify system processes and their decomposition into subprocesses. The process interfaces define the data that flows among them. DFDs are used in structured analysis to guide the functional decomposition process. DFDs are typically represented as bubbles depicting processes and arcs between bubbles depicting data flow. DFDs are especially useful for representing batch processing systems but are less expressive for representing the behavior of interactive systems. In object-oriented methods, use case models and sequence diagrams supplant DFDs.

Information/Data Models

In this view, the data that is created and retained by an application and the relationships among that data are represented. It is not uncommon for the data model to be the most complex aspect of a system. Data modeling methods were developed in response to the need to automate data-intensive, paper-based systems. Commonly, a data-intensive system involves automated database systems, but it is possible to automate paper-based legacy systems by capturing the complex interrelationships among large amounts of retained data. Not all of the data in a system may be retained electronically, yet it is still necessary to model that data.

Data modeling began with the formal mathematically-based relationship modeling. This method was derived from set theory and relied on simple structures; relations with attributes; and basic operations, such as union, set difference, Cartesian product, projection, selection, and join. Relational database technology is based on this method. Semantic data models, such as entity-relationship models (ERM), were introduced to accommodate increasingly complex structures.

The entity-relationship diagram is the basis of modern information modeling. Object-oriented modeling methods extend the ERM concept by combining data and behavioral modeling. Object-oriented analysis can be thought of as an inversion of functional decomposition. DFDs describe the system as a hierarchy of functions and the data model is interleaved in the functional structure. In this method, the only data relationship is aggregation. Object-oriented analysis starts with a decomposition of the data decomposition and interleaves a functional model through it. Object orientation supports a wide variety of data relationships, including aggregation and inheritance.

UML class diagrams are commonly used for information models, even if the eventual implementation is in a relational database. In modern software systems, a lot of the procedural logic that was implemented in the database system is being replaced with a middle-tier object layer. This explains the rich collection of types of models in the UML. Databases are becoming more of a persistence mechanism for objects.

Models of Form

Models of form represent the structure of the system. In simple systems, the structure could be inferred from its function and the behavioral and information models were sufficient to specify the architecture. Today, with more systems being distributed and utilizing commercial technologies, the structure can no longer be simply inferred from the functional model. Models of form include scale models (or prototypes), components and connectors, and source code.

Scale Models

Scale models (prototypes) in other engineering disciplines are models that have reduced functionality or reduced size. Prototypes are typically used as exploratory or provisional models that allow architects and engineers to test designs when it is most cost-effective: early in the design phase. For example, dimensionally accurate models of aircraft can be tested in wind tunnels at less expense than building a full-scale prototype. For software we have user interface prototypes, functionally limited models to test performance, and performance-limited models to test proof of concepts.

Working user interface prototypes allow the architect to validate system objectives, and they can also be used to solicit requirements, test different approaches to the user interface design, and solicit user feedback for requirements and usability.

An example of a performance-testing model is a component that simulates database access from a middle-tier object. You may need to know how fast you can access data concurrently from several distributed objects before you commit to a design. These kinds of models help you empirically test assumptions and compare design approaches.

Proof-of-concept models are useful for validating a novel design approach. For example, suppose you would like to consider using XML as a way of transferring data between a client (such as a Servlet) and a server (such as a Session Enterprise Java Bean [EJB] running in an application server). The design is intended to satisfy modifiability and adaptability requirements. It looks good on paper, but will it really satisfy the requirements? Implementing the critical portion of this mechanism and testing it may provide enough validation that it is a good approach or it may uncover hidden problems. This example is taken from a real project in which the concept was used but hadn't been proven to really satisfy the modifiability and adaptability requirements. As it turned out, the design was no more modifiable or adaptable than a basic Java API approach, yet performed much worse. A proof-of-concept may have saved the development team a large amount of work, since the XML mechanism would have required much more effort to implement and maintain than the API approach.

Components and Connectors

Component and connector diagrams account for the vast majority of software design models of interest to the software architect. This category of models includes the usual UML diagrams such as classes, object collaboration, and component diagrams. In electronics, for example, block diagrams represent physically identifiable elements of the system. In software design, the common component and connector style diagrams are class and object diagrams, component diagrams, and deployment diagrams.

UML component diagrams represent software components and their dependencies. The dependencies are based on the interfaces that are exported or implemented by the component. In RM-ODP, the computational, engineering, and technical viewpoint models are all component and connector style diagrams. The computational models represent logical distributed objects and their logical interrelationships. Engineering models represent the computational objects, but their relationships are in terms of either generalized distributed object services or local method invocation. In the technology model, the connectors represent concrete implementations such as RMI or blocking method calls.

These types of diagrams represent a system at many levels of abstraction. A class diagram can be used to represent the logical relationship between objects, or it can be used to represent the actual programming language objects.

Models of activation represent how information flows through the components of a system, as well as how control is passed from component to component along connectors. Activation models may be logical such as depicting interactions between objects as messages, or they may be physical depicting the interaction between objects as blocking method calls. In UML, a logical data flow is represented as objects passing messages to objects. The message types include synchronous, balking, timeout, and asynchronous. In the technology-independent models, these messages are not assumed to be method calls. In the technology-dependent models, the implementation is represented.

The types of activations include:

Soft push.   The sender sends a message, which may be lost if the receiver is off-line or not explicitly waiting to receive the message.

Hard push.   The sender sends a message, and the act of sending interrupts the receiver who must react to the message.

Blocking pull.   The receiver requests the data and waits until the sender responds (also known as synchronous in UML).

Non-blocking pull.   The receiver requests the data and continues on without it if the sender does not send it. This includes blocking for a period of time (also known as balking or timeout in UML).

Hard pull.   When the receiver requests the data, the sender is interrupted and must send it.

Queuing channel.   The sender pushes data onto a channel without interrupting the receiver. The data can be stored in the channel so that the receiver can pull it later.

Source Code

Source code can be considered an architectural view. A programming language is a type of modeling language. Recall that we considered implementation to be part of the detail design phase. The source code is not the system itself, but rather a machine-readable representation that can be compiled into the executable system. We think of source code as a model because the problem-solving activities of coding are, in general, the same as the problem-solving activities of creating other models.

Nonfunctional/Performance Models

Performance models, in classic systems architecting, describe or predict how effectively an architecture satisfies some function. These models are usually quantitative. Performance models are often called nonfunctional requirements because they do not define a functional thread of operation, which is what the behavioral models represent. The term nonfunctional is a misnomer, however, because some system attributes of the nonfunctional variety really are functional or behaviorally related.

There are three general categories of performance models in classic systems architecting. These are analytical, simulation, and judgmental. Only the last one is relevant to software architecting. Analytical (mathematical) and simulation models are typically infeasible in software design and therefore human judgment is necessary. This judgment can yield reliable performance indicators. For example, using explicit or implicit design heuristics can often rate one architecture as superior to another. We will explore this in more detail in Chapter 12, where we address architectural evaluation.

Summary

Creating models requires experience, insight, and creativity and is something that you must practice continually in order to improve your skills. Understanding the types of models you can create helps frame your modeling activities. A model type is like a canvas; it provides a boundary and a form in which to create. The techniques I present can help you get there by giving you practical instruction on how to practice.

In this chapter, we learned about what models are and why they are important to software design. Models can help save time and money, and increase the odds of achieving the quality attributes by not only facilitating communication but also by facilitating an understanding of the problem to be solved. There is a challenge that the architect has: how to decide which models to build and how many details to put in them. The architect is the key decision maker in these decisions. In the next chapter, we will discuss some specific architectural views and architectural description languages.

Architecture Representation

In the previous chapter, we explored models and their roles in the software design process. Models are used to represent many aspects of a system, including its function and form. In this chapter, I present a type of model for representing the form (the component structure) of a software system, which can be used to model a software architecture in terms of components and connectors and even generate a system or parts of a system. This representation model is known as an *architectural description language.*

In this chapter we look at the concept of architectural description languages. An architectural description language (ADL) has a formal, usually textual, syntax and can be used to describe actual system architectures in a machine-readable way. Some ADLs also have a graphical notation. Some ADLs are associated with particular architectural styles (such as pipes and filters), and almost all embody the concept of components and connectors. ADLs are not commonly used in industry but are the subject of research. My treatment of the topic in this book is intended to introduce you to ADLs as well as to provide some ideas as to how you may apply the concepts of ADLs in your own system designs.

The structure of this chapter is as follows:

Goals of architecture representation. An architecture description is a representation of a system that can be used to design a system, analyze a design, and generate or instantiate a system.

Foundations of software architecture representation. The elements for describing an architecture are components, connectors, and architectural constraints.

Architecture description languages. ADLs are design languages that are used to describe a system using components and connectors instead of programming language constructs. These higher-level constructs can be projected onto component technologies or programming language constructs. ADLs should exhibit some basic design language properties, including composition, abstraction, reusability, configuration, heterogeneity, and analysis.

Goals of Architecture Representation

Architecture representation goes beyond the intermediate models that support the design process. The goals of architecture representation using architectural description languages are not only to facilitate the design process but also to represent the actual architecture of a system in a machine-readable format that can be analyzed and used to instantiate an instance of a system. Although there are no standard ADLs, they do have some elements and goals in common. ADLs describe systems in terms of components and connectors, which can be projected (or bound) to existing technological components. For example, the pipes-and-filters syntax of UNIX shells can be thought of as a simple ADL. It supports the specification of an instance of a system in terms of components (filters) and connectors (pipes).

Some goals of architecture representation are:

- Prescribe the architectural constraints of components and connectors to any desired level of granularity
- Separate aesthetics from engineering
- Express different aspects of the architecture in an appropriate view or manner
- Perform dependency and consistency analysis
- Support system generation or instantiation

An architecture description prescribes the constraints on a software system. These constraints are really requirements imposed on individual modules of the system. Anything not constrained in the description is not at the architectural level of design and is therefore free to be designed independently from other modules.

An architecture description should separate aesthetic concerns from engineering concerns. Aesthetic concerns are those aspects of the architecture that do not directly affect the architecture-related quality attributes. An obvious example is the layout and colors of a user interface. However, the term *aesthetics* can transcend the graphical user interface (GUI) to include the feel of the application as well, such as how intuitive the user interface is. These concerns, although important, need to be considered separately from other quality attributes. The aesthetics should be more easily changed than other aspects of a system and should therefore be isolated. As we'll see in later chapters, the human/computer interaction (HCI) concerns can be separated from the application or functional core concerns to create more robust architectures that are also easier to understand.

Architectures cannot be described from one particular view or aspect. The architecture of an application can be viewed as data, processing, or as a module structure for design or project planning. An architectural description must be multiviewed in order to provide enough information about its operational characteristics (function, performance), its nonoperational characteristics (modifiability, buildability), and its business-related characteristics (time to market).

An architect must be able to perform dependency and consistency analysis on the architectural design of an application to ensure to some degree that it is complete and correct. An architectural description must express enough information in order to perform analysis using software tools as well as to perform manual assessments (as discussed in Chapter 14). Ad hoc notations and informal textual descriptions do not address the problem of complexity and lack of precision in describing design. Ad hoc mechanisms cannot be automated and can lead to time wasted in ineffective discourse among team members. Mathematical descriptions are usually too time consuming to produce. There are only a limited number of practical software views that can be described mathematically.

The architecture description must be machine-readable. Not only does this support analysis but also the ability to generate a system or portions of a system from existing technological components. An architecture description describes a system in terms of components, connectors, and their arrangements. An ADL may be used to instantiate a system or a portion of a system from existing technology components, and it may also be used to generate the code for the system or portions of the system.

Foundations of Software Architecture Representation

A paper by Wolf and Perry (Perry, 1992) identified the foundational elements of an architecture representation language. The primary objective of their research was to support the development and use of software architecture specifications. They identified three types of constructs necessary in a software architecture representation:

- Elements
- Form
- Rationale

Their *elements* are what later authors called components and connectors (which is the terminology that I'll also use). Their elements are classified as:

- Data
- Processing
- Connecting

Data elements are components that contain the information that is used in the system and transformed into other data elements. *Processing elements* are components that supply the transformation on the data elements, transforming one data element into another. *Connecting elements* are the connectors or the glue that hold the components of the system together and are the mechanism for moving data elements between processing elements. A connecting element may be a data element, a processing element, or a hybrid of the two. Several similar architectures (characterized as using the same set of processing and data elements) are distinguished primarily by their connecting elements, which can be thought of as forming the topology of the design. The choice of connecting elements has a profound impact on various operational and non-operational quality attributes.

The architectural *form* is composed of weighted *properties* and *relationships*. The weighting may either indicate the relative importance of the property or relationship or it may indicate the necessity of selecting among design variations. Weighting may be useful in distinguishing between design concerns that are aesthetic or required, providing engineers with some degree of freedom in making detail design decisions.

Properties may be used to define constraints on the selection of architectural elements. *Relationships* may be used to constrain how different architectural elements may interact and how they may be organized in the architecture. The architect uses properties and relationships to define the minimum desired constraints on the architecture. Engineers must respect these properties as they make detail design decisions. A specific quality attribute requirement may map to several properties on a set of elements. For example, a specific performance requirement that is related to data throughput might map to properties on several processing elements that implement the function. Relationships define the synthesis of elements to form new functions (purposes).

Integral to the specification of the architecture is the *rationale* for design decisions. Rationales capture the motivation behind various decisions, such as the partitioning of the system into discrete elements and the formation of the architecture in terms of connecting elements. Rationales are *inferences* that can be structured as an argument with the design decision being the conclusion.

Fundamental Software Design Views

The three types of architectural elements provide two fundamental views or representations of a software design. Probably the most common view of software is the *data view*, which represents the relationships between data elements and the flow (processes) between them. Object orientation and entity-relationship modeling are data view-centric methodologies. Another popular view is the *processing view*, which emphasizes the data flow through processing elements. Structured analysis is a modeling methodology that emphasizes the processing view of a software design. We know from experience that both views are interdependent as necessary. Modern methodologies, including object-oriented analysis and design, are comprised of techniques for generating models of both views. Class diagrams model data elements and object collaboration diagrams, and sequence diagrams model processing and connecting elements.

A processing element may map a data element into an entirely new data element, or it may change the state of an existing data element. A compiler is an example of a system that maps data elements to new data elements (character stream to object code). A banking application operating on a customer account is an example of a processing element that changes the state of a data element (such as disabling an account).

Wolf and Perry use a multiphase compiler for illustrating the architectural components. The processing elements of a multiphase compiler are a lexical analyzer (lexer), a parser, a semantic analyzer (semantor), code optimizer, and a code generator. The data elements of a multiphase compiler are characters, tokens, phrases, correlated phrases, annotated phrases, and object code. The connecting elements differentiate two compiler architectural styles, which are sequential and parallel process and/or shared data.

Weighted properties and relationships express the form of the multiphase compiler architectural style. The optimizer processing element and the annotated correlated phrases data elements must be used together, but the combination is optional within the architectural style, since optimization is not necessary to transform program text into object code. There are relationships between the data elements as well. The character string that comprises a program's text is linearly related to tokens and tokens are linearly related to phrases. There is a nonlinear relationship between the phrases and the correlated phrases. The linear relationships are expressed as properties of the processors. The lexer, for example, has an order-preserving property. This property is dependent on the property of the tokens, which are linearly related to (they appear in the same order as) the sequences of program text characters they represent.

In the sequential architectural style, the connecting elements are procedure calls and parameters. Each phase of compilation runs to completion before the next phase is invoked. Each phase is represented by one of the processing elements, which transforms data elements of one type to data elements of another type. The lexer transforms program text (characters) into tokens, the parser transforms tokens into phrases, and the semantor transforms phrases into correlated phrases. The optimizer is optionally invoked, which transforms correlated phrases into annotated correlated phrases. The code generator transforms correlated phrases (annotated and nonannotated) into object code. The processing elements may be hooked-up to call each other directly or they may be invoked from some main program.

In the parallel processing architectural style, the connecting element is the shared representation of the data (a repository). Each process performs eager evaluation (when enough data is available for it to process). Each processing element can be modeled as a standalone process that operates on a shared data representation.

Architecture Description Languages

In this section, we discuss the requirements for architecture description languages as defined by Shaw and Garlan. "The problem of describing structural decompositions more precisely has traditionally been addressed by the modularization facilities of programming languages and module interconnection languages. These notations typically allow an implementor to describe software system structure in terms of definition/use and import/export relationships between program units" (Shaw, 1996). These programming language structures are inadequate for describing architectural elements, especially because they provide only an implementation view of connecting elements.

Furthermore, there is no way to model a strict separation of concerns between architectural-level design issues and detail design (implementation) issues. In Java, data elements and processing elements are modeled as classes and connecting elements are typically either method calls or remote method calls. To implement an asynchronous message passing connection requires the use of new data elements (messages and queues) and remote method calls to place read messages from and write messages to queues.

Garlan and Shaw observed that commonly used architectures contain similar patterns or idiomatic constructs that rely on a shared set of common element types including connecting elements ("common intermodule connection strategies"). Languages in general serve the purpose of describing complex relationships among primitive elements and element combinations (assemblies). Therefore, having identified semantic constructs, it makes sense to define a language around them.

Common architectural description elements include:

- (Pure) computation (processing elements)
- Memory (data element)
- Manager
- Controller
- Link

Computation elements represent simple input/output relations and do not have retained state. These are processing elements. Memory elements represent shared collections of persistent structured data such as databases, file systems, and parser symbol tables. These are data elements. Manager elements represent elements that manage state and closely related operations. A manager provides a higher-level semantic view on top of primitive processing, data, and connecting elements. A controller governs time sequences of events, such as a scheduler or resource synchronizer. This use of the term *controller* is different than the use in the context of model-view-controller (MVC) or presentation-application-control (PAC). Links are elements that transmit information between other elements. A link may be a communication channel between distributed processes or it may represent a user interface (HCI element), since a user can be considered another element in the architecture that produces and consumes information. The link is similar to a connecting element.

Some common component interactions (forms of connecting elements) are:

- Procedure call
- Data flow
- Implicit invocation
- Message passing
- Shared data
- Instantiation

Design Language Elements

The elements of a programming language are components, operators, abstraction rules, closure rules, and specification. *Components* are the primitive semantic elements and their values, such as an integer data type and its range. *Operators* are functions that combine components, such as arithmetic operators. *Abstraction rules* allow for the definition of named expressions of components and operators, such as the creation of macros and procedures, so that the expression may be reused in multiple contexts. *Closure rules* determine which abstractions can be added to the classes of primitive components and operators, effectively making constructs like procedures or classes first-class entities. Closure allows a compiler to perform type checking on user-defined types. The language *specification* associates semantics to the syntactic forms; that is, it specifies the meaning of the language elements.

Shaw and Garlan define similar elements for an architectural design description language. Their elements of an architectural description language are components, operators, patterns, closure, and specification.

Components are the modules (possibly logical) that compose the architectural level of design. A module in this sense may be a physically discrete software element or compilation unit (such as a shared library or a program executable) or it may be a logical package of software elements (a set of classes that perform some logically coherent function). It may also be a more abstract concept that is particular to an architectural style. For example, the components in the pipes-and-filters-style architecture are filters (processing elements) and data (data elements), including the standard input/output streams. In a client-server style, the components may be clients and servers and the data that the servers provide.

Operators (that is, connectors) are the inter-component connection mechanism. Operators are like functions that combine architectural elements to form higher-level components. In the pipes-and-filters-style architecture, the operator is a pipe. A pipe can be thought of as a binary operator that connects two filters. In a client/server style the operator is a client/server communication protocol that connects a client process with a server process. For example, Java Data Base Connectivity (JDBC) or Open Data Base Connectivity (ODBC) are operators that combine clients with database servers. In a three-tier system there may be several operators: the client to application server operator (such as a distributed process communication mechanism like HTTP, CORBA's Internet Inter-ORB Protocol [IIOP], Remote Method Invocation[RMI], or Remote Procedure Call [RPC]), and the application server to database server operator described above. In this style, there are still only server and client components, but a given module may be both a server and a client.

Patterns are like programming language named expressions in that they are reusable compositions of architectural elements. The term pattern here is only indirectly related to the design pattern concept. A design pattern (or architectural pattern) is a design template that solves a particular set of problems and that must be implemented within a particular design. That design pattern describes the kinds of elements that should be in a design and how they interact. A given implementation of classes may embody several design patterns, even though they are not obvious or even visible (and sometimes they are applied unknowingly). In the ADL context, a pattern refers to an archetypal composition that serves as a framework for an architecture description that is expanded. For example, an ADL pattern may identify a particular component B as separate from another component A to support reliability and performance. The pattern may be expanded in a particular architecture instance (an executable system) to include multiple instances of the component B.

Closure defines the conditions under which a particular assembly of components (a set of components and operators) may also be used as an atomic component. For example, in our three-tier architectural style, the composition of a client and application server itself is a client component that can be composed with the database server component, similar to the pseudo mathematical expression db_client + db_server = (app_client + app_server) + db_server. Likewise, the app_server and db_server can be composed to form another component that can be composed with the app_client. In the pipes-and-filters example, two filters composed together can be reused as a single filter, the input of which is the input of the first filter and the output of which is the output of the second filter.

The design language *specification* associates semantics such as functionality and other quality characteristics, such as modifiability, reliability, and performance, to the syntactic forms.

Shaw and Garlan identify six classes of properties that should characterize an ADL (their desiderata for architecture description languages). These classes are composition, abstraction, reusability, configuration, heterogeneity, and analysis. Shaw and Garlan use the term *architectural description* to refer to an artifact that conforms to an ADL syntax and which can be transformed into (compiled to) an implementation or an executable simulation. In this book, I am using the term in the IEEE 1471 (IEEE, 2000) sense (see Chapter 12). Therefore, I will substitute the term *architecture specification* to mean such an artifact.

Composition

An ADL should allow for the description of a system as a composition of components and connectors. As we have already seen, composition (describing a system as a hierarchy of simpler subsystems) helps us manage the complexity of a design or a design process. An ADL must support the ability to split a system or module into two modules. A series of splitting operations can be applied to form a hierarchy of modules that is easier to build, modify, and understand. Similarly, an ADL must support the ability to synthesize or combine modules to create new forms. The splitting or synthesis operations should be independent of implementation design decisions such as choice of algorithms; data structures; or connecting technology, such as whether the connecting element is an RPC/RMI or message queue.

The closure rules of an ADL must allow an architect to view or use a composition of elements as a single component. In mathematics this composition would be considered a *term*. A term can be treated as a single atomic thing to be added, subtracted, multiplied, or divided, but when it is necessary, the term itself can be viewed as an expression of smaller terms. Similarly, the architect should also be able to operate on the individual components of the composition.

This notion of composition corresponds to our design operators of decomposition and synthesis-aggregation.

Abstraction

A programming language provides an abstract view of the underlying hardware. A programmer does not need to think in terms of registers and binary machine instructions, for example. This abstract view allows a programmer to focus on higher-level concerns without having to think in terms of low-level implementation details. A programming language is considered an abstraction because it removes nonessential details for solving a problem at a particular level of granularity. At this level a programmer can work with more complex elements with greater ease. A for-loop in C++ or Java is simpler to comprehend, create, and use than the equivalent in assembly or binary machine instructions.

Likewise, an ADL should allow a designer to focus on still higher-level concerns without having to think in terms of programming language constructs such as for-loops, classes, and methods of related technologies such as RPC/RMI. Just as a for-loop is an abstraction of a certain pattern of machine instructions, architectural abstractions are patterns of programming language constructs. An architect can think in terms of components and connectors, thus focusing on architectural-level concerns such as modifiability, reliability, and performance without having to map these concepts to specific programming language elements.

Reusability

It should be possible to modularize a specification written in a particular ADL just as it is possible to modularize software components so that they may be reused in other system or application instantiations. However, an architectural module is not a reusable executable module like a reusable programming language library. Rather, it is a reusable pattern of component compositions. Garlan and Shaw call these patterns *shared properties*. A family of products may share common properties such as canonical structures of components or common constraints on particular components.

For example, a certain client-server pattern may identify a database server component with a particular database table structure (a reusable data model). This pattern could be implemented on several different database server products and used in many different instantiations of a system with a variety of different client applications. Each physical database implementation might look different but would contain the same core data and enforce the same semantic rules.

Configuration

Configuration is related to composition. It should be possible with an ADL to describe a composite structure separately from its elements so that the composition can be reasoned about as an atomic element and support the dynamic reconfiguration of a system in terms of restructuring compositions without knowing about their internal structure. During execution, a system may need to instantiate redundant processes in order to improve throughput or to handle a fault. Compositions that can be instantiated at run time are like objects in an object-oriented programming language.

The actual number of objects that may be instantiated is not necessarily predetermined. In a client/server system, an indefinite number of clients may be executing at any time. The number of clients and when they will be instantiated is not described by the architecture specification. Every time a client starts executing or stops executing results in a new system configuration.

Heterogeneity

Heterogeneity refers to the ability to mix architectural styles within a single architecture specification. At one level, the architecture may exhibit a particular pattern of compositions but the structure of each composition may follow a different pattern. In a client/server system, the server component may be a composition organized as layers, with each layer structured as interacting objects. An ADL should allow for this kind of hierarchy of component patterns. It should allow different compositions to be compiled to different languages. For example, a particular component may be compiled to Java while another is compiled to C++. The operator (connector) between the two components would have to compile to something that supported multiple languages, for example, a message-queuing system or a middleware-based distributed object broker based on CORBA.

Architecture Analysis

An ADL should support the ability to analyze an architecture. Analysis of this sort goes beyond type checking such as may be performed by a programming language compiler. Analysis of architectures includes automated and nonautomated reasoning about quality attributes of a system. The difficulty in validating a program statically (by parsing it) applies to an architecture specification as well. Analysis, or reasoning about the properties of an architectural design, is currently best accomplished by producing models that address specific quality attributes and then applying heuristics-based techniques of reasoning.

ADL research aims to automate this analysis by providing machine-readable specifications of specific quality attribute requirements and then analyzing the architecture specification to see if it conforms to the quality attribute specification. As we have also seen, there are qualities that are bound to the executable system (such as performance and reliability), and there are qualities that are bound to the source of the system (such as maintainability).

First-Class Connectors

One of Garlan and Shaw's main points about architectural representations is that connectors, the elements that operate on components, should be considered equal to components. Wolf and Perry recognized this need as well when they included connectors as one of the main component types, along with processing and data elements. Most ad hoc architecture descriptions tend to gloss over connectors, typically representing them in a diagram as lines, arrows, or just adjacencies between component boxes. This is indicative of how connectors are typically not treated as significantly as processing and data elements. However, it is the connectors that often embody the nonfunctional quality attributes and that bring form to the architecture.

Modules and Components

In programming languages such as Java and C++, a module is informally a set of classes that are somehow related (such as using Java packages or C++ namespaces). Typically, a module is considered to be a set of elements that exhibit high internal cohesion or are treated as a single compilation unit. "A module is a unit whose structural elements are powerfully connected among themselves and relatively weakly connected to elements of other units. Clearly there are degrees of connection; thus there are gradations of modularity" (Baldwin, 2000). In C++, a module could be a shared library or dynamic link library (DLL). In Java, this may be a single package or a collection of packages with a common parent package. A module in an object-oriented language is some set of elements such as classes and interfaces that is treated as a unit. The unit has an external interface and is dependent upon other interfaces. The module's interface is all publicly visible connecting elements such as C++ classes or Java classes and interfaces. The module's dependencies are all imported elements (which are visible connecting elements of other modules). In Java, this is all imported packages or classes (even the implicit ones like java.lang). In C++, these are all included files.

A module in a modifiable design can be changed without affecting other dependent modules. Thus, the changes do not affect its externally visible connecting elements. It may also be desirable to replace a module with another module of the same type. This kind of modifiability of adaptability requires a facility for replacing implementations but keeping the interface the same. In programming languages like Java and C++, this means providing a different implementation of the same externally visible classes. This is partly a limitation because a module imports connecting elements from other modules by explicit element naming. In Java, a package is imported directly by name. In C++, a class is included by filename and referenced by name. To achieve some modularity, software developers can use patterns and idioms that provide a level of indirection between the imported connecting element and the implementation. For example, in C++ a module can be designed so that it only makes abstract base classes visible. In Java, the use of interfaces accomplishes the same thing. However, these techniques still rely on explicit naming.

In order to obtain an instance of an implementation of an abstract connecting element, there needs to be some boot object like a factory. This is easier to achieve in Java because classes can be dynamically loaded and instantiated via the `Class.forName` technique. In C++, this is commonly accomplished by providing a different implementation of a factory class, compiled into a stand-alone shared object that is linked at run time. The indirection is achieved by changing the application's path so that it finds the different library. Java's reflection application program interface (API) (also a module) can be used to decouple other modules. A Java object can invoke a method on an object without prior knowledge of the other class's definition. The only assumption that must be embodied in the first class is the signature of a method. The name of the class and the name of the method can be parameterized.

Java supports modularity a little better than C++. In Java, you can create a module, (a package), and hide classes and methods to outside classes while still making them visible to classes within the package itself by using the protected keyword. This is one way to achieve high-internal cohesion and low-external coupling. The Java compiler prevents classes from outside of the package from linking to protected methods and data. In C++, the friend keyword can be used to grant some classes access to private and protected members, thus including the friend class in the module. Of course, a module can be defined by policy or convention by stating which connecting elements may be legally used.

Another kind of connecting element is the user interface and the common data representation. Two applications can be connected by shared data that is stored in a file or database. The connection is not physically between the two applications but rather through the user. For example, consider a configuration file for an application. The configuration file may be a simple text file that stores name-value pairs. The user can edit this file directly in any text editor. The application doesn't care which editor is used, as long as the configuration data is in the right format. XML is becoming a popular data interchange format. A user can create or edit an XML file using an XML editor or even a standard text editor. The application that consumes the XML is indifferent as to what software was used to create the XML. Thus, this connection does not link one activity to another; rather, two different activities (providing data for an application and editing the data) are considered connected simply because they use the same information store.

As you can see, programming languages are insufficient for representing architectural level designs because they lack explicit connecting elements. Connecting elements are typically embodied in import/export mechanisms by the use of local or remote method invocations, by the use of shared data representations, or a combination of the two. However, connecting elements are just as important from the architectural level of design as processing and data elements. Furthermore, the ability to abstract the implementation of a connecting element within an architecture specification is what makes an ADL so powerful.

We will not discuss ADLs much more in this book, since they are not commonly used in enterprise application architecting. However, understanding the concepts of ADLs is important to understanding the architectural level of design, as well as understanding the elements necessary for representing architecture design decisions.

Example: C2 SADL

C2 SADL is the C2 Software Architecture Description Language currently under research (Taylor, 1996). C2 is an architectural style as well as an ADL. The C2 architecture is intended for designing a flexible, extensible component- and message-based system that has a graphical user interface. A C2-based system is structured as a hierarchy of concurrent components that communicate via connectors, which are message-routing mechanisms. A component can have, at most, two connectors, a *top* connector and a *bottom* connector, which attach it to components that are in the immediate higher-up level or the immediate lower level in the hierarchy, respectively. The top connector of one component is coupled with the bottom connectors of other components, and vice versa. There is no limit to the number of connectors that may be coupled with a single connector. A C2 component is only aware of the components above it, but not below it, in the hierarchy. Requests go *up* the hierarchy, and notifications go *down*.

A C2 architecture is an arrangement of C2 components. It is a specification of the coupling of the connectors of components, which form a hierarchy of components with one component being the topmost component of the hierarchy (a component that cannot make requests of any other component).

A system conforming to the C2 architectural style relies on a programming language-neutral event mechanism, such as a message queue. C2 components may be written using different programming languages since they are physically decoupled and communicate only via events or messages.

C2 SADL is composed of three parts:

- Interface Definition Notation (IDN)
- Architecture Description Notation (ADN)
- Architecture Construction Notation (ACN)

The IDN supports the textual specification of C2 component interfaces. A component interface is composed of a top domain and a bottom domain. Each domain has inputs and outputs. The component specification also consists of specifications for parameters, methods, behavior, and context.

The ADN supports the textual specification of a C2 architecture, which consists of a hierarchy of components that are coupled via their connectors. It also supports the textual description of a C2 system (an instance of a C2 architecture), which specifies the bindings of components and connectors to implementations.

The ACN supports the textual specification of architecture changes, such as for expressing dynamic architecture changes. Systems that are C2-compliant can be self-adaptive, changing their own architecture at run time, such as by changing bindings to implementations.

This ADL is currently a prototype language, and there are no commercial tools at the time of this writing that support it.

Applying ADLs

Architectural description languages are not commonly used in the development of enterprise applications. ADLs are mostly experimental. However, there are two benefits to understanding the problems that ADLs attempt to solve. The first benefit is that an understanding of the problems addressed by ADLs can help a designer to think about the solution to his particular system. The second benefit is that in some circumstances the designer may need to design an ADL for a particular enterprise problem space or as a tool for a software product line.

Understanding the problems addressed by ADLs can help elevate the designer into a higher-level context or granularity of problem solving. The architect, for example, should not be concerned with the implementation of connecting elements when first formulating an architecture design concept. When applying design operations like decomposition or abstraction to a design, the architect should not be concerned with how the components or elements are physically connected, but rather about the nature of the connection (whether it is synchronous or asynchronous; whether it must support run time or compile time decoupling).

An approach to architecting a line of products could involve a proprietary or custom ADL. An ADL could be as simple as a language for describing a deployment configuration of a system. Unlike a configuration file, the ADL would provide much stronger semantics that could require the system to be compiled before deployment. Such a language could simplify the customization of a product framework. Many enterprise software applications are really frameworks that must be customized by the customer. Sometimes this customization can take the simple form of configuration files or the creation of object attributes, business processes, workflows, and business rules. Some customization, however, must occur before the system is actually instantiated or deployed. For example, in some forms of an adaptable system, the basic business entities of the system need to be extended to support customer-specific attributes, entities, and entity relationships. An ADL, possibly a simple one, could be used to describe the entities and their relationships in a nonprogramming language. Compiling this system description could generate the Data Definition Language (DDL) for the database tables and generate the Java or C++ classes that represent the entities in the program, as well as generate all of the code necessary to map the data between the two representations.

Summary

In this chapter, we looked closely at the fundamental concepts of architecture design representation, specifically at the component level of design. The component level of design allows us to reason about properties of the system without first constructing the entire system. The fundamental language of specifying architecture design is composed of elements, form, and rationale. Elements are processing, data, or connecting. A connecting element couples data and/or processing elements and itself may be composed of data and processing elements. Form is composed of weighted properties and relationships. Rationales capture the reasons why certain design decisions were made over other decisions.

Architecture description languages, or ADLs, are high-level languages for describing the component view of a software system. ADLs have been researched, but they have not been applied much in practice. Unified Modeling Language (UML), according to some authors, is used as an ADL, even though some feel that it is inadequate for expressing architecture-related designs. By studying the nature of ADLs, you should have a good idea as to how difficult it is to describe the architecture of an application at a level higher than a programming language. Most ADLs are a language for describing a system from a physical view in terms of components.

The dependency structure matrix (DSM) introduced in Chapter 5 is still one of our most powerful representation tools. It allows us to describe our system and reason about it from a modular or design task point of view. However, the DSM does not provide us with the runtime view that ADLs do. The ideas from ADLs (components and connectors) along with DSMs provide us with a powerful set of tools for capturing architecture knowledge. In Chapter 8, we elaborate on quality attributes and quality models. Quality attributes are the properties of a system that we are attempting to achieve in our design. Modular and component views of a system allow us to understand and reason about many quality attributes before implementing the application. In Chapter 9, we discuss the component-level equivalent of the modular operators, called the *design operators*.

CHAPTER 8

Quality Models and Quality Attributes

The quality of a system is directly related to the ability of the system to satisfy its functional, nonfunctional, implied, and specified requirements. A system has many characteristics such as functionality, performance, and maintainability. The quality of each of these characteristics comprises the total quality of the system. Each characteristic can be specified as an attribute of the system. For example, the throughput of a system operation can be measured in terms of amount of data per unit time or number of operations per unit time. Measurable or observable qualities of a system are called *quality attributes*. Quality attributes are not mutually exclusive; rather, they tend to interact with each other. The value of one quality attribute, such as performance, may depend on the value of another quality attribute, such as modifiability. A standard taxonomy of quality attributes is called a *quality model*. A quality model serves as a framework for system specification and testing.

Quality attributes serve as a framework within which to analyze requirements, stakeholder concerns, and design decisions. The purpose of this chapter is to present a set of common quality attributes and describe how some of these are directly influenced by the architectural design of a system.

Quality in software is subjective due to the lack of formalism and consensus in defining software quality. Quality is inherently difficult to measure. Usually it is associated with the absence of defects in application function (for example, it passes functional testing). It also includes some notion of performance and reliability and even the quality of the source code. Performance and reliability can be measured to some degree, but even those numbers do not guarantee that a customer will have the same results. Other aspects of quality are even more difficult to measure, such as maintainability, and stakeholders tend to have different ideas of what these qualities mean. As an example, I've been in various discussions with other developers where I've inquired about a particular design choice and the response was that it was a "better quality design." But when I've inquired about the meaning of "better quality design," I've usually gotten vague responses. This is indicative of the state of the practice in using quality attributes to specify requirements and drive design.

In this chapter, I discuss the fundamentals of quality attributes and how they relate to software architecture. The topics in this chapter are:

Process and product quality.   Quality techniques are applied to the process as well as the product. Improving the quality of the process can have a positive impact on the quality of the product. However, quality must also be designed in. Process quality improvements can help with the construction of a sound, durable system that passes many types of verification tests (for example, has a high reliability measure or high throughput). Process quality does not, however, address other qualities, such as the modifiability of a system or even the validity of the system (that is, whether the functions of the system correspond to the problem that is being solved).

Specifying quality requirements.   Quality attributes are specific characterizations of a system that can be measured or observed. Some quality attributes have numeric values, such as attributes related to performance and reliability, which can be measured by executing the system. Other quality attributes have qualitative values, which are observed by either executing the system (such as for usability testing) or by performing other nonoperational scenarios (such as identifying the steps necessary to introduce a new function into the system).

Understanding quality models.   There are several quality models from which software developers can choose. Most of them are very similar and all of them are fairly informal. A quality model is a taxonomy of quality attributes and their relationships. This serves as a framework for detailed system specification, design evaluation, and system testing.

Architecting with quality attributes.   There are several quality attributes that are influenced by the architecture of a system and which can be (partially) evaluated from the architectural design models. These attributes are functionality, performance, modifiability, and reliability. Usability, which is a quality of the executable system itself, can be influenced to a lesser degree by the architecture.

Process and Product Quality

Quality permeates all aspects of software development from the initial requirements gathering process to the operation of the executable system. Qualities can be attributed to two basic things: process and product. *Process qualities* are a measure of an activity the end result of which is a product. Some methodologists compare software development with manufacturing and try to measure and control it accordingly. The philosophy is based on the premise that if a process is of the highest quality, the products will be of high quality as well. This is why there are so many standards for software engineering that focus on quality management.

A classic measurement of software development is the lines of code (LOC) or thousands of lines of code (KLOC) written per person per unit time. Other classic attributes include bug discovery rate and bug fix rate: The ratio of the two measured over time can be a good indicator of whether bug-fixing activities are effective. The McCabe complexity measure can indicate how complex a software routine is and therefore how modifiable it is. These processes and measures are largely nonarchitectural. There is currently only limited information available on quality models for software architecting processes so we won't discuss process quality any further.

Product quality is a measure of a tangible product itself, such as a technical specification, or a running system. Products are the result of some activity or process. An intermediate product is any model, specification, document, or source code that is prepared or created in support of constructing an executable system. An intermediate product's quality attributes are measured using internal metrics. The attribute values may be quantitative or qualitative. The results of evaluating an intermediate product provide a reasonable prediction of some of the target system's quality attributes.

The ultimate product is, of course, the executable system itself. Intermediate products are products used in designing the final system. Intermediate products include specifications, models, plans, and source code. Architecting is a model-building activity and as such there are many intermediate architecture products, which collectively form the architectural description. The architectural description is the intermediate product that we measure early in the system's life cycle to validate the design against the quality requirements.

Specifying Quality Requirements

Here are some sample questions that provide ways to discover information about quality attributes. How does the application fit into the enterprise's objectives, processes, and other information systems? How does it relate to other systems including manual business processes? Is the application suited to its intended use? Is it intuitive and usable or does it sit in a virtual corner collecting cyber-dust? The answers to these questions are embodied in an application's characteristics.

An application is characterized by several quality attributes. *Quality attributes* are specific characterizations or properties that can have some quantitative or qualitative value and are measurable or observable. A *quality attribute* is a property of a process or product that can have some qualitative or quantitative value and can be measured or observed. Quality attributes are sometimes referred to as the "ilities," as in *maintainability, portability, functionality,* and *usability.* A *quality requirement* is a specification of the acceptable values of a quality attribute that must be present in the system.

The types of quality attributes that an application has and the values they must hold can be specified in a requirements document; although often in practice these types of requirements go unstated. A requirements document may specify that the application must exhibit some minimal throughput measured in terms of the number of transactions per unit time. By leaving certain attributes out of the requirement specification, the acquirer may be stating that the particular quality is not required. More often than not, these requirements are left out due to lack of understanding of the quality or how to specify it. An architect must understand the implicit quality attribute requirements in order to produce a design for a durable system.

The external view of an application's qualities is called its *characteristics.* These are quality attributes that can be viewed by a user, such as usability and performance. Internal characteristics, or *subcharacteristics,* are quality attributes that are viewable by the developers. External characteristics are a manifestation of several internal characteristics. For example, performance is an external characteristic that may be internally measured by throughput and load balancing. Reliability may be externally measured by observing the number of failures in a given period of time. It may be internally measured by inspecting specifications and source code to assess the level of fault tolerance. One internal attribute may influence one or more characteristics. A characteristic may be influenced by more than one attribute. Improving performance tends to reduce the maintainability of a system.

Measuring Quality Attributes

A quality attribute has an associated set of metrics. A *metric* is a qualitative or quantitative measurement or scale of a specific quality attribute together with a method or technique for observing or measuring the quality. Metrics are applied at different phases of design and development. Different metrics may be applied to the same quality attribute at different phases. For example, design-related metrics may be applied to the design specifications for performance and when the system is executable, runtime metrics may be applied.

Internal metrics are applied to the executable system or its source code during the construction phase. Examples of internal metrics are the complexity of code logic, and the performance of specific functions or components, which compose a single, externally-visible system function.

External metrics (such as functionality or performance) are applied to a software product by executing the system and observing it. The most common external metrics are tests of the system's functions (whether it behaves according to specifications), reliability (how long the system remains operational before it must be repaired or restarted), and performance (whether it handles the specified user loads within the specified time constraints).

Quality requirements should be specified along with functional requirements as unambiguously as possible. With the exception of performance and availability qualities, most other nonfunctional qualities are not typically specified quantitatively. These qualities may be specified with scenarios. Scenarios are the context in which some nonquantitative attributes can be evaluated. These scenarios are similar to internal metrics because they are applied to the design models of the system and possibly its source and may be specified by the software designers and architects, with assistance from the acquirers and users.

Quality Requirements and Architectural Design

This chapter is concerned with product qualities that can be measured and evaluated with respect to the architecture of an application. These measurements are performed primarily on the architectural description but can also be performed on the executable system. Some measurements can be quantitative, but most architectural qualities are evaluated qualitatively. Qualitative evaluations, although not as rigorous as quantitative ones, can still be fairly objective and provide useful predictions about the success of the system in meeting its quality requirements.

Architecture styles and patterns are two ways to address quality attributes. Different architecture styles address different sets of quality attributes and to varying degrees. Thus, specifying the desired quality attributes of an application is central to the design process because it affects the architectural style of the system.

Not all quality attributes are addressed by the architectural design. Quality attributes must be considered in all phases of design, implementation, and deployment. Usability, for example, has nonarchitectural aspects. Choosing between various widget types and their placement in a window is localized to a single component and is considered detailed design. However, the overall usability of the system, which is represented by the conceptual design of the system, does have some architectural implications such as what the system does and how its functionality is partitioned across components and associated with user roles (actors). Performance is affected by the architectural design as well as implementation details. The way a system is distributed can affect performances as well as the selection of implementation details such as choice of algorithms or data structures in the implementation of a class method.

Systems Knowledge and Quality Attributes

Let's consider how quality attributes fit into our hierarchy of systems knowledge. Quality attributes are like variables or dimensions of a thing and can have a quantitative or qualitative value. In terms of levels of systems knowledge, the identification of quality attributes is equivalent to the source level (level 0) of systems knowledge. Quality requirements are specific values or ranges of values for these attributes. This is data level knowledge about the system (level 1). Recall that systems design moves from lower levels to higher levels. Requirements specifications produce data level knowledge. Software architecting begins with creating models (generative level of systems knowledge, or level 2) that can generate this data level knowledge.

We evaluate the architecture to see if it indeed does produce the same data as specified in level 1. According to our systems knowledge model design, evaluation is itself a form of systems analysis; in this case, we are analyzing the design models and the output is another set of data that is compared to the original data.

Barriers to Achieving Quality

Software quality attributes can be difficult to specify, address by design, measure, and test. Therefore, most software applications typically lack in those areas that are not functional. Common reasons for failure to meet high levels of quality in all aspects of a system include:

- Misunderstanding of the importance of quality attributes
- Inadequate languages for expressing and specifying quality requirements
- Inadequate modeling methods and notations for expressing solutions that address specific quality attributes
- Difficulty in designing for quality attributes
- Lack of documented design and architecture patterns for addressing quality attributes
- Quality control as an afterthought in most projects

Common Quality Attribute Misunderstandings

Quality attributes are commonly misunderstood. Eberhardt Rechtin (Rechtin, 1991) said, "The ilities are condemned as extraneous, as unnecessary gold plating, and as superfluous paperwork, adding to a program cost and micromanagement." He cautions the architect: "The ilities are the imperatives of the external world as expressed at the boundaries with the internal world of the system. Reliability is the imperative of the user, affordability that of the client, maintainability that of the operator, and accountability that of the auditor."

NOTE The costs of maintaining and extending an application will account for most of the cost of the application over its lifetime.

Specifying Quality Requirements

Until recently there has been little work in the field of formal specification for nonfunctional requirements. There is a considerable amount of work in the area of formal specification for functional requirements. For example, the Z specification language is based on the solid rigorous foundations of mathematics, but is useful for specifying functional requirements only. The problem is that specifying quality requirements is difficult. Yet the acquirer needs to understand clearly their requirements to be able to communicate them to the architect and development organization. The architects and developers need to understand these requirements unambiguously in order to assess whether they are possible to achieve in the final product.

Modeling Methods Don't Address Quality Attributes

Design methodologies are strong in representing functionality but weak in representing the nonfunctional requirements. Some methodologists feel that object orientation can effectively represent some of the quality attributes such as maintainability, understandability, and reusability. But object-oriented methodologies do not directly model these qualities; rather, the designer must use heuristics and design patterns to address them. Designing for quality attributes is difficult and takes experienced architects.

Designing for Quality Attributes

Quality attributes are interdependent and cannot be achieved in isolation. Every design decision potentially impacts multiple quality attributes. This makes designing difficult. Each design decision would have to be evaluated to see its impact on existing quality attribute values. A new design decision may invalidate a previous one, causing the designer to vacillate between them until an effective balance is achieved. A good design is a balanced design that addresses all of the quality attributes within tolerance.

The difficulty in designing to meet these various competing quality attributes is why modeling and design methodologies usually don't address them. Each quality attribute is like a variable. In other engineering disciplines where problems can be stated mathematically, a good design is a solution that satisfies all of the variables. If a problem can be represented with linear equations, then the solutions are easy to find. Some classes of nonlinear problems also have solutions but most do not. Software design is like a nonlinear problem, expressed mathematically.

Solution Catalogues and Quality Attributes

Since the seminal work *Design Patterns* (Gamma, 1995) was published, there has been a fervent effort to catalogue software design solutions. Patterns can be used to address some quality attributes. For example, the original *Design Patterns* addressed some aspects of reusability and extensibility. Mapping quality attributes to a design pattern's context and problem statements is not easy and there is no automated way to do this. The growing body of patterns does not make the designer's life any easier because there is no effective way to organize this knowledge that makes it easy to search and retrieve. Most design patterns start with a design problem or set of forces that must be balanced by the design. For example, the design problem for the Singleton pattern is how to control access to a single instance of some resource (Gamma, 1995). But if you are unable to articulate your design problem, then a pattern may not be of much use. How would you map a specific reliability requirement to some problem statement about global synchronized access to a resource? The difficulty in using patterns, as we will see in Chapter 10, is in mapping a quality requirement to a pattern's problem and context statements.

It may be worthwhile for practitioners and researchers to begin cataloguing patterns with respect to standardized quality attributes to facilitate their adoption and to contribute to a better understanding of quality attributes in general. Some of this work has already begun at the Software Engineering Institute (SEI) with Attribute-Based Architectural Styles (Clements, 2002).

Quality Control Is an Afterthought

Testing almost always occurs late in projects, usually when the system is close to being complete. Most modern methodologies incorporate testing early and often, and this is one of the hallmarks of the iterative approach to software development as seen in process models like the Rational Unified Process (RUP). In my experience with small and medium-sized organizations, testing is still put off until the end, and engineering management assumes that engineer-driven unit testing is sufficient until the end. Putting testing off until the end of a project is, in a way, a statement that quality is not important enough to be assessed early. Furthermore, almost all of this testing is strictly on the functional characteristics of the system and not on the other quality attributes.

This is especially true in in-house development where there seems to be a tacit assumption that the users will test the system while it is in production (and that they will tolerate a buggy system). This implies that usability is also not considered to be important. I have also seen acquirers balk at project schedules and budgets that included lengthy test phases and technical documentation activities. This is also a consequence of not realizing the importance of quality requirements.

Understanding Quality Models

In this section, I present some well-known quality models and then compare them. I give overviews of quality attributes defined in each model, but reserve more detailed discussion of specific quality attributes to the following section. Quality models are systems that relate various quality attributes and, in some cases, identify key engineering practices to address them and metrics appropriate for measuring or observing them. Each model uses different terminology; the terminology that I use is represented in the quality metamodel in Figure 8.1. The quality metamodel can be used as a basis for describing various quality models. A quality model is a specific instance of the quality metamodel and defines specific characteristics, quality attributes, and metrics.

A quality model is a specification of the required characteristics that a software system must exhibit. Architects can use existing documented quality models as templates and derive a quality model for a specific system. Sometimes a particular class of application may not need to exhibit all of the characteristics or quality attributes as specified in a generic quality model. It may not even require use of all of the metrics specified. The architect should prepare as part of the requirements specification a specific quality model that identifies the characteristics, the quality attributes for each characteristic, and the metrics for those quality attributes. The architect may have to produce such a specification for each product of the development effort, such as the executable system itself, and some intermediate products, such as the architectural description.

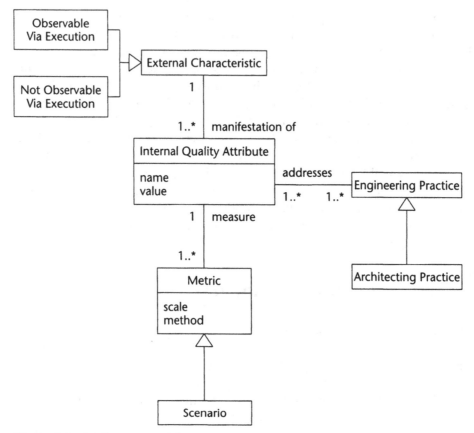

Figure 8.1　Quality metamodel.

There are various quality models that have been developed over the years. The earliest, most recognized is the McCall/GE Quality Model that was published in 1977 (McCall, as cited in DeGrace, 1993). The model organizes quality around three uses of software: product revision, product operations, and product transition. Each of these uses is associated with a set of quality characteristics. Product revision includes maintainability, flexibility, and testability. Product transition includes portability, reusability, and interoperability. Product operations include correctness, reliability, efficiency, integrity, and usability.

Barry Boëhm (Boëhm, as cited in DeGrace, 1993) presented a similar model that was composed of 19 essential quality attributes. The Boëhm model shares a common subset with the McCall model and identifies additional quality attributes. DeGrace and Stahl (DeGrace, 1993), refine the McCall model and add the notion of engineering practices that address specific quality attributes. A joint technical committee of the International Organization of Standardization (ISO) and the International Electrotechnical Commission (IEC), called the

ISO/IEC JTC1/SC7, prepared a standard for software quality characteristics and metrics called ISO/IEC 9126-1:2001 (ISO/IEC, 2001). This standard identifies six external quality characteristics—functionality, reliability, usability, efficiency, maintainability, and portability—that are further subdivided into several subcharacteristics or internal quality attributes. For example, functionality consists of the internal characteristics: suitability, accuracy, interoperability, and security. Recent work at the Software Engineering Institute at Carnegie Melon University has produced a framework for specifying quality models by adding more precision to quality attribute definitions and introduced metrics and analysis techniques for measuring software and architecture descriptions.

Early development of quality models was based on the assumption that it would be possible to produce objective measures of quality attributes for any system and that a function could be applied to the quality attribute values to produce an overall quality indicator. Years of practice have revealed that objective measures of the internals of software are elusive. There have been some metrics, such as McCabe's measure of code complexity, that produce useful information, though not entirely objective. Increased complexity of the logic of a software module can make it more difficult to understand and maintain, but if the design is based on a well-known pattern or algorithm, then the complexity is reduced because the logic is well documented.

Most small and medium-sized development organizations do not employ formal metrics for nonfunctional requirements. Instead they typically rely on ad hoc testing, code inspections, design walk-through, and subjective assessments of quality attributes. If done right, these can be effective means of predicting the quality of a system. The antitheses of formal metrics are heuristics and best practices. Following best practices can result in improved quality. We will see some of these less formal techniques applied in Chapter 14 on architectural assessment.

The McCall/GE Model quality model is one of the first recognized quality models. It is sometimes referred to as the Factor Criteria Metric model. The model organizes quality around three uses of software: product revision, product operations, and product transition. Each of these uses is associated with a set of quality characteristics called factors, a set of criteria of things to build, and a set of metrics for measuring and controlling factors in a given application. *Factors* (characteristics) describe the external view of the software as viewed by users of the application. A factor is associated with a set of *criteria* (quality attributes) that describe the internal view of the software, as seen by software engineers. *Metrics* are a scale and a method of measuring a particular attribute.

Product operation relates to qualities of the system while it is operational. The criteria for product operation quality are:

- Accuracy
- Reliability

- Efficiency
- Integrity
- Usability

The factor called reliability has simplicity as one if its criteria. Simplicity is a desired internal characteristic of software and describes aspects such as the structure of the software in terms of module interconnection and the program logic of individual modules. The complexity or simplicity of the structure of the software in terms of module interconnection can be measured in terms of the amount of coupling between modules, the complexity of the communications between them, and whether there are cyclic dependencies between modules.

Product revision relates to the source code and development aspect of the system. The criteria for product revision quality are:

- Maintainability
- Flexibility
- Testability

Maintainability is partially affected by the complexity of the source code. Code complexity can be measured in terms of the possible number of execution paths through a given function or method (determined by the number and types of loops and conditional branches) and by the coupling of internal structures such as classes.

Product transition relates to reusing or re-purposing some or all of the system's components. The criteria of product transition quality are:

- Interface facility
- Reusabilty
- Transferability

Another early quality model is attributed to Boëhm and is similar in identification of criteria to the McCall. Boëhm performed a study for the National Bureau of Standards Institute for Computer Sciences and Technology, the purpose of which was to identify a set of characteristics of quality software and to define metrics for each of those characteristics. The goal of the metrics was to provide a quantitative measure of the degree to which a software program possessed the associated quality characteristic and to define the overall quality of a software application as a function of the values of those metrics. The Boëhm model consisted of criteria similar to the McCall model and also included:

- Validity
- Clarity
- Understandability

- Modifiability
- Modularity
- Generality
- Economy
- Resilience
- Documentation

DeGrace and Stahl (DeGrace, 1993) identify 11 characteristics of good software that are based on the McCall model, with a few modifications in terminology. DeGrace and Stahl emphasize software engineering practices that address one or more characteristics. Software engineering practices include coding practices, management practices, and the use of design heuristics. For example, the engineering practice of modularity addresses rat killing (maintainability), flexibility, testability, portability, reusability, and interoperability. Applying a software engineering practice does not guarantee that a quality will be satisfied, but is a necessary tool for addressing the quality.

These early models did not specifically target the architecture of an application but rather the entire process and product of software engineering. The term architecture wasn't really applied to software design until the late 1980s. One of the earliest books on the subject was Laurence Best's *Application Architecture* (Best, 1990). Best identified several *architectural characteristics* that must be present in large-scale applications for them to be completely successful in supporting the sponsoring organization. Those characteristics are:

- Accuracy and comprehensiveness
- Simplicity of use
- Operational flexibility
- Ease of development, maintenance, and extension
- Security and control
- Resource efficiency
- Recovery

Qualities that are specific to the architecture of an application are treated a little differently than software engineering quality attributes. For one thing, quality attributes that can be addressed by the architecture can be evaluated or measured against the architecture (as represented in the architectural description). This means that many important characteristics of the application can be evaluated before the application is implemented. Measuring intermediate products such as design specifications is not new; the prior quality models encompassed those activities. However, the idea that there is a level of design higher than the usual functional and data design and that this design can be evaluated is relatively new. This higher level of design is, of course, the architectural level of design. Best's treatment of characteristics is not rigorous and does not define a set of architecting practices or metrics for the characteristics. Rather, he relied on the intuitive understanding of the characteristics.

Bass, Clements, and Kazman (Bass, 1998) state that architecture addresses more than functional requirements. Some requirements are implicit in the business or organization objectives: "Business considerations determine qualities that must be accommodated in a system's architecture. These qualities are over and above that of functionality, which is the basic statement of the system's capabilities, services, and behavior." Their quality model does not use the terms *functional* and *nonfunctional requirements* because they find that the terms are archaic and imprecise. Basically the term *functional* in the mathematical sense means a relation that maps program state and input to program state and output. Because there are many nondeterministic behaviors of applications, the term isn't fully appropriate.

Furthermore, many nonfunctional requirements technically are functional in the above sense. Instead, they prefer two broad categories in which qualities are contained and systems measured. These are *observable via execution* and *not observable via execution*. A system can be tested or measured against many qualities by executing the system. Typically, this is how functional or behavioral requirements are validated. It is also how performance-related requirements are validated. Many qualities cannot be observed by executing the system. This includes validating whether it is easy to integrate or modify or determining whether it has met its time-to-market requirements.

The quality model is organized by three categories: system attributes (both observable via execution and not-observable via execution), business qualities, and architecture description qualities. They do not distinguish between characteristics and quality attributes as in the quality metamodel of Figure 8.1. The following quality attributes may be observed by executing the system:

- Performance
- Security
- Availability
- Functionality
- Usability

Usability is composed of six quality attributes:

- Learnability
- Efficiency
- Memorability

- Error avoidance
- Error handling
- Satisfaction

The following quality attributes are not observed by executing the system; rather, they are qualities of the source of the system and its architectural design:

- Modifiability
- Portability
- Reusability
- Integrability
- Testability

Some quality attributes are business related. These include qualities concerning cost and schedule, such as:

- Time to market
- Cost

Some business-related quality attributes concern the market and marketing:

- Targeted market
- Rollout schedule
- Extensive use of legacy systems

In the SEI quality model, quality attributes have three characterizations: *external stimuli, architectural decisions,* and *responses* (Clements, 2002). An architecture responds to stimuli, such as a modification to functionality. The requirements need to be specified in such a way as to be observable. For example, maintainability should be specified as concrete change scenarios that a software developer would do in order to modify the system. These scenarios can be observed. This model provides the most precise framework in which to specify quality attributes and to address them in an architectural description.

The SEI approach to characterizing quality attributes can lead to reusable quality attribute templates that may compose a library of such attribute specifications. Quality attribute characterizations are a treelike structure that can lead questioning for evaluations or analysis and design activities. Quality attributes are associated with specific scenarios that address the concern of specific stakeholders. The quality attribute characterization has associated general questions that can be asked of any design. The system-specific scenario itself defines the stimulus and the response. The general questions can be applied to the specific scenario. These questions then lead to questions concerning the ability of the architecture to fulfill the scenario (see Chapter 14).

The ISO/IEC 9126 (ISO/IEC, 2001) standard organizes software quality into six characteristics or goals, each of which is composed of several quality attributes or subcharacteristics. External qualities may be experienced by users of the system and subcharacteristics are the internal quality attributes, which, when properly balanced, achieve the external qualities. The six external characteristics are:

- Functionality
- Reliability
- Usability
- Efficiency
- Maintainability
- Portability

The responses of a quality attribute characterization of the SEI quality model correspond to the subcharacteristics of the 9126 model. For example, in the 9126 model, the reliability characteristic has three subcharacteristics: maturity, fault tolerance, and recoverability, each of which can be measured. In the SEI quality model, availability is the quality attribute and mean time to failure, reliability, levels of service, availability, fault detection time, and fault recovery time are the responses. In the SEI model, the quality attribute is the external characteristic, and the response is an internal measurable characteristic.

Benefits of Quality Models

Before we look at some detailed quality attributes, let's consider some of the benefits of using a quality model and the benefits of a standardized approach. The ISO/IEC 9126 specification identifies the following uses:

- Validate the completeness of a requirements definition
- Identify software requirements
- Identify software design objectives
- Identify software testing objectives
- Identify user acceptance criteria for a completed software product

Specifying quality attributes unambiguously is difficult. However, by applying a quality model, we can address many of the issues associated with achieving quality. A quality model that defines quality attributes precisely improves communications between acquirers, architects, and developers. This can result in quality requirements being specified more precisely and more frequently. A quality model that specifies usable and practical metrics can improve the quality of design models. Effective application of a quality model, especially in evaluating architectural design decisions, adds more quality control earlier in a project's life cycle where it is typically needed most. Quality models, unfortunately, cannot communicate the importance of quality attributes. Convincing acquirers or management of the importance of quality attributes beyond functionality and performance is left as an exercise for the reader.

Architecting with Quality Attributes

In this section, I present descriptions of the quality attributes identified in the quality models that can be addressed by an application's architecture:

- Functionality
- Performance (efficiency)
- Modifiability
- Availability and reliability
- Usability
- Portability

Functionality

Functionality is the ability of the system or application to satisfy the purpose for which it was designed. Functionality is related to validity, correctness, interoperability, and security. Some of these quality attributes are more affected by the architecture than others. Functionality drives the initial decomposition of a system architecture into a set of components that together perform the functions of the system. An architecture cannot easily be evaluated using functional criteria. Functionality is the basis upon which all other quality attributes are specified because the decomposition of the system is partly affected by functionality. Performance must be measured with respect to certain functions. Designing for performance requires an understanding of the functionality in order to distribute it or modularize it appropriately. Maintainability must be measured with respect to modifying or adding functions in a particular functional component or set of components.

A functional specification is a common document used to describe functionality-related requirements. This is quite often the only specification produced for a system or application. An architecture based solely on a functional specification will typically suffer in the other quality attribute areas. Maintainability, for example, is quite often never specified and as a result most systems are more difficult and costly to maintain than they probably would have been had the architecture taken this quality attribute into account.

Interoperability

Interoperability is the quality of a system that enables it to work with other applications, systems, and technologies, even those that have not been foreseen during original development. In modern information processing, business system interoperability is becoming a major necessity. In in-house development a system or application will eventually need to interoperate with other systems in the same organization and even with systems outside of the enterprise (Business to Business [B2B] integration). Systems may interoperate in order to accomplish some higher-level, higher-value function, such as the integration of the manufacturing supply chain, in order to improve responsiveness while lowering costs associated with maintaining excess inventory. They may also interoperate in order to achieve other quality attributes. For example, in order to manage security for many systems it becomes paramount that new systems and applications fit within the Information Technology (IT) architecture's existing security model and components. A common integration requirement for systems is the ability to leverage an existing directory of user information and security credentials.

Interoperability also affects commercial software developers. An enterprise software vendor that has an open system or one that has prebuilt adapters for existing technologies and systems has a better chance of selling its product than a competitor that has a closed, standalone architecture.

Security

Security is the ability to enforce authorization, authentication, and, in some cases, deliberate denial of service attacks. Authentication is the action of establishing the identity of a user or system. Authorization is the action of allowing or preventing a user or system access to some resource. Security is commonly addressed in the architecture using techniques like authentication and authorization servers (security gateways), network log monitors, firewalls, and other components that provide security services. The ISO/IEC 9126 model specifically does not include safety as a software quality attribute because it relates to the entire system, not just the software.

Security requirements can affect the functional decomposition of the system. Some operations and resources may need to be secured differently than others, and therefore need to be split apart from other components.

Performance (Efficiency)

Performance represents the responsiveness of the system, which can be measured by the time required to respond to events (stimuli) or by the number of events that are processed in a period of time. Typically, performance quality attributes are expressed as the number of transactions per unit of time or the length of time required to complete a single transaction. The external characteristic is usually measured as the number of concurrent users and the relative responsiveness of the application under user load.

Some aspects of performance are architectural. Specific choices of algorithms or data structures in code are not considered architectural decisions, but decisions such as how computations are distributed across components and the patterns of communication among components (intra- and interprocess) are architectural decisions. Intercomponent communication is usually more time consuming than internal computations (interprocess communication is commonly the bottleneck in systems performance). Performance is partially a function of how much communication and interaction occurs among system components. Performance can be modeled at the architectural level in terms of things like arrival rates and distributions of service requests, processing times, queue sizes, and latency (the rate at which requests are serviced).

DeGrace and Stahl refer to this quality as efficiency. *Code execution efficiency* is the economy required by the customer, such as the run time, response time, and memory used. They tacitly identify an architecture decision: minimize module-to-module and module-to-operating system communication. The characterization presented by DeGrace and Stahl focuses on the implementation (nonarchitectural) practices such as taking advantage of various compiler optimizations, keeping loop constructs free of unnecessary computations, grouping data for efficient processing, indexing data, and using virtual storage facilities (relational databases) to optimize data storage efficiency.

Performance has typically been a driving factor in system architecture and frequently compromises the achievement of all other qualities. However, with the price/performance ratio of hardware dropping and the cost of software development rising, other qualities are emerging as important competitors to performance.

Resource Efficiency

One aspect of performance is the efficient utilization of resources. Some authors refer to this attribute of performance as *resource efficiency*. Computational resources are becoming more powerful and cheaper (Moore's law). Processors are always getting faster, and systems have increasing memory capacities. The kinds of design idioms practiced in the past to save computational cycles and reduce memory usage become less relevant as system capabilities improve.

Performance (processor efficiency) affects the decomposition of a system and the design of the connecting protocols between components. A system may be decomposed into a set of layers in order to improve the modularity of the system (and therefore the maintainability and reusability), but this decomposition may impede the system's ability to satisfy performance requirements. The architect will have to make quality attribute and design trade-offs in situations such as this where quality attributes conflict. Performance qualities and software architecture are discussed in Chapter 14.

Modifiability

A modifiable architecture is one that can be added to or grown over time, possibly by other developers or customers in a straightforward way. In other words, it is more cost effective to add features to the existing application than to build a new application. Modifiability is sometimes called maintainability. A modifiable application can have new features added without requiring architectural rework, such as changes to how functions are distributed across components. The measure of modifiability is the cost and effort required to make a change to an application.

The types of stimuli related to modifiability are change requests for functions, platforms, quality attributes, or operating environment. Function change requests are probably the most common event. The architectural response to modification change requests may be the addition, modification, or deletion of components, connectors, or interfaces, as well as a cost and effort measure.

Availability and Reliability

Availability is an attribute of the system that measures the proportion of time the system is up and running usually by measuring the mean time to failure and the mean time to repair a system after a failure. Reliability is a closely related attribute and is often considered together with availability. Reliability is an attribute of the system that measures its ability to continue operating over time. Both attributes are partially addressed by the architecture.

The stimuli related to availability are hardware and software faults, which are measured using responses such as mean time to failure. The architectural decisions that affect availability include hardware and software redundancy and various fault-detection techniques such as retry and watchdog.

Recoverability

Recoverability (also known as repairability) is related to availability. If your system is one where processing is long running and the application must pick up where it left off after a shutdown or a crash, then you need to consider this property. This property isn't unique to transaction-based information systems; it is also appropriate for desktop applications. Consider a word processor that crashes while you are in the middle of writing some long important document. People cope with this case by saving frequently, but that isn't always successful. Modern word processors automatically save intermediate drafts or deltas between drafts of documents to the hard drive. Then if something crashes (the application or the operating system), when you launch the application, it recovers from its last state, allowing the user to save the modified document and continue working.

Simple applications tend to repair themselves, but more complex systems may require manual repair efforts to reset the state of the system so that it can start up correctly. This might involve launching a diagnostic program to check the integrity of the system before the actual system or application launches. Sometimes applications launch such diagnostic programs automatically every time the system restarts, regardless of whether or not it was shut down correctly.

One system that I worked on had a queue-based request processing architecture. Requests could not be lost so they were persisted in message queues and temporary workspaces. The system scaled using software and hardware redundancy but the queues were global. In order to prevent multiple processors from working on the same request, the state-of-the-request meta data was toggled to "in process." During normal shutdown, every process that could not complete a request would change its state back to "needs processing" so that it would be picked up again upon restart. However, if the system crashed in process, requests were orphaned. To solve the problem, we ran a diagnostic service as the first service during restart. This diagnostic service resets all orphaned requests so that they would be processed normally.

> **TIP** A common formula for availability is MTTF / (MTTF + MTTR), where MTTF is mean time to failure and MTTR is mean time to repair. Reliability is commonly considered to be the mean time to failure although some texts define it as mean time *between* failure (MTBF), which is the sum of MTTF + MTTR.

Usability

Usability typically refers to the usability with respect to the end user. However, usability also addresses other system users such as system maintainers, operators, and porting engineers. The 9126 model calls each of these aspects of usability *quality in use* with respect to a user type. End users (modeled as actors) are concerned with functionality, reliability, usability, and efficiency. Maintainers (often not modeled) are concerned with maintainability. Quality in use is the overall subjective quality of the system as influenced by multiple quality attributes. Quality in use is measured using scenarios.

Portability

Portability is the ability to reuse a component in a different application or operating environment such as hardware, operating systems, databases, and application servers. Portability can be considered a specialized type of modifiability. The measure of the portability of a system is based on how localized the changes are. The ideal is a single component. Like modifiability, portability is really a measure of the cost in terms of time and money to port a system. The portability benchmarks are specifications for specific system configurations on which the system must run. The ISO 9126 model identifies four portability-related attributes: adaptability, installability, conformance, and replaceability.

Another word for portability is *extensibility*. In my experience, this quality attribute is commonly ignored because I believe that it is misunderstood. Portability is often associated with porting the source code of an application from one operating system, such as Windows, to another operating system, such as Linux. Modifying a system or application so that users can access it from a Web interface is an example of extensibility. The change might not introduce new functionality into the system; rather, its operating environment has changed. Best says extensibility is "important because application designers can never foresee all the changes that will occur in an organization's operating environment." The costs of maintaining and extending an application will account for most of the cost of the application over its lifetime.

One example from my experience was seeing a product largely reworked because it didn't work within a standard Java 2 Enterprise Edition (J2EE) application server environment; it had been written using a proprietary application server platform. The application didn't have the quality of extensibility. Had the original designers anticipated that their proprietary application server would be obsolete in a year or two, they probably would not have gone through the headaches to make the migration when customers started demanding that it work on standard J2EE application servers. It was managing database connections explicitly, and end users of the application, who were developers using the proprietary application program interface (API), were required to use the database connection objects from the application to perform application-related database functions. Had the application been designed to isolate the component responsible for managing database connection, the end users would have had an easier time integrating the application into their J2EE environment and the software vendor would have had an easier time transitioning as well. There are two issues with the un-extensible approach:

- The end-user applications and the vendor-supplied platform have to be configured with the database connection information. This complicates the configuration, violates the Simplicity of Use quality, and makes it generally harder to troubleshoot.

- It is not possible to take advantage of transactions (performing updates on both the end-user's Enterprise Java Beans (EJBs) and the application's data objects) introducing a functional issue in the end-user's application. Consequently, data integrity can not be guaranteed.

As we saw in Chapter 6, one way to partially satisfy the extensibility requirement is to produce a set of platform-independent architectural models.

This is the premise of the Object Management Group's (OMG's) MDA approach. Platform-independent models represent the architecture independently of a particular middleware technology and can be reused when building similar systems. This doesn't ensure that the application itself is extensible, but it leaves behind as a tangible artifact a set of design documents that can drive future development efforts because the difficult work of producing an abstract architectural description has already been done. Producing implementation-independent architectural models forces the designer to consider the architecture from a platform-independent point of view.

Architecting and Quality Models

In the DeGrace and Stahl model, quality attributes are called *software engineering practices*. The SEI model calls these techniques architectural decisions. Of course, the former model emphasizes addressing quality attributes through implementation-level practices such as programming idioms. In the later model, which can be thought of as a specialization of the former, the specific software engineering practices are architectural decisions. The types of architectural practices include the use of patterns and heuristics to address the quality attributes.

In *Evaluating Software Architectures* (Clements, 2002), the authors use Attribute-Based Architectural Styles (ABAS) as a means for addressing particular quality attributes with specific architecture styles. Quality attributes, architecture styles, architecture patterns, and multiview architectural descriptions are all interdependent. An architecture style is a high-level architecture pattern that addresses a specific set of concerns or quality attributes.

For example, a classic pipes-and-filters style addresses quality attributes such as modifiability and reusability but at the expense of performance. We will look at architecture styles and patterns in Chapter 10. Different views in an architectural description address different stakeholders and their concerns. Some views, and hence some models, will address particular quality attributes and not others. Use cases, for example, address functionality but not performance.

Some quality attributes cannot be entirely evaluated by inspecting the models alone; some require additional context information such as scenarios. For example, modifiability cannot be measured without specifying what is to be modified. A set of modification scenarios must be supplied in order to make the evaluation. We will learn more about evaluation techniques in Chapter 14. The relationships between all of these concepts will unfold throughout the remainder of this book.

Summary

Quality attributes are measurable or observable characteristics of products and processes and are source-level knowledge. The quality requirements specification gives quantitative or qualitative values for these attributes that must be satisfied by the executable system. Building a system and then observing it to determine its quality attribute values is expensive, especially if any architectural rework needs to be performed. It is more cost effective to evaluate intermediate products, such as design models and source code, to get a reasonable prediction of the quality of the final system itself. Not all quality attributes can be satisfied by architectural decisions.

There are many reasons why the use of quality attributes is not found in most applications. These include misunderstanding of the importance of quality attributes, inadequate languages for expressing quality requirements, inadequate specification of quality requirements in projects, inadequate modeling methods and notations for expressing solutions that address specific quality attributes, the inherent difficulty in designing for quality attributes, the lack of documented design and architecture patterns for addressing quality attributes, and the fact that quality control is an afterthought in most projects.

Architectural Design Principles

In this chapter, we look at the general design operators of software architectural design and how they help the architect decompose the system into components and connectors that achieve desired quality attributes. Applying design operators transforms the architectural design of a system into one that is functionally equivalent but which exhibits different quality attributes. Each design operator effectively modifies a set of quality attributes associated with a given design affecting some positively and some negatively. Design operators apply to the component view of the architecture. Common design operators are decomposition, replication, compression, abstraction, and resource sharing.

I present the following topics in this chapter:

Architectural level of design. The architectural level of design is the design of the system in terms of components and connectors and their arrangements. It is at this level of design that the architecture design operators are applied.

Architecting with design operators. The design operators are explicit transformations of a design. The common design operators are decomposition, replication, compression, abstraction, and resource sharing. The application of a design operator may introduce new components, divide an existing component into two components and a connector, or compress two components and a connector into a single component.

Functional design strategies.   Design operators help us achieve the first principles of design (such as modularity, information hiding, and overall management of complexity). Architectural designs can also be transformed by applying higher-level "macro" operations such as design patterns and other design strategies. Two common functional design strategies, self-monitoring and recovery, are presented.

Architectural Level of Design

The architectural level of design focuses on the system at the level of components and connectors and their arrangements that address quality attribute requirements.

Applying Design Principles

Design methods by themselves are difficult to apply. For example, when applying the method of systematic variation, how do you decide which attribute to focus on and how to transform the design to some variation of that design? Understanding quality attributes helps you reason about specific characteristics of the system. Design principles guide the decisions that must be made during the application of design methods.

Systematic variation is a technique that helps the architect discover or create a solution field to a given problem. From this solution field, the architect can evaluate the design candidates and pick the most appropriate or at least reduce the field to a smaller set of more suitable candidates. But how does the architect go about creating and evaluating each design?

The architect applies some design operation or transformation to either generate a new design or to refine an existing design. This transformation may decompose the solution into more components, or abstract a part of the system to make its internal workings transparent to other components. Each operation preserves the functionality represented by the architecture, but changes its structural architecture and thus changes some of the quality attributes of the system being described. Each application of a design operation transforms a small portion of a design with respect to some given quality attribute such as reliability. For example, replicating one component potentially improves some reliability attributes and may negatively affect performance.

Each transformed design can undergo further transformations, thus producing a path through a set of potential solutions (see Figure 6.3). The architect can also go down multiple paths forming a solution tree. The set of nodes of the solution tree is called the solution field. From any given design variation, the architect may create two branches and apply different design operations to each branch. For example, the architect may apply the operation of abstraction on one branch and the operation of resource sharing on another. At any time the architect may apply design evaluation techniques to test the quality attributes of the design. Thus, we can see how the methods and principles of architectural design can be applied with the problem-solving design methods to find solutions.

The transformation of designs is not limited to first principles. You can also apply architecture styles and patterns as operations. You can think of these types of operations as macro operations. For example, if you were to apply the model-view-controller (MVC) pattern as individual first principles (retracing the steps that originally led to the advent of the pattern), you would produce a solution path containing several nodes. You may apply the principle of decomposition to separate the data (or application objects) from the presentation objects in order to improve reusability so that other presentation objects may use the objects. Then you may apply the principle of abstraction to hide the implementation details of the data object so that changes to its implementation do not affect the presentation objects, thus improving modifiability.

Operations are not necessarily transitive; that is, the order in which they are applied may matter. Applying a design pattern like MVC followed by an abstraction to improve modifiability may result in a different design with different quality attributes than applying the abstraction first followed by the MVC pattern. Fortunately, many designers have traversed the same path and have documented these patterns.

Using Systems Thinking

This section on systems thinking will help us to understand the scope of architecture design. One thing that distinguishes software architecture design from detail design is the scope of the problem being addressed. Software architecture design requires systems thinking, considering the entire view of the problem, not just subproblems. Subproblems help us to tackle complex problems, but the architect must continually synthesize the solutions to the subproblems in order to evaluate the overall system solution.

Systems thinking requires a balance between looking at the big picture and looking at the subpictures. It is easy to become overwhelmed with the big picture and fall victim to analysis paralysis. The experienced software architect can change perspectives from system level to component level as necessary. There is a heuristic for this implied in the last chapter: move between different levels of abstraction and scope. A related heuristic is "don't filter or formalize on the first pass." That is, don't interrupt your intuitive thinking in order to be entirely discursive or artificially systematic. It is important to not interrupt the flow of ideas as they come to you. So perform at least a two-pass approach solving a problem. On the first pass capture what comes to you and don't filter it or try to formalize it. On the second and subsequent passes, remove, revise, and refine as necessary.

This is similar to the writing process. The most important aspect of the first step is to get your ideas out. Once your ideas are out and on paper (or in a modeling tool), you can start formalizing the ideas. It is easier to see the larger picture this way.

Example

This is an example based on a publishing system that processes XML documents. An XML file may include other files called external entities, much like a C++ source code file may include a header file or a Java class file may import a Java class or package. One way to do this is to associate the entity reference with a filename. Sometimes the filename is a full Uniform Resource Locator (URL), but it could also just be the filename without any path information. An XML document is defined as the entire set of data contained in all of the files that compose the document.

When processing an XML document, an XML processor must be able to find the referenced external entities and load them into memory in the correct location within the XML document being processed. This is called *resolving an entity*. In our example, a design decision was made for the sake of portability that external entities would only contain a filename without path information so that documents could be processed on different machines with different configurations and different operating systems.

Suppose during detail design, the engineers have a problem resolving XML entities in the XML files. Upon analysis, they discover that the solution, which we'll simply call the Entity Resolver Component, potentially impacts adversely some specific architecture quality attribute such as modifiability. The architects must analyze the problem to see if it does have an impact on the architecture design and what other specific quality attributes it affects. They may discover that since XML files are processed frequently, that resolving entities may have an impact on overall system performance, which may require that entities be cached in memory.

Since external entities are external, there is the possibility that they may not be available, thus affecting the availability of the system. Caching the entities for performance may cause the system to behave incorrectly if the entity is modified (this is sometimes called a cache coherency problem). The solution must be portable, modifiable, and satisfy required performance constraints. The Entity Resolver Component design is compared with other potential designs to see if a solution that satisfies the three quality attribute requirements can be found. In the event that no satisfactory design can be achieved, the architects must either rework the requirements with the acquirers so that at least one of the designs satisfies them, or else they need to step back and review the design decisions that originally led to the Entity Resolver Component and perhaps go down a very different path. It is also likely that they may need to perform both actions, both lowering (weakening) the requirements and taking a different design approach.

If the Entity Resolver Component did not impact the required quality attributes regardless of how slow, nonportable, and nonmodifiable it was, then the design decisions made while designing this component could not be considered at the architectural level. Another example is in a repository-style architecture where the entire system's architecture is unaffected by the design of the individual tools used to operate on the repository. The quality attributes of the repository system such as performance, availability, modifiability, and functionality are largely unaffected by the design of individual tools (unless the repository is unstable and could be crashed by a single tool).

Architecting with Design Operators

Design operators are a fundamental design tool for creating an architectural design. The design operators can be used together with the modular operators discussed in Chapter 5. The application of design operators starts with a representation of a system as a single component that has externally visible characteristics and functions. The architect initially decomposes the system into two components, each with a well-defined purpose and which interact via some connectors. In terms of the modular structure, the system would now appear as two modules that share a set of global design rules, which define the connectors.

Common software design operators are:

- Decomposition
- Replication
- Compression
- Abstraction
- Resource Sharing

You'll notice that abstraction appears as both a design method (Chapter 4) and a design operator. The abstraction design method is a problem-solving technique that allows you to focus on the essentials of a problem while ignoring the nonessentials. Abstraction as a design principle is about representing abstractions in the solution in order to improve quality attributes such as modifiability and integrability.

There are other categories of design principles, such as for graphical user interface (GUI) design, user interaction design, object-oriented design, Java programming, Java thread programming, application domain analysis, and requirements analysis. You will probably identify some first principles of your own that are specific to your application domain or architecture. These statements of first principles form your design goals or objectives, to which all team members must abide, only to be deviated from with the consent of the architect.

Decomposition

Decomposition is the operation of separating distinct functionality into distinct components that have well-defined interfaces, for example, decomposing a system into a client and a server using Open Data Base Connectivity (ODBC) or Java Data Base Connectivity (JDBC) as the interface to the server. Decomposition is the most important and often-used principle in any engineering design field. From a systems view, decomposition separates a system into two or more systems (called subsystems). Decomposition is used to achieve a variety of quality attributes including modifiability, portability, performance, and buildability.

The two types of decomposition are part/whole and generalization/specialization. Part/whole composition can be divided into uniform and nonuniform decomposition. Part/whole decomposition divides a system into a set of subcomponents that do not overlap functionally. Part/whole decomposition can be performed recursively to form a hierarchy of functional components. Uniform decomposition divides the system into a set of components that are themselves structurally similar. For example, each component has a presentation component, application logic component, and data storage access component. In a generalization-specialization decomposition, there is potential overlapping functionality among components such as between a child and its parent component or between sibling components.

Each application of the decomposition operator divides a unit component into two subcomponents. The choice of where to draw the line between components is driven by what quality attributes you are trying to improve or emphasize. If you are trying to improve the ability to exchange some functionality for a different implementation in the future, then separate the set of functions that are likely to be replaced with those that are not.

For example, you may plan to use files for persistent storage and anticipate needing a document repository. To support future modifications as well as potential future requirements such as document version control, separate the functionality that interacts with file storage from other functions in the same component to produce two components. If you will need to add multiple presentations of some data in the future, then divide the component into a component that represents the data and another component that represents its presentation. The choice of how or where to apply any design principle is aided by heuristics (which are often embodied in design patterns). The separation of data from presentation is one such heuristic that can be accomplished by applying first principles or by applying design patterns like MVC. We will see more of this in later chapters.

In the next section, we look at some examples of component decomposition techniques useful for identifying components.

Identifying Functional Components

The identification of system components based on the initial functional specification of the system utilizes decomposition. The system components form the highest-level functional decomposition view of the structural architecture of the system. This approach starts from the view of the system as a single component within some environment or context. Components are identified in several ways (Bosch, 2000):

Interfaces.   The interfaces between the system and external entities should be associated with components. You can associate one component per interface or possibly associate more than one interface to a given component, but you shouldn't fragment a single interface across multiple components. When you first start creating a component model, take the simplest route and assign one component per interface. You can refine the associations, remove components, combine components, and decompose components during subsequent design steps.

Domains.   There are two types of domains: application domains and solution domains. Both are sources for identifying components. A software application may address more than one application domain. Each of those domains may be modeled by a separate component. For example, in a publishing system you may identify a Content Authoring component, a Publishing component, and a Marketing component, each being separate but related domains. In the solution domain you may identify components like Content Repository, Content Delivery, Project Management, and Royalty Management. You will eventually identify lower-level components in the solution domain such as File Systems and Process Schedulers.

Functional abstraction layers.   Functional abstraction layers decompose the system into a functional hierarchy. From this functional hierarchy it is possible to identify common functions that can be represented by shared components. For example, the Content Authoring and Publishing components may use a shared Project Management component. The Project Management Royalty Management components may use a shared component such as a Workflow Engine.

Domain entities.   Just as we may represent a domain as a component, it may also be useful to represent specific domain entities as components. These entities can be found in the literature of the application domain and in the application object model (if one was created) as part of the requirements analysis activity. However, it may not always be appropriate to model these entities directly as components. The application domain models describe the application or problem domain and may not be appropriate in this solution domain model.

In the publishing domain, there is an entity called a Content Reviewer. This might be a person or a group responsible for content review. It may be appropriate to model this entity as a Content Review component, but then again, it may be more appropriate for that entity to be modeled in some process and not explicitly in the structure of the system.

Composition/Aggregation

Composition (or *aggregation*) involves synthesizing components into a larger whole, hiding the lower-level components. It produces new behaviors that are not inherent to the subcomponents individually. Composition is related to decomposition, but is not exactly the opposite of decomposition. Decomposition involves subdividing a component into two, possibly distinct, functional components. Composition involves assembling components to form new components. Sometimes the two are indistinguishable from one another. You may realize that your component could be assembled from a relational database, Web server, and some custom component (your application logic). In this sense you composed the system using three components: two with well-known properties and a third that is the remaining functionality not achieved with the first two. But this composition could also be thought of as a decomposition of the system into three components.

The true opposite of decomposition is compression, which is addressed later in this chapter.

Component Communication

When a component is divided into two components, there is an implied communication channel introduced between them. The communication—which takes place via the interface—can be synchronous or asynchronous. Asynchronous communication decouples the processing of two components, making them concurrent. This may improve performance and reliability. However, it adds complexity to the system, making it harder to build and debug, and requires additional nonapplication domain functions.

Replication

Replication, also known as redundancy, is the operation of duplicating a component in order to enhance reliability and performance. There are two flavors of runtime replication:

- Redundancy, where there are several identical copies of a component executing simultaneously.

- N-version programming, where there are several different implementations of the same functionality.

N-version programming involves simultaneously running redundant components to perform a function and using some algorithm to determine which of the multiple results is correct (sometimes using voting, sometimes using the first result received). There are two variants of replication: static replication and runtime replication (Bass, 1998). Runtime replication involves replicated components executing the same function simultaneously, improving reliability at the expense of performance. Static replication involves backup components that do not perform any work until needed (such as when a primary component fails). Static replication tends to have better performance than runtime replication for nominal operation, but is slower when responding to failures. An example of a static replicated component is a database with a mirror (or slave). The purpose is to minimize or prevent downtime from a database server software or hardware crash, thus improving the mean-time-between-failures. A database with a slave mirror must also have some sort of replication server that handles the synchronizing of the data, as well as a component for activating the slave when the master fails and a means of configuring and managing the additional components. This introduces additional functionality to the system for replication, self-monitoring, and component switching, and may negatively affect performance.

A static replication variation of N-version programming, called backup (or failover), involves a primary implementation, a secondary implementation, and so forth with only one component active at any given time. The secondary component is activated when the primary component fails. A static replication variation of redundancy is called clustering, which involves multiple instances of the same component, each running independently from each other. A cluster of components may appear as a single component to other components. Clustering can improve performance by boosting throughput and improving reliability. If one component in the cluster fails, the remaining components compensate.

There is some overhead involved in managing client sessions within a cluster when a client must continuously interact with a single instance of a clustered component. Clustering is a popular way to improve performance and reliability and is a native capability in many application server platforms, making its use nearly transparent to programmers. It is used often in the presentation and middle tiers of Web-based applications.

Some real-time systems use backup components that are implemented using different algorithms (N-version programming). The use of a backup component requires additional functionality for configuring and managing the seamless switching of components. With N-version programming there is a potentially heavy performance hit since the redundant components are all consuming computational resources. In the primary-secondary version of backup, performance is not as adversely affected since it is possible that a component is never switched and, if it is, the demand on computational resources may not be large. However, there is always some amount of computational overhead in self-monitoring.

> **NOTE** A good design approach to redundancy and backups is to make component switching transparent to the other components that are using it. If a database goes offline, its slave should start handling all requests without interruption of service to client applications and without client applications realizing that a switch has occurred.

Redundancy is related to the self-monitoring pattern. The self-monitoring system is capable of detecting some component failures and can notify an operator or perform a component switch itself. Different replication strategies can be used with different sets of components in a system. For example, clustering can be used in the middle-tier and backup can be used in the persistent data tier simultaneously.

Compression

Compression is the opposite of decomposition, although composition is not exactly the opposite of decomposition. Compression involves merging components into a single component or removing layers or interfaces between components. Composition involves coupling or combining two components to form a new system. In the former, there is no trace of one or more original components. In the latter, the individual components still exist as subcomponents. Composition is a form of synthesis used to find new behaviors or functions by combining different components in an attempt to simplify a solution or find new solutions reusing existing solutions.

Compression is intended to improve performance by eliminating a level of indirection. This may involve removing an interface between two components (effectively merging the two components into one), or it may involve removing some middle layer between two components so that the two components interact directly instead of through another layer. For example, a presentation component may interact directly with a database instead of using middle-tier objects. This is common in some servlet-based Web applications where performance outweighs the need for a middle-tier abstraction layer. In this case, the presentation tier servlets make direct JDBC calls to the database.

Compression does not have to be applied uniformly. For example, you may remove some middle-tier components, allowing the presentation layer direct access to the database to improve performance of bottleneck areas. This sort of nonuniform compression can make the solution more complex because there are two ways of interacting with the database. It also makes the component more difficult to maintain, such as when there are changes to the database structure that otherwise do not affect the interfaces of the middle-tier components.

A form of compression called *layer straddling* is often used in communication protocols to reduce the performance overhead associated with layered protocols. This is different than the use of the term compression to improve communication performance by reducing the amount of data transmitted, which is called *data compression*.

Abstraction

Abstraction hides information by introducing a semantically rich layer of services while simultaneously hiding the implementation details. It is also referred to as creating a virtual machine (Bass, 1998). A virtual machine is not necessarily a complex interpreter of programming or scripting languages. In the general sense, anything that hides the implementation of some system is considered a virtual machine. This includes interfaces such as JDBC or ODBC.

Hiding an underlying implementation and providing an abstract representation makes other components portable with respect to the component that has been abstracted. The Java virtual machine (JVM) abstracts the operating system and hardware, making Java programs portable across both. JDBC abstracts the interface to a relational database, making a Java program portable across database platforms. The XML document object model (DOM) abstracts an XML parser implementation and allows a program to be portable with respect to XML parser implementations. As you can see, the portability quality applies to many aspects of a system. A single portability quality attribute is specific to a component or technology. If your application needed to be portable across operating systems, relational databases, and XML parsers, then those requirements would be expressed as three distinct portability quality attributes.

Abstraction—particularly the virtual machine—can also be used to improve adaptability, as we explore in the next section.

Virtual Machines and Adaptability

A virtual machine makes a system more adaptable to end-user business processes. The idea is to convert adaptability quality attribute requirements into a language for describing the semantics of an application or system. The virtual machine exposes nonapplication domain functions that can be synthesized into new application domain functions. Sometimes this is referred to as end-user programming, scripting, or configuring.

Virtual machines can be implemented with a text-based interpreted or compiled language (like Java or Visual Basic), or a simple scripting mechanism that has a GUI design environment (like a database report design tool or a workflow designer). This approach adds to the complexity of a system by adding not only the functions of the virtual machine itself, but also functions for creating or modifying configurations or scripts.

A variation of this technique is the *command interpreter*. A command interpreter allows a system to be controlled by the execution of commands. For example, start, stop, suspend, and restart are typical system functions that have nothing to do with the application domain but are necessary in order to achieve other quality attributes. These types of commands help make a system more usable because an operator can restart after making some important configuration changes to improve performance or security. It can also help make a system more reliable by allowing the operator to suspend parts of the system that are failing or close to failing and fix them before other parts of the system are affected. This technique can be used along with asynchronous communication so that portions of the system can be stopped and started without immediately affecting other parts of the system.

Resource Sharing

Resource sharing is encapsulating data or services in order to share them among multiple independent client components. The result is enhanced integrability, portability, and modifiability. Resource sharing is useful when the resource itself may be scarce, such as during processing or threading. Persistent data is a common shared resource such as that stored in databases or directories.

For example, a repository of user information—such as security credentials—can be accessed by multiple independent applications. Several independent Web applications can share clusters of Web servers to take advantage of computational resources and even a single Internet Protocol (IP) address. This can simplify the deployment of applications, since it is not necessary to install a new Web server and configure it every time a new Web application is created. A relational database server is also a shared computational resource. Different applications can store their own data on a single database server sharing the computational resources. This is useful when the collective demands of individual applications do not tax the single database server. Resource sharing can simplify some aspects of systems configuration and management.

Another example of resource sharing is a server-side presentation manager, such as used in X-windows or Web-based applications. In Java Web applications, servlets and JPSs are responsible for handling user requests and generating presentation from responses. A single servlet instance will handle all user requests to a given URL. Each user's state is stored in a session object that the servlet has access to within the context of that user's handling thread. This sharing of presentation logic simplifies client applications (in this case, the browser) because changes to the presentation logic do not affect the client application itself.

Resource sharing is commonly applied with abstraction, as we have seen in databases and with application program interfaces (APIs) like JDBC and ODBC. An enterprise application vendor may also expose some components as shared resources so that a customer can build his or her own applications to leverage the capabilities and data of the commercial components. If enough vendors build similar components and if enough customers start demanding standards, then a standard API or interface may emerge that allows end users to exchange or even mix heterogeneous shared resources.

Functional Design Strategies

Functional design strategies are more complex than individual design principles. A strategy cannot be applied to a design to yield a new design. Nor are strategies patterns in the strictest sense, because they don't suggest any concrete forms. Rather, they suggest a functional decomposition strategy to achieve specific quality attributes. These strategies can help guide the architect as he or she decomposes a system based on functional and nonfunctional needs. Two strategies are presented here: self-monitoring and recovery, both related to achieving reliability.

Self-Monitoring

A system that is self-monitoring is able to detect certain types of failures and react to them appropriately, possibly without involving an operator or by notifying an operator about a specific condition (Bosch, 2000). The functionality added to the system is not in the application domain, and should be documented as such. There are two basic approaches to self-monitoring:

- Process monitoring
- Component monitoring

A process monitor is a layer "above" the application or system that watches over the system. The component monitoring involves a monitor hierarchy that mirrors the component hierarchy where each component monitor is responsible for monitoring its own component and reporting issues to the next higher level component monitor. A simple example is a script that restarts a Web server when an event detects that the Web server is no longer running.

Self-monitoring is intended to improve reliability, but it introduces additional computational overhead that can affect performance. This impact can be reduced by using distribution patterns and asynchronous communication patterns. For example, if a monitor is running on a different processor reading messages in a queue, then the overhead to the application itself is the generation of messages. However, logging is such a common component in business systems that the overhead is usually assumed. Self-monitoring can be used to introduce more intelligence to a basic logging system.

Maintainability can also be negatively affected by the increase in size and complexity of the system. Quite often monitoring code, such as logging, is embedded within application objects making them more complex. There are other noninvasive ways to monitor objects, but they may have an even greater negative impact on performance. One technique is to use code generation or some runtime reflection technique that allows you to keep the business logic separated in the source code. A code generator could combine the various pieces to form a binary object that has both business logic and logging code, thus potentially making the code easier to maintain but adding performance overhead.

Recovery

Recovery functions are related to the quality attribute of recoverability. Recoverability is usually a quality that is introduced based on certain design decisions; it is typically not a product requirement based on the application domain. Recovery is related to reliability because it can affect the mean-time-to-repair (MTTR), which is a factor of the mean-time-between-failures (MTBF), a common measure of reliability. It may be necessary for a system or application to restore itself to some stable prior state by resetting some flags in a database or possibly restoring a database from a backup. Both are functions introduced to help the reliability of the application. Each component may need to address recovery differently and some not at all.

Instrumenting

To instrument a component is to hook it up to some instrument in order to measure it. This strategy is similar to self-monitoring. A component that can be instrumented can have some code, such as logging code, hooked on in order to diagnose or troubleshoot a problem. A component can be instrumented so that performance measurements can be taken or it can be instrumented so that a test harness can be hooked up to it.

A common practice in Java development is to use a unit-testing environment such as JUnit to help automate component or class-level testing. Testing code can be kept separate from the actual component logic. Instrumenting an application can be very useful when the user interface is not available for testing.

Summary

General design methods combined with quality attributes and design principles yield an architectural design method that is heuristic and participative. The design principles in this chapter address the functional and structural aspects of software architecture. Specialized principles such as those for usability and user interface design, object-oriented design, and database design were not covered. Those specialized design areas, while possibly overlapping into the architectural level of design, are the subjects of numerous other books.

In the next chapter, we look at a general architecture process that extends the engineering design process to form a framework for design methods and principles.

CHAPTER 10

Applying Architectural Styles and Patterns

Our initial view of a system is typically of a single component that exports a set of use cases that represents the system's required functions and interacts with other external entities, such as users and other software systems. This single-component view is the system in its enterprise context. We then decompose the system into multiple parts, maintaining the function of the system but adding structure to the system in order to achieve the other nonfunctional quality attributes that are required or desired. We can decompose a system by the application of first principles (including the design and modular operators).

The search for a good solution can be a slow process if we rely solely on the application of design operators. We would like to improve our design productivity while not sacrificing the quality of the design (and the resulting system). One way to improve design productivity is by leveraging existing design experience from the software engineering community.

There are two types of reusable architectural products: product families and architecture patterns. Product families, or domain-specific software architectures, define a family of applications within a common application or problem domain such as banking or human resources management. These *domain-specific software architectures* classify software systems by *function* (*utilitas*). Applications within a given domain solve related problems. *Architectural styles* define classes of software systems based on the *form* (*venustas*) of the solution and which can be applied across problem domains. For example, the *client/server* architectural style can be used for health care systems and content publishing applications. Applications that share the same architectural style share common organizational principles. Architectural styles and patterns are reusable design principles that can be applied to a design much like the design operators (Chapter 9). Styles and patterns can be thought of as macro operators that embody some set of quality attributes.

Shared or reusable design solutions identify a set of problems that are solved within a context or set of obstacles. Design patterns are such shared design knowledge that can be represented in more or less formal ways. They allow us to think about design at a higher level. There is some debate over whether styles and patterns are different concepts or whether they are fundamentally the same. I will avoid fueling this debate in this book, but I will present styles and patterns as separate concepts. The topics of this chapter are:

Defining architectural style.   An architectural style is a type of metamodel (see Chapter 11) that prescribes a set of elements and their relationships that characterize a system based on the style. These elements are commonly expressed as components and connectors and their relationships are the constraints on how components and connectors may be combined.

Common architectural styles.   Several architectural styles are presented. These are organized as dataflow systems, call-and-return systems, independent components, virtual machines, and repository systems.

This chapter ends with a case example.

Defining Architectural Patterns and Style

Christopher Alexander developed the concept of a pattern language in *The Timeless Way of Building* (Alexander, 1979). A pattern is a design solution to a problem within the context of other problems. Problems or requirements may be interdependent, as described in Chapter 5. This means that a single problem cannot be solved in isolation but rather must be solved in the context of other competing forces or obstacles. Thus, a pattern is a solution that strikes some balance between competing forces. The better we understand the problem, the better our chances of discovering or creating a solution. Alexander argues that if we find the right decomposition of the problem, then the form of the solution will reveal itself and the final solution is the synthesis of solutions to generate a form. Decomposing the problem is not only a matter of finding the problem constituents but also understanding their interdependencies (modeling the requirements as a graph or a design structure matrix (DSM).

A pattern is more than a solution to a set of problems in a context. What makes a solution a pattern is the fact that it is *recurring*. If a design solution in its essential distilled form is found in multiple systems and is a successful design, then this solution is a pattern.

A *pattern language* is a set of patterns, together with the rules for describing how patterns are created and how they must be arranged with respect to other patterns. The patterns are the vocabulary of the language, and the rules for their implementation and combination are the grammar. Patterns in a pattern language can be constructed from other patterns in the language.

Most architectural styles are described in such a way as to solve some initial set of quality attributes or problems. Thus, one can argue that styles are patterns. However, styles are not solutions but rather a framework for solutions. The selection of a style limits the scope of the solution space, thus reducing the complexity of the process for discovering a suitable form. Some architectural styles could even be considered small pattern languages.

There are many definitions and applications of architectural style. According to Ivar Jacobson (Jacobson, 1997), the architecture style of a software system is "the denotation of the modeling languages used when modeling the system." Jacobson equates architecture and architectural style with the entire modeling approach of the system development effort. This definition is based on building construction, where the architecture of the construction approach is the "foundation of concepts and techniques" that "defines the characteristic structure of all buildings designed using the approach." Architecture (style) is seen as the foundation of a philosophy of building. Upon this foundation rest methods, then process, and at the top are tools. The method is the detailed procedures that are followed in order to apply the architecture. Process adds the elements of time and people in order to scale the project across multiple parties. Tools support and enable the activities of the architecture, method, and process.

Richard Hubert's *Convergent Architecture* (Hubert, 2002) extends this model. It is composed of four elements: an architectural metamodel, a development life-cycle model, a tool suite, and formal technology projections. The architectural metamodel is equivalent to Jacobson's architectural style and includes the guiding principles and prescriptions that the other development model elements must satisfy. The development model defines how the vision established by the architectural metamodel is realized. The model transports the principles into concrete software structures, development organizations, and development processes. Tools support the development model. The fourth element can be seen as an extension to the tool suite. This element is introduced to support model-driven architecture (MDA), in which design models are compiled to a variety of middleware platforms much the same way source code is compiled to hardware platforms. The compilation of a model (Unified Modeling Language [UML] or C++ source code) to a technology (middleware or hardware instructions) is called *formal technology projection*. A model compiler that generates a system from reusable software components is called a GenVoca generator.

Hubert refers to this four-element model as the Information Technology (IT)-architectural style. Our use of the term *architectural style* in this book is closer to Jacobson's use, but also resembles Hubert's definition of architectural metamodel.

Architectural styles are commonly described in terms of abstract elements (components and connectors) and their canonical forms (relationships and properties). The architectural style prescribes in part the method of construction. In software, we don't actually construct a system as much as we design the specification for construction (for example, source code). The order in which we create the source level design elements and the manner in which we go about designing them is based in part on the architectural style. If the architectural style is object-oriented, then we apply object-oriented design methods to produce the source code.

Some styles overlap or can be classified in more than one way. However, the architectural style still conveys a lot of information to all stakeholders. If we describe the architectural style of a given application as pipes and filters or as an interactive system, a stakeholder has a good sense of the architecture from a high level. Of course, naming an architectural style does not communicate the details of the system, but it establishes the basic form. Along with this basic form are inherent quality attributes. A pipes-and-filters architectural style exhibits high adaptability and modifiability. Stakeholders that know the architectural style know of these qualities. If we say that our application is based on a pipes-and-filters architectural style, then knowledgeable stakeholders know that the system is composed of multiple filters that can potentially be reconfigured or reused in other systems. They also know that development work on each filter can go somewhat in parallel as long as the global design rules have been created, such as the format of data passed on the pipes and whether the data is a stream of characters or is passed in batches.

According to Shaw and Garlan, "An architectural style defines a *vocabulary* of components and connector types, and a set of *constraints* on how they can be combined" (Shaw, 1996). As you look at the classification you may notice that most applications, especially enterprise business applications, are a combination of styles (that is, they have a *heterogeneous* architectural style).

There may be many parameters that we can use to characterize software architecture. One such parameter is the style in which control is passed from component to component (what we might call the *control principle* or *activation model*). Another parameter is the general quality attribute emphasis of the style. Different styles emphasize or de-emphasize certain quality attributes like maintainability and performance.

Activation Model

The activation model (control principle) of a system describes how components are activated in order to process information and how information is passed between components. This is also referred to as the *control principle* of the architecture.

In dataflow systems, the components read data from input ports and write data to output ports. Control is implicit in the underlying data passing mechanism. In call-and-return systems the control is explicit in the application structure where there is a main routine and thread from which all other functions are invoked. Control within independent components is similar to dataflow systems; a component or object reacts to the arrival of a message from another component or object. A virtual machine controls the execution of instructions or the execution of rules-based triggers.

In an object-oriented programming language, a given object's methods or operations execute within the context of an activation. "An activation (also known as a focus of control) represents the period during which an object performs an operation either directly or through a subordinate operation. It models both the duration of the execution in time and the control relationship between the execution and its callers. In a conventional computer and language, an activation corresponds to a value of the stack frame" (Rumbaugh, 1999). Rumbaugh's definition is of a UML activation, which is a model of an object's activation, hence, the phrase "It models both the duration of the execution in time and the control relationship between the execution and its callers."

An activation model describes how a component is activated, or how its logic is executed. The activation model that I present is split into two levels, the technology level and the design level. The technology level describes how method invocation and method execution are coupled at the language (runtime) level or how middleware is used to activate remote objects via remote methods or message queues. In classic procedural languages (such as C) and their object-oriented derivatives (such as C++ and Java), there is a procedural activation where method execution is bound to method invocation. In other words, invoking a method on an object from within another object's method's activation causes the method to be activated immediately and for the method activation of the client object to be suspended until the invoked method returns. In these languages, *method invocation* and *method execution* are bound. Method invocation in a procedural language is a local procedure call that causes a new stack frame to be created and for the program pointer to be positioned to the new method. Method execution then follows immediately within the same thread of control.

In languages like Smalltalk, method invocation and method execution are decoupled. A client object sends a message to another object, which executes the appropriate method possibly within a different thread of control. The client invocation of the method does not necessarily result in an operation being executed within the same thread of control. A *message* is an object that contains data. The arrival of a message is called an *event*.

At the design level, you can simulate activation models in the language level. In Java or C++, you can use patterns like Completion Callback, Notification, and Futures to simulate synchronous or asynchronous activations.

Communication patterns can be classified as synchronous, asynchronous, or delegating. *Synchronous* communication means that the client component activates a server component and then waits for a response. In object-oriented languages like Java and C++, this is the equivalent of invoking a method on an object: The act of calling the method causes the current executing method to be suspended while the called method executes in the same thread of control. Synchronous communication does not necessarily mean that the invoked operation is performed in the same thread. Generically it just means that once an operation is invoked, the caller waits until a response is returned. In a distributed application, a remote procedure call (RPC) or remote method invocation (RMI) can be synchronous even though the invoked operation is actually performed in a different process space and hence on a different thread of control.

A variation of the synchronous model is the balking model. In the *balking model* the client or server component may reject a request immediately for any reason. For example, a server component may reject a request because it does not have enough resources available to handle the request immediately (for example, a Web server does not have any available threads to handle a client request or a database connection pool is depleted of available connections). The client component may also balk if it detects that the server component cannot handle its request immediately.

Another variation of synchronous communication is the timeout. Timeouts are a strategy where a client component waits for a response and if the response does not arrive within a certain time, then the caller continues on assuming that the server component failed to process its request. The client component can even send a "cancel" message to the server object in the event that the server may be still processing the original request. This sort of message could be asynchronous without a response. Balking can be thought of as a degenerate case of timeout where the timeout is zero.

Asynchronous communication between components means that the client component invokes an operation on a server component and, before receiving a response, continues performing other operations. The client eventually retrieves the response. If the response is not ready, the client may wait for the response or perhaps continue performing more operations while periodically checking for the availability of a response. Asynchronous communication is a powerful pattern for building high-performance distributed applications but the price is that the application is more complex and possibly less fault tolerant. When using asynchronous communication, you need to determine how to detect an error. If a response never arrives, at what point should the client component give up and signal an error?

In the *delegating* pattern, a client component invokes a server component and also passes an address to which the response is to be sent. Examples of *addresses* are a Uniform Resource Locator (URL) to which a response is posted, a reference to another object the methods of which will be invoked by the server component, or the name of a message queue to which a response is written. Delegating is similar to asynchronous communication because the caller component invokes a server component operation and then continues doing other work. The difference is that the caller component doesn't necessarily receive the response. In the asynchronous model, the response is eventually processed within the same activation as the original operation invocation (that is, the client component needs the response in order to finish its processing). In the delegating model, the response may be processed within a different activation and perhaps in a different software process. Delegation when coupled with persistent messages (messages that persist between software processes) provides a powerful decoupled fault-tolerant architecture.

Another aspect of activation and communication is the patterns of information passing. The common language-level model is to pass information in the form of parameters in an operation invocation. Data elements can be passed directly between processing elements such as in the pipes-and-filters style. Data elements may also be shared in a central store and accessed by different processing elements, in what is known as a repository style. In the repository style, the activation model becomes very important because processing components may not be directly invoking operations on other processing components. In one model a component updates a shared data element and then invokes another component, but instead of passing the data, it simply informs the other component of the availability of the data. The activation of the second component can happen in a traditional method invocation and/or execution style, but the information is not passed as a parameter. However, the address of the information could be sent as a parameter if the second component does not know where to locate the information.

The activation model (communication patterns and information passing patterns) can be used to compare different architectural styles. Understanding the activation model needs of the subsystems in your application can help you identify the appropriate architectural style for the entire system or the best combination of architectural styles.

Later in this chapter, intercomponent communication patterns are covered. These extend the primitive concepts presented here.

Styles and Quality Attributes

Each style emphasizes a set of quality attributes while de-emphasizing another set. Pipes-and-filters-style systems emphasize reusability and adaptability but usually sacrifice maintainability with respect to changes in data representation. Object-oriented systems tend to emphasize maintainability with respect to data representation changes because they hide internal representations, but object-oriented systems are not easily reused due to the *subjectivity principle* (no one interface can satisfy the needs of all potential users). Repository-based systems emphasize adaptability and performance (time and resource efficiency) but are not highly reusable or maintainable in terms of changes to algorithms or data representations (since the data representation is shared by many autonomous clients).

Architects combine styles in different areas of a system in order to exhibit different quality attributes. For example, a repository approach may be combined with an object-oriented approach. This allows the representation to change, but at the expense of performance and design complexity of the object. This heterogeneous style can be seen as the application of three styles because there is an implicit layering style (the object layer and the repository layer).

Common Architectural Styles

The following is an informal taxonomy of architectural styles adapted from Shaw and Garlan:

- Dataflow systems
    - Batch sequential
    - Pipes and filters
- Call-and-return systems
    - Main program and subroutine
    - Object-oriented systems
    - Hierarchical layers
- Independent components
    - Communicating processes
    - Event systems
- Virtual machines
    - Interpretors
    - Rule-based systems
- Repositories
    - Databases
    - Hypertext systems
    - Blackboards

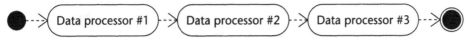

Figure 10.1   Activity diagram representing a dataflow architectural style.

Dataflow Systems

Dataflow systems are characterized by how data moves through the system. Dataflow architectures have two or more data processing components that each transform input data into output data. The data processing components transform data in a sequential fashion where the output of an upstream processing component becomes the input of the next processing component. This style can be seen in the UML activity diagram in Figure 10.1. This model shows three processing components but does not describe the nature of the data being passed (as represented by an object flow association). This example is called a *pipeline* because it is limited to a linear sequence of filters.

It is common in a pipes-and-filters architecture that a processing component has two outputs, a standard output and an error output and a single input called standard input. Generically, the input and output mechanisms for a given processing element are called *ports*. Thus a typical filter has three ports. The error output can be connected to a different processing component, as depicted in Figure 10.2.

It is possible to define more complex processing elements to produce even more complex arrangements and data flows. For example, a processing component may contain decision logic that routes data to two different subprocesses (as in Figure 10.3).

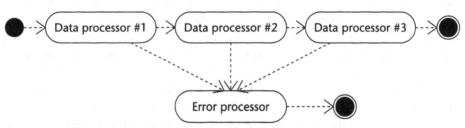

Figure 10.2   Pipes-and-filters architectural style.

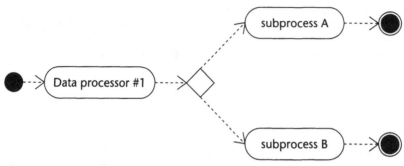

Figure 10.3   Dataflow with complex processing components.

Dataflow systems resemble program logic flow where each processing element is like a programming statement. Workflow logic is also modeled as data flow. It is common to informally represent the processing model of an application using diagrams that resemble activity or data flow diagrams. A true data flow architecture, however, is characterized by how the data actually moves through the system. There are two basic dataflow models: streams and objects (or *entities*). In a streams-based dataflow, the data moves between processing elements as a stream of binary data. This data must be parsed by each processing element as it reads it from the input port and serialized as it is written to the output port. In an object-based dataflow, the data moves in logical chunks. In this style, the term *object* is more general than a programming language object. When objects are being moved between processing elements, the entire object is consumed and transformed. It is possible to have a mix of the two types of filters in a single configuration, as long as the connected ports receive and send the appropriate type of data. Some filters can be configured for both styles.

A *bounded pipe* is a pipe that restricts the amount of data that can reside on the pipe. For a stream-based pipe, this refers to the amount of binary data that may be on the pipe before the pipe rejects further data write requests. An object-based bounded pipe can restrict the number of objects that may be in the pipe.

Our XML-based publishing system example utilizes a dataflow architecture for part of the system. Data is authored in XML and stored in a repository. The repository may store the data as raw XML in a database table or it may store it as individual elements and a description of their hierarchical relationships, or some combination. However, to outside components the data is read and written as XML. In order to publish a static work such as a book, the XML is retrieved from the repository and then a formatting process is invoked. In our example, the XML is based on a proprietary Document Type Definition (DTD), and we want to publish the content in a variety of formats including HTML and Portable Document Format (PDF). The basic processing model, a pipeline architecture, is depicted in Figure 10.4. In this example, the source input conforms to a proprietary XML vocabulary. The first filter transforms this XML data into XML based on the DocBook XML standard. The data is then sent to two parallel processing elements. One of the processing elements transforms DocBook-based XML into HTML.

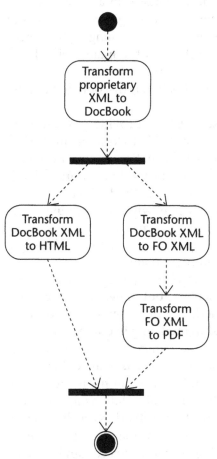

Figure 10.4   Dataflow for the content publishing application.

Call-and-Return Systems

Call-and-return systems are characterized by an activation model that involves a main thread of control that performs operation invocations. The classic system architecture is the main program and subroutine. "The primary organization of many systems mirrors the programming language in which the system is written" (Shaw, 1996). Object-oriented languages like C++ and Java still have vestiges of this architectural style present. However, a Java-based system may have many "main" entry points. A Java-based system is invoked by specifying a class name. The system locates a public static method named main, and gives it the primary thread of control. In a C or C++ executable, there is one entry point named main, which is a global function and not the method of an object or a class. A common programming style in these languages is to instantiate several active objects from the main method and then either to exit or block waiting for the active objects to exit. Adding any sort of application logic to the main method or function is discouraged but not enforceable.

Object-oriented and data abstraction-based systems provide capabilities to encapsulate portions of the system so that it is possible to localize implementation changes. The class is the basic unit of encapsulation in object-oriented languages like C++ and Java. A class allows data to be hidden within an object so that other objects must request information via methods. Java interfaces also allow implementations of objects to change without affecting other dependent modules. Similar capabilities can be simulated in C++ using abstract base classes with abstract virtual methods and some sort of component system for solving the binary compatibility problem.

Object-oriented systems are not only characterized by the ability to encapsulate information and isolate system changes, but they also embody a methodology that encourages the direct modeling of real-world concepts or entities as objects, much like entity relationship modeling in database systems. In dataflow systems, the dominant view of the system is about the process and not the data. Object-oriented or data abstraction emphasizes the data view of the system while still allowing for a strong process view in the form of data-specific operations (methods) and the hierarchical relationship between classes allowing for processes to be customized by method overriding. There is a growing body of design patterns and design idioms that allows systems of many forms to be assembled from objects. For example, objects can be reified processes as well as data entities. Also, objects can be used to solve the problem of *subjectivity*, which is the principle that no single interface can adequately describe an object through design patterns like façade, wrapper, adapter, and bridge. Process-oriented styles that do not promote data encapsulation suffer from subjectivity.

The hierarchical layers style is a commonly misunderstood architectural style. The difficulty arises in the interpretation of the layers. All complex systems are hierarchical in nature. A system can be depicted as a hierarchy of components or modules, which are further decomposed into more primitive components. I argue that the layers style is not really a style or pattern at all, but an attribute of all complex software systems. Since all complex systems have hierarchy, then this implies that there is a fundamental architectural view that represents this aspect of a system's organization. There is a design style that also uses layers, such as the often-cited ISO seven-layer model for network communications protocol stacks. This layering strategy is more like a design pattern than an architectural principle.

When designing a system, instead of asking yourself if you should use the hierarchical layers style, you should ask yourself what the layers are. We will see more use of layers and hierarchical decompositions in the next chapter on metamodels. Many metamodels present canonical hierarchical decompositions of systems, such as the arch/slinky metamodel for interactive systems. This model presents five layers from the lowest level abstract function core to the concrete physical presentation. This is not so much an architectural style as it is a metamodel that describes possible layers, depending on what quality attributes you are trying to achieve.

Another classic hierarchical layer depiction is the technology stack. The model in Figure 10.5 shows a classic architecture. This view is often confused for the architecture of a system where each technology layer is mapped to an architectural layer. In some simple cases, the logical layers of an application do correspond to a technology. However, this kind of decomposition of a system is never very useful except perhaps in marketing literature. Most complex applications have layers that are orthogonal to the technology stack. We explore the hierarchical decomposition of a system and technology stacks in more detail in Chapter 11.

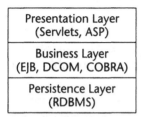

Figure 10.5   Architectural layers versus technology stacks.

Independent Components

Communicating processes and event-based architectural styles rely on an implicit invocation of operations. In other words, the invocation of an operation is decoupled from the execution such that the caller and called can exist in separate software processes and possibly distributed across multiple processors. In an event-based system, the various components are decoupled and usually unaware of each other. Activation is based on arrival of events. An event system can be based on a publish-subscribe communication pattern. Implicit invocation is different from remote procedure calls or remote method invocations. Those are still explicit invocations, even though execution is still decoupled from invocation. The implicit invocation style is an example of message-oriented communication.

The components of an implicit invocation style are operations (procedures) and events. A component associates operations with events (for example, an event handler). This style is seen in application integration. Two existing systems (components) may be connected by means of messages and therefore become communicating processes. If an application or system is not designed with integration in mind, then there may be a need for an adapter that converts message-oriented communication into a simulation of connection-orientation (where a message or event handler becomes an agent for the other system).

A characteristic of this style is that the components are not aware of each other. The component that generates events is not aware of the components that subscribe to or react to events. Triggers are an example where an event (such as a data update event) may cause many triggers to be activated, which in turn cause other processing to happen. The originator of the event is unaware of the triggers. An event is not necessarily a physical object. Recall that, abstractly, an event is the arrival of a message and the invocation of a method is a specialization of a message. Therefore, a client object may invoke a method on another object and the invocation of this method (an event) may cause some other objects and methods to be activated, hidden from the original client object.

Systems based on independent components tend to be more modular and hence provide more opportunities for reuse. However, the running system itself is more complex and can be difficult to configure, operate, troubleshoot, and debug.

Independent components are a form of a distributed system and therefore incur potential performance penalties. At the architectural level of design, performance is addressed at the component boundaries (as opposed to optimizing implementations). The patterns of communication can affect the performance; therefore, when designing around independent components, consider the overhead of the communication itself. If the components are using delegation or asynchronous communication, then the communications between components are probably few and contain more data. However, for an interactive system that is driven by user commands, the communications between components may be more frequent and of smaller amounts of data.

Virtual Machines

The interpretor architecture is comprised of four main components: an interpretation engine, a memory that contains a pseudoprogram, the interpretation engines control state representation, and the representation of the program's current state (Shaw, 1996). The pseudoprogram is composed of a program and the program's activation record.

Recall that the layered style is also considered a type of virtual machine by some authors where each layer provides a different semantic interface than the lower-level layer. Interpretors and rule-based systems share the same essential characteristics because they provide a semantic layer on top of some other technology. The activation model of interpretors is based on an interpretation engine reading and executing instructions. In a sense, the interpretation engine is activating each instruction.

As with all styles, interpretors and rules engines can be combined with other styles. For example, an interpretor can be activated when a rule or trigger fires. An interpretor, like a workflow engine, can control the state of a system causing rules to trigger. A client or server component can be written using an interpretor style.

Instead of supplying an out-of-the-box application, an enterprise software vendor can provide an application platform based on the virtual machine style. This approach allows for maximum adaptability because the system is customized using a programming language or user-defined business rules instead of through static configuration via parameters. This kind of flexibility comes at a price. Interpretor systems are difficult to design and test. You cannot produce every possible program that can be executed and therefore you cannot ever fully test your interpretor. Some systems are designed using an interpretor approach for only some parts of the system. For example, a system can be configured or customized using a workflow component, which is a type of virtual machine. The typical workflow language is usually not general-purpose and therefore has a limited or fairly simple grammar. However, end users may customize the processing rules of the application and model their own business processes and rules. Any vendor of enterprise applications must provide some virtual machine as part of the architecture.

In-house systems are less likely to enjoy the benefits of the virtual machine approach. If you control the source code for your system and you only need to maintain your own business rules and processes, then the cost of developing a general-purpose virtual machine can outweigh the return on the development investment. However, if you are developing in-house systems, then you are most likely using enterprise systems from various vendors. In that case, you are relying on their virtual machines to build some applications or application parts.

Repositories

Repository-style architectures involve a shared data source approach to information passing. However, different repository-based styles vary in terms of the communication and activation styles. One of the motivations for repository-based systems is the need to store persistent application data, which is a requirement of more enterprise business systems. A degenerate form of a repository style is a shared file system together with office productivity tools that manipulate the shared files. Human users perform the activation of individual tools and the synchronization of data access is usually ad hoc. Some file systems and applications will detect that a file is in use and block an application from opening it or will allow a read-only view of the file.

The repository-style architecture is characterized by two primary components: a central data element and multiple potentially independent processing elements. The central data element represents the current state of the system and the processing elements operate on the data element. Different activation models characterize different flavors of the repository style. The blackboard is a style in which multiple independent processing elements called *knowledge sources* operate on the shared data store called the *blackboard*. Knowledge stores do not directly interact with each other. Knowledge sources operate on the blackboard opportunistically, when the blackboard is in an applicable state. The actual activation logic may exist on the blackboard, in the knowledge sources, or in a separate component. Blackboards are typically applied in systems where there is no deterministic algorithm for solving a problem.

A database is the most common form of the repository style and is utilized in most enterprise applications. A database can be combined with a rules-based system so that changes in the state of the central repository cause different rules to trigger. Very sophisticated and adaptable applications can be built using this approach along with a workflow engine.

Example of Applying Architectural Styles

Let's consider a typical enterprise application with a Web-based user interface. Web-based applications are commonly depicted as a layered or tiered architecture, as shown in Figure 10.6. We know that our initial components are a browser, a Web server, and a database. We see in the figure that we already have a default client/server pattern—actually two overlaid client/server patterns—which produce a three-tier architecture. The first client/server pattern instance is the browser (client) and the Web server (server). The second is the Web server (client) and the database (server).

Figure 10.6 Tiered view of a Web-based application.

But just because we have to use this platform doesn't mean that we have to conform to a true client/server architecture or three-tier architecture. There isn't much we can do about the browser and the Web server, but since we are not writing those components we don't care. Anyway, that architecture works well (and is really our best choice when building a Web site). Another choice might be to use browser-related technologies such as applets. Notice that our above model is actually only partially correct. While browsers do communicate with Web servers, Web servers don't communicate with databases (this is not a typical Web server function). Web servers invoke, at the browser's request, some module like a Common Gateway Interface (CGI) program, servlet, or some other plug-in. Let's suppose that the module in our example is a servlet. The corrected model is depicted in Figure 10.7.

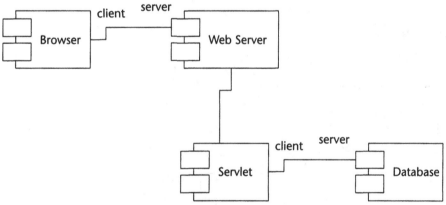

Figure 10.7 Corrected tiered view of a Web-based application.

To complete the model, we note that the browser is communicating with the Web server using HTTP, the Web server is communicating with the servlet via the HttpServlet application program interface (API), and the servlet is communicating with the database via Java Data Base Connectivity (JDBC). The updated model is depicted in Figure 10.8. One might argue that this is a four-tier model, but other architecture patterns fit the description. The browser/Web server part is client/server. The servlet/database is also client/server. The Web server/servlet is not easy to classify. It fits the description of layered systems (Shaw, 1996), but so do all four components when taken together. The servlet is far from being ignorant of its activation context, rather the servlet knows that it is being invoked from a servlet container and that it can query the servlet container for details about the request and other information about the environment and client. However, some definitions of the layers pattern have variations that relax the one-way knowledge constraint (Buschmann, 1996). In this variation, the Web server/servlet relationship can be characterized as layered.

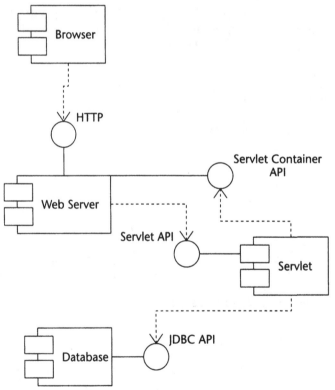

Figure 10.8 Detailed physical view of tiered Web-based application.

Our model is still not entirely accurate, because servlets are not invoked directly by Web servers, but rather by a more generic component called a servlet container. A Web server may implement a servlet container directly or a servlet container may plug into a Web server via the Web server's proprietary plug-in API and the servlet container may also implement a set of callback procedures that are also proprietary to the Web server. The model in Figure 10.9 expresses this. Note that the models in Figures 10.8 and 10.9 both depend on the choice of Web server component.

To make things more generic we can show the servlet's context, or view of the world. To a servlet, anything invoking its `javax.servlet.http .HttpServlet` interface is a servlet container. This means in Figure 10.8 the Web server was in the role of servlet container. In Figure 10.9, we represent an explicit servlet container.

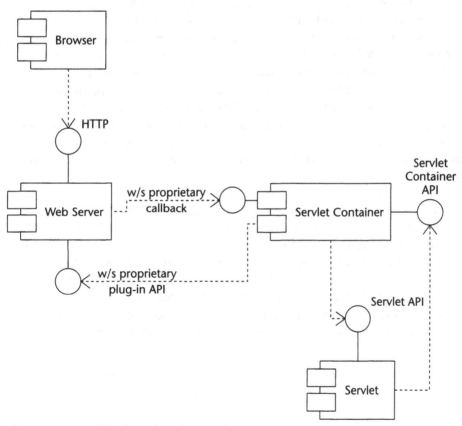

Figure 10.9   Explicit view of servlet container.

The Web server/servlet relationship is not client/server in the architectural style sense because they are not separate (distributed) software processes, though generally the servlet container is the client and the servlet is the server in a general caller/called sense. The Web server is really a broker (Buschmann, 1996) for the servlet or any other resource that it can serve, such as static HTML pages. The browser gives the Web server a URL that the Web server uses to look up the servlet class.

The servlet can gather information about the Web server (or rather from the servlet container) and its environment and state information so the servlet is then making requests of the Web server (servlet container) using Java API objects like HttpRequest and HttpSession. In a Web server/CGI context, it could be characterized as client/server because the CGI application is an independent application that the Web server invokes. The CGI application cannot make requests from its caller; all of the information available to it is passed in as command line variables and environment variables.

The servlet is an object in the sense of Shaw's object-oriented organization architecture style. That is, it is a data abstraction. The data is what is returned to the Web server in the form of character output writing to a Java OutputWriter object obtained from the HttpResponse object.

From the context of the servlet, the servlet container is the only thing invoking it. We could say that the servlet cannot distinguish between one servlet container and another, and hence servlet containers are generic servlet clients. But physically the servlet's activation context is within the servlet container's process space so the servlet is not a server in the distributed sense: It is an object.

The Java package javax.servlet.http is an example of global design rules. We can view a servlet and a servlet container as modules sharing a set of design rules, as depicted in the package diagram in Figure 10.10 and the DSM in Figure 10.11. We see that the javax.servlet package and its subpackages represent a module of design rules. A servlet and a servlet container have implementations that are completely independent. They only rely on the global design rules specified in the javax.servlet package.

In Figure 10.12 we see our final decomposition of the application with a Web-based user interface with various architectural styles overlaid.

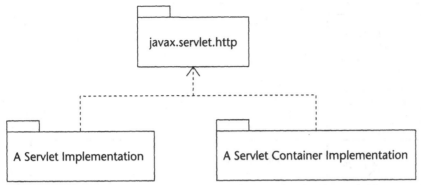

Figure 10.10   Servlet container and servlet design rules (package view).

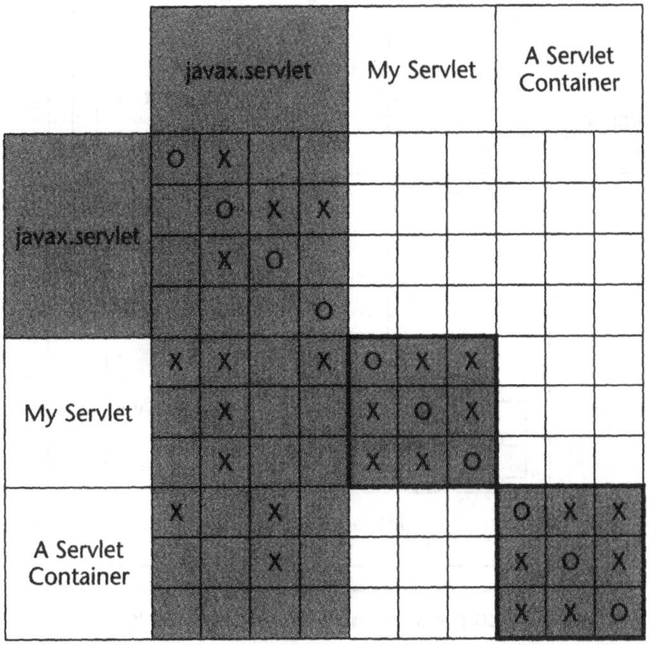

Figure 10.11   Servlet container and servlet design rules (DSM).

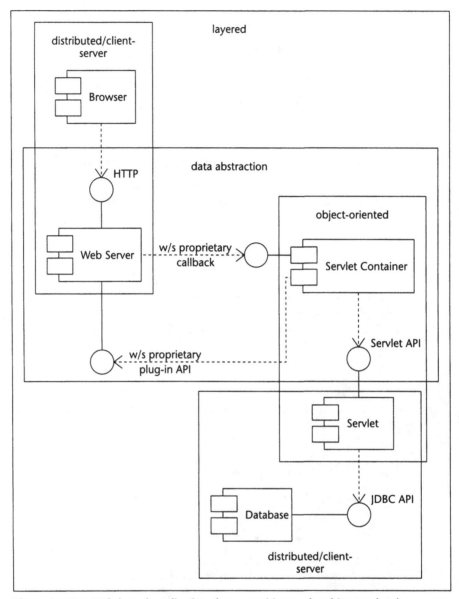

Figure 10.12 Web-based application decomposition and architectural styles.

Summary

Architectural styles allow us to reason about the high-level design of a system before we start to implement it. They are applied early in the architecture process to narrow a potentially large solution field. Selecting an architectural style also helps us to choose finer-grained design patterns. Architectural styles and patterns address many nonfunctional quality characteristics such as performance, reliability, and modifiability. The selection of architectural styles and patterns is largely driven by the required or desired quality attributes. The application of architectural styles and patterns can help us to decompose or split our system more effectively.

Understanding Metamodels

Metamodels are literally "models of models." A metamodel is a language for describing another model. For example, the Unified Modeling Language (UML) metamodel describes the syntax of diagrams expressed in UML. Every model has a metamodel that describes it, although the metamodel may be implicit. A metamodel is like the grammar of a formal language, and a model expressed in that grammar is a sentence or set of sentences expressed in the language of the metamodel. The UML metamodel defines the grammar of a class diagram. A particular class diagram conforms to this syntax. Metamodels are models and therefore may also have metamodels (in this case, you might refer to such a model as a meta-metamodel). Metamodels regress infinitely, but for practical purposes we typically see metamodels applied only once or twice. A system may use a metamodel to describe itself so that other applications may discover information about it (in this case, the metamodel is called meta data).

We will look at two applications of metamodels in this chapter. The first application has to do with describing software architectures using domain-specific metamodels. A metamodel in this application is used to help create an architectural description for a system within a specific domain. A metamodel for content management applications is presented. The second application is to actually implement a metamodel in an application in order to build a flexible, adaptable architecture (referred to as reflective architectures).

The topics of this chapter are:

Understanding metamodels.   Metamodels are a powerful concept but can be difficult to apply. Metamodels are fairly abstract tools for creating, understanding, and evaluating models. The relationship between metamodels, models, and data corresponds to the three layers of knowledge representation (ontology layer, domain layer, and technology layer). An example of this model is applied to modeling business applications.

Applying reference models.   A reference model is a type of metamodel that contains domain knowledge in the form of architectural components and connectors that can aid in the decomposition of a system. Two types of reference models are presented: the Seeheim and arch/slinky metamodels for user interface architectures and the enterprise application reference model for enterprise application architectures.

Fundamental metamodel for describing software components.   This metamodel example describes software components in terms of primitive software building blocks (data entities, Input/Output [I/O] servers, transformation servers, and data flow managers).

Content management system reference models.   A set of reference models for describing content publishing systems is presented. These reference models capture domain knowledge about content management and publishing systems.

Understanding Metamodels

Models and metamodels form a hierarchy of models. Each higher-level layer (the *meta* layer) describes the structure (syntax) of the next lower-level layer. The term *metamodel* can be considered a role that a model assumes with respect to other models. Another way to think of a metamodel is as a set of instructions for creating an instance of a class of models. Metamodels are like design languages; they are a domain-specific, self-contained design ontology.

For example, the UML has a notation for describing object models using class diagrams. An object model has an operational projection that is comprised of actual data (objects) in an operational system. For example, an object model consisting of customer and purchase can have an operational projection consisting of any number of customer objects and related purchase objects. The UML class diagram notation itself is a metamodel; you cannot interpret the class diagram accurately without understanding the class diagram notation. The class diagram instance (object model) is also a metamodel. You cannot interpret the runtime objects without understanding the object model. Interestingly, UML can be described in terms of itself (an interesting property of some languages), which means that the UML metamodel is itself expressed in UML. This relationship between models and metamodels is represented in Figure 11.1(a), and an example of the UML metamodel and its relation to object models and objects is represented in Figure 11.1(b).

Three-Layer Model of Knowledge Representation

The models of Figure 11.1 correspond to the three layers of a model of knowledge representation (Figure 11.2):

- Ontology layer
- Domain layer
- Technology layer

This is a common data model design for representing knowledge in knowledge management systems and lends itself nicely to interpreting architectural descriptions as well. Although more layers or fewer layers are possible, three seems to be a common pattern.

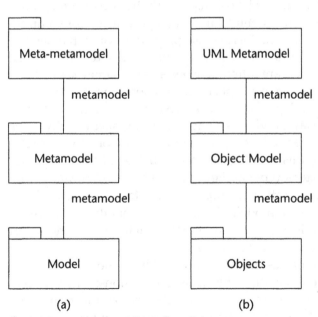

(a)   (b)

Figure 11.1 Metamodels and models.

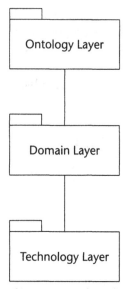

Figure 11.2   Three-layer model of knowledge representation.

These layers of models should not be confused with the succession of models you may build to describe the architecture of an application from requirements to implementation. Those models are also projections of each other, but along a different axis. Each of those models is interpreted as a different aspect of the same *system*. Metamodels are different aspects of the same *model*.

The *ontology layer* contains core concepts or abstractions and their relationships. An example of an ontology for software design is three core business abstractions presented by Dave Taylor as Convergent Engineering (Taylor, as cited in Hubert, 2002) and extended by Hubert's notion of a Convergent Architecture. I am representing this ontological model using UML metaclasses (classes with the *metaclass* stereotype) in Figure 11.3. This is not meant to represent an implementation, but rather to emphasize the fact that I am using a class diagram to represent a metamodel. (Recall in UML that the metaclass, in an implementation model, is meant to represent a metaclass in the target implementation language, such as in Smalltalk.)

Richard Hubert's version of this model (Reduced Abstraction Set Computing, or RASC) is based on the three business abstractions: organization, process, and resource (OPR). All application objects (that is, functional core objects) are one of these three abstractions. Human/computer interaction (HCI) and application integration objects and logic are not part of the OPR model and are represented by a fourth concept called *accessors*. System-related objects and logic, such as security and logging, are represented by the fifth concept called *utilities* (or services). The interpretation of the OPR is simple. An organization manages the life cycle of processes and resources. Processes use, consume, and produce resources (that is, they transform resources). This is a simple but very powerful ontology of designing business applications. One immediate application of this ontology is in the separation of concerns. Accordingly, the implementation class must be one of these five abstractions.

The *domain layer* contains domain models, such as models of specific business domains. These domain models are described in terms of the ontology abstractions. A domain model that conforms to the OPR can describe any business application (and those that are not traditionally considered to be business applications). Note that the domain model is only in terms of the three business abstractions. The other two, accessors and utilities, are not part of the application domain but are part of the operational, or solution, domain. We can represent this domain model using a UML class diagram with stereotypes applied to the classes. Recall that a UML stereotype is a way to specialize the semantics of a class without actually specifying any implementation details.

An example of a domain model is shown in Figure 11.4. In this model, Enterprise X (an organization) manages the product development process, which consumes money (a resource) and uses engineers (a resource) to produce Product Y (a resource).

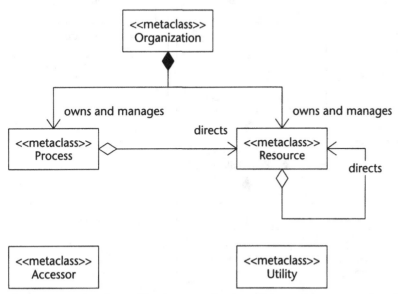

Figure 11.3   Ontology of business applications (from convergent engineering).

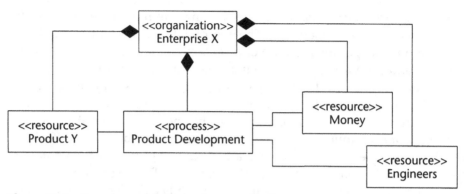

Figure 11.4 Domain model of a business application.

The *technology layer* is composed of models that are the technology projections of the domain layer. An example of a technology model is represented in
Figure 11.5. This example is a simplified model relying on the class names to
suggest the technology involved in each object, as well as the domain object
being represented. The mapping of ontology abstractions is represented using
additional boxes and text around groups of classes.

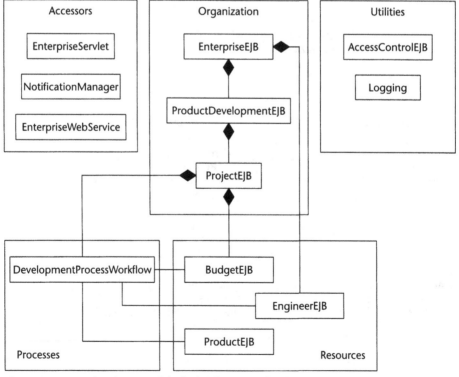

Figure 11.5 Technology model of a business application.

A design pattern is similar to a metamodel. It describes a working principle, which in turn implies the structure of source code. An architecture pattern is like a design pattern but describes the higher-level physical structure of an application or system. The proxy pattern describes a class design that addresses specific design concerns. By introducing the proxy design pattern (Gamma, 1995) into a source code, the system will contain the characteristics of that pattern.

A metamodel is more general. It is used to describe the logical relationship or responsibilities of elements in a design or solution formulation, but the meta-model elements are not necessarily visible in the source code or structure of the application or system itself. Metamodels define a language for a very special-ized domain and are a basis for discussing or describing a problem or design. Metamodels exist or can be created at all levels of information from the very abstract, such as object orientation, or the very specific, such as user interface design using arch/slinky. A design pattern can be thought of as a template for a design within the context of a metamodel. The proxy design pattern is expressed as a class diagram in UML and therefore itself conforms to the UML metamodel.

In Chapter 13, we will show how an architectural description can be composed of sets of architectural views that address specific shareholders and specific con-cerns. In Reference Model for Open Distributed Processing (RM-ODP) terminol-ogy, each view is described using a viewpoint language (see Chapter 14). These languages are in terms of elements and relations with respect to the viewpoint concerns.

Applying Reference Models

A *reference model* abstracts software components and expresses the system as connectors and components. Reference models are common in mature domains such as HCI, compiler design, and database system design. A refer-ence model may be created as a result of domain analysis, whereby a problem domain is analyzed (decomposed) until a canonical form is achieved.

The Seeheim metamodel and the arch/slinky metamodel are reference models for the architecture of interactive software applications that have a graphical user interface (GUI) element. Both models specify a canonical form for designing an application and are based on several years of research in the field of HCI. In order to understand these models, you must mentally separate the concept of a user interface from an application. Recall that a user interface is a type of connecting element and the user and the application are compo-nents (see Figure 11.6). This use of the term *application* and the term *user inter-face* may not compare with some common uses. I have seen the term application used to describe the user interface component of a system where the underly-ing objects and database were not considered part of the application.

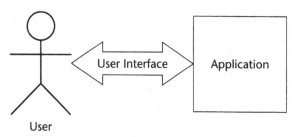

Figure 11.6 User interface as connecting element.

In these models, and in subsequent discussions, I use the term application to refer to the abstract problem being solved and also to refer to the underlying software system that models the problem. The term *functional core* is also used to mean the latter. I will use both terms interchangeably when the context is clear. The user interface is not part of the application proper, but is one type of connecting element that can be removed, replaced, or changed without actually changing the problem being solved or the internal model of the problem.

A metamodel can be considered the most basic decomposition of a problem domain. By mapping quality attributes to a metamodel you can compare or evaluate design patterns and detail design solutions by first mapping the design components to the elements of the metamodel. The properties of the metamodel are then transferred to the design. Some authors have used the arch/slinky metamodel as a means of performing architectural analysis. A comparison of the arch/slinky model to a design for an interactive system is one approach to validating quality attributes (Bass, 1998).

Seeheim Model

The Seeheim reference model for interacting applications is composed of three software elements: application, dialogue control, and presentation (Figure 11.7). A fourth element, the user, interacts with the presentation element only. The Seeheim reference model originated as an architectural style, a way of splitting a system into three software modules such that the system exhibited the qualities of portability and modifiability. It is the result of applying two decomposition or splitting operations to a design problem. The splitting operations result in the three components represented in Figure 11.7.

In Figure 11.7, presentation logic is separated so that this type of component is only aware of presentation technology. A presentation module contains lexical knowledge (for example, how to display various data controls and respond to user actions on those controls). Application logic is separated so that this type of component is only concerned with the application level (knowledge). An application component contains semantic knowledge: It represents the problem domain. In between is the dialogue control, which translates user interface commands (lexical actions) into application commands (semantic commands). The dialogue control is the syntactic component that ensures the lexical elements (user interface components) are used in the correct context. The dialogue control knows what commands can be executed in which modes and in which contexts. The application logic understands the meaning or interpretation of the commands that change the underlying problem data representation.

The Seeheim model recognizes the potential performance degradation related to the dialogue control layer and allows for a shortcut between the application and the presentation for "rapid semantic feedback." The trade-off in allowing the application to return data directly to the presentation component is reduced modifiability of the system. This is a classic example of the kind of trade-off (performance versus modifiability) that an architect needs to make.

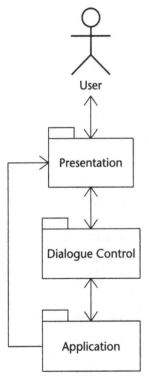

Figure 11.7   Seeheim metamodel.

The Seeheim model was intended to address modifiability and portability qualities. By separating the presentation layer, the logic could be ported to a different user interface technology or windowing system. The presentation component could even use a shared resource (such as the X-Window system server). The separation of the dialogue control from the application logic allowed for changes in the interaction model without having to modify the application logic itself. The same semantic model could have many different syntactic representations (there are potentially several interaction models for a given application model). One interaction model may break user tasks into many fine-grained tasks that are executed in a particular order (such as a wizard-style user interface). The application component is not aware of the exact user tasking or interaction model. The dialogue control and presentation could be changed to support a different task model or even multiple models (for example, the wizard for inexperienced users and a different interface for experienced users). This flexibility is a result of the very limited set of responsibilities that each component has.

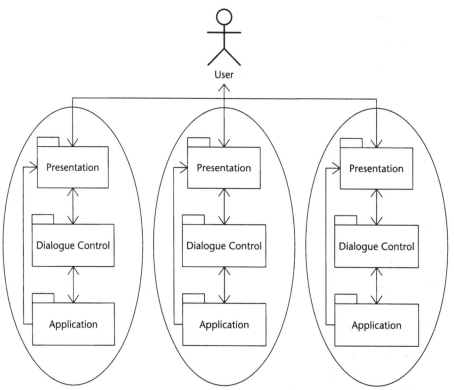

Figure 11.8 Part-whole decomposition and the Seeheim model.

The Seeheim model can be applied horizontally to a system decomposition as well (using uniform decomposition). A system could be decomposed into a set of components (part-whole decomposition) where each component is further decomposed according to the Seeheim model, resulting in the decomposition shown in Figure 11.8.

Arch/Slinky Model

Arch/slinky is another metamodel for interactive applications that evolved from the Seeheim model. Arch/slinky, like the Seeheim model, separates the user interface (presentation) and user interaction logic (dialogue control) from the application functional core. The arch/slinky reference model is composed of five elements, as shown in Figure 11.9:

- Presentation
- Virtual toolkit
- Dialogue control
- Virtual application
- Application

The term *arch* in arch/slinky is based on a common view of the model as an arch. The term *slinky* comes from the fact that an architecture that is based on this model does not necessarily explicitly contain the five elements. Some elements may be compressed into a single module (the analogy being like the toy spring of the same name compressing somewhere along its arch).

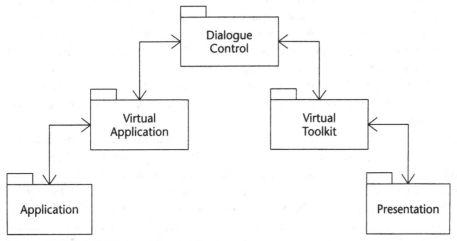

Figure 11.9   Arch/slinky metamodel.

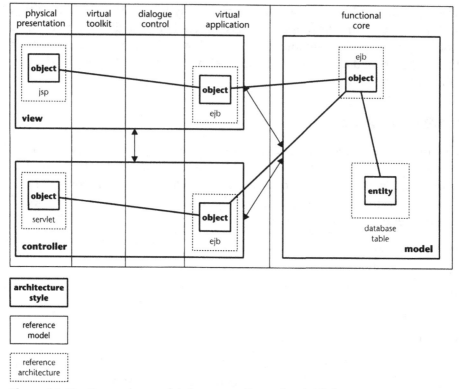

Figure 11.10   Comparing model-view-controller and arch/slinky.

At first glance, the Seeheim and arch/slinky models appear to be design patterns, but they are not exactly patterns. You would not necessarily create five classes, each mapped to the elements of the metamodel; rather, you would describe your design and design choices using the language of the metamodel and use the metamodel to guide the decomposition of your solution. The Model-View-Controller (MVC) pattern, on the other hand, is directly implemented in your source code. You can describe the MVC pattern in terms of the arch/slinky metamodel.

The arch/slinky decomposition emphasizes portability and modifiability. The arch/slinky presentation and virtual toolkit components together correspond to the Seeheim presentation component. Together, these two components have the same quality characteristics of the Seeheim model. A benefit of separating the toolkit from the actual presentation component is that the separation allows a presentation component to be ported to a variety of presentation technologies without theoretically changing the dialogue. The virtual toolkit presents a virtual presentation layer and maps user interface archetype objects to physical presentation objects. HTML can be thought of as a realization of the virtual toolkit. A Web application user interface can be described using HTML, and the physical presentation is constructed (dynamically, in this case) on any system that has a browser that supports HTML.

Arch/slinky is commonly contrasted with the model-view-controller and presentation-abstraction-control patterns. See Bass (Bass, 1998) for a detailed discussion of this contrast. A comparison can be seen in Figure 11.10.

Enterprise Application Reference Model

Enterprise applications have a common set of archetypal components: a data store, an application logic layer, and a presentation layer. This is nothing new; we are all familiar with the three-tier model of distributed enterprise applications. The application layer accesses and updates the data store. The presentation layer interacts with the application layer and requires potentially multiple technologies such as email, Web, client applications, Personal Digital Assistants (PDAs) using browsers or clients, and integration technologies such as Web services. The presentation layer provides input and output services to external entities such as human users and other systems. The three-tier model can serve as an architectural style or reference model. In this section, I present this set of common archetypal components as a reference model.

Let's look at our ontology of business applications again and how it relates to the classic three-tier model and the arch/slinky. Three metamodels are depicted in Figure 11.11. The presentation layer of the three-tier model contains components that are either accessors or utilities. The first four elements of the arch/slinky model also overlap the presentation layer. Objects that implement or map to the arch/slinky elements may either be pure accessor (handling human-computer aspects of the application) or they may be system-related (such as authorization components or logging components). The arch/slinky application element encompasses the business layer and persistence layer of the three-tier model. The business layer is composed of organization, process, and resource components and, optionally, utility components, such as access control and logging components. Note that the OPR elements may have accessor representations (for example, Data Transfer Objects) that are passed between the business layer and the presentation layer. These accessor components might be part of the virtual application. If the façade pattern were being used, the façade would be part of the virtual application layer in the presentation layer and would also be an accessor. The data persistence layer also has representations of the OPR elements.

The presentation layer may also be substituted with an integration layer, but the relationships remain the same.

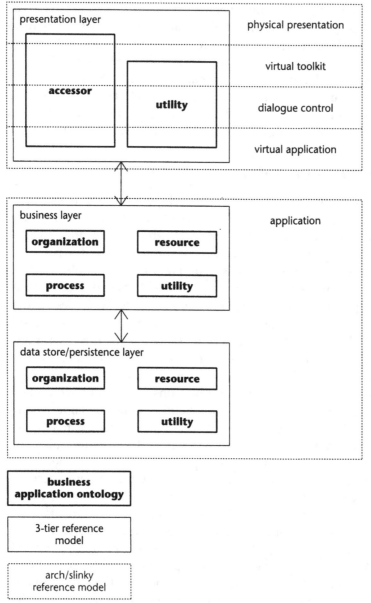

Figure 11.11 Enterprise reference model.

Technology Stacks and Architectural Layers

I commonly see depictions of technology stacks used as architectural descriptions, such as shown in Figure 11.12, where each application layer is associated with a single technology or a set of technologies that is only applied to that layer. The problem with this view is that technology stacks can be orthogonal to the layers of an architecture. Architectural layers may sometimes line up with specific technologies, but the layers do not typically form a technology stack. This is especially true in the presentation and business layers. Technologies and their interrelationships can suggest system decompositions but should not be confused with system decompositions.

The presentation layer is responsible for end-user interaction as well as rendering of information. As we have seen in the arch/slinky metamodel, what we traditionally think of as presentation involves physical presentation and logical interaction. In Web-based software applications, the presentation layer may need to store its own state information in order to perform the logical interaction. It is also likely that much of the information for constructing the presentation pages is stored in a database. Therefore, our presentation component or layer could also use Enterprise Java Beans (EJBs), Java Data Base Connectivity (JDBC), and Structured Query Language (SQL), as depicted in Figure 11.13.

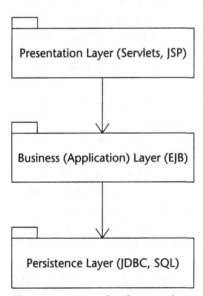

Figure 11.12   Technology stacks as architectural layers.

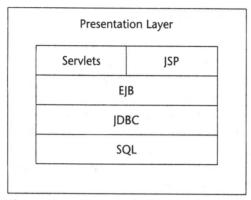

Figure 11.13   Presentation layer technology stack.

The use of a technology stack as an architectural description is the source of a lot of confusion and requires a change in the way we view the relationship between technology and software architecture. In the design process, the application of technology should come later rather than sooner, so the decomposition of a software application into layers occurs before assigning technologies to layers, instead of assigning layers based on technologies. This should be the case even if we have already selected a technology platform before architecting the application. We can see how technology stacks could be aligned with architectural components in Figure 11.14. Here, the same technologies can be used to implement the dialogue control, virtual application, and application components.

Let's consider a nonsoftware example of a reference model. Consider the architecture of a cell phone. This device has a liquid crystal display (LCD) screen for viewing information and getting input from the user and a keypad for entering information into the device (the screen and keypad are the terminal for the device and are responsible for interacting or dialoguing with users). The device also has a receiver, a transmitter, and a battery. A phone has many other components, but let's just consider these main components for the sake of this discussion. An engineering designer can order these components from a catalogue of such components that some electronic component vendor may produce. The engineer doesn't have to design these components from scratch, but rather can work with existing components that satisfy the functional need.

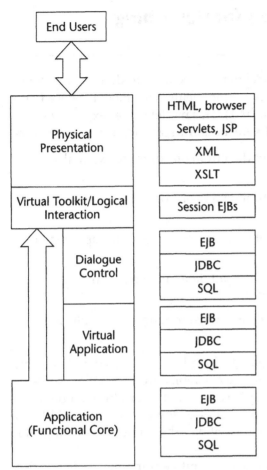

Figure 11.14   Architectural layers with technology stacks.

The phone has a basic architecture that is well understood and duplicated across many vendors' cell phone designs. Although the details vary and different vendors may use different manufacturer's components or variations of standard components, the architecture at a certain level of abstraction is the same: keypad, screen, battery, transmitter, and receiver. This abstract description is referred to as a reference model (it is a metamodel for a particular architecture). A given vendor's cell phone design has an architecture, which is a projection of the reference model onto a set of hardware (and software) components.

Fundamental Metamodel for Describing Software Components

In this section, I describe a metamodel that can be used to describe functional components in terms of four primitive components. This model is based on a fundamental design pattern (Buhrer, 2001). This model makes explicit the relationship between hardware and software. Buhrer's software design axioms are:

- The software must obtain input data from one or more external (hardware) interfaces.

- The software must deliver output data to one or more external (hardware) interfaces.

- The software must maintain internal data to be used and updated on every execution cycle.

- The software must transform the input data into the output data (possibly using the internal data).

- The software must perform the data transformation as quickly as possible.

The first approach is to think of a single thread of control as defining a software machine. Software machines may be assembled from "smaller" software machines. Two software machines can be connected to produce a more powerful software machine. The connection requires some amount of additional code in most cases, unless the parts were written to be connected via pluggable interfaces.

Buhrer defines four design elements, or primitive components, that satisfy the above axioms:

Data entity.   Data entities represent the software system's input data, output data, and internal data. This is a *data element*.

I/O server.   I/O servers encapsulate the external (hardware) interfaces with which the software interacts. I/O servers can also be pure input or output servers. The I/O server interacts with the hardware. Two software machines interact by passing data back and forth using I/O servers. This is considered interacting with the hardware because data is stored somewhere like random access memory (RAM), registers, or on disk. This is a type of *connecting element*.

Transformation server.   Transformation servers perform the transformation from input data to output data, while possibly updating internal data. The transformation server represents the algorithmic aspects of a system. This is also known as a *processing element*.

Data flow manager.   Data flow managers obtain input data from the I/O servers, invoke the transformation servers (which transform input data into output data), and deliver output data to the I/O servers. Data flow managers also own the internal data. This is a type of *connecting element*.

The data flow manager is like an integrated circuit (IC) board and etched circuits between the other three components. This element is like the object that orchestrates block diagram interactions but is hidden or implicit. Buhrer describes this model as a pattern upon which other patterns can be described. This makes it a candidate as a metamodel. We can use Buhrer's model as an ontology for implementation components. Certainly, all software embodies these capabilities, but they are not always explicitly identified as separate modules, objects, or functions.

Examples: Content Management System Reference Models

In this section, we look at metamodels for a content management and publishing application and several reference models that are useful for designing a publishing system. The content publishing metamodel example illustrates an application that is fairly complex in terms of the number and types of users and the complexity of the process that is automated. The challenge of this type of application is in designing around the large amounts of semistructured data and how to process potentially different data formats to produce a variety of content-based products. The metamodels presented here are applicable for designing a variety of content-oriented systems.

One application is the automation of the authoring of Web site content for an organization whose Web site is the primary tool for communicating valuable information to customers. Rich, timely, relevant, and accurate content is essential to maintain customer site loyalty. To support better communication, the Web site should encourage the user to visit more frequently and increase customer and visitor retention. To support the goals of the organization, the solution should reduce system and site maintenance costs, utilize Information Technology (IT) resources more efficiently and more effectively, improve department relations, leverage existing assets more effectively, and increase revenues.

Another application is the automation of the authoring of content that is sold to customers (such as online leading applications and products, as well as printed book versions of the same content). The value of the system is in increasing the company's revenue by reusing intellectual assets and lowering the cost of the creation, management, and delivery of those assets. A more specific example is a distance learning application such as Web-based tutorials offered by professional societies or software technology vendors.

Domain Model

In this section, I present a simplified domain model for publishing electronic and print content. The basic domain of content management and publishing includes the process of authoring intellectual content (that is, information resources for human consumption and which are an asset to the selling company). In terms of the OPR ontology, content management and publishing consist of the basic abstractions represented in Figure 11.15. A publishing enterprise is comprised of several business divisions, each of which may be responsible for publishing different content types. A business division owns the basic processes of content authoring, content publishing, and content delivery.

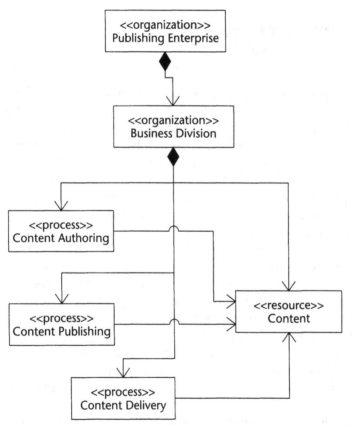

Figure 11.15   Content management and publishing domain model.

In book publishing, the term *publishing* basically means producing the product up to, but not necessarily including, printing (manufacturing) the book. It doesn't necessarily include the authoring, either, since a manuscript may be delivered to a publisher in (fairly) complete form. A publisher may publish a work once but may reprint it several times. Publishing electronic content doesn't require a manufacturing (printing) stage like traditional books. A term commonly used in electronic publishing is *delivery*. Content delivery can be considered a generalization of manufacturing and distribution for print products and electronic delivery (via the Web). This model focuses on electronic content publishing but can be extended to include print products. The content authoring and publishing process can be described in terms of several activities:

Authoring/editing/assembling.   This is the process of creating content and source code for an electronic content product and assembling it into a collection. The term *assembly* is borrowed from the magazine publishing domain, where an editor assembles a journal or magazine from content to produce an edition.

Snapshot (edition).   This is the creation of a snapshot of the repository content that defines a product, but not the generated content. This is also known as creating an *edition*.

Compilation/production.   This is the process of creating a ready-for-delivery product. For an electronic product, this optionally includes formatting the content (for example, from eXtensible Markup Language [XML] to HTML). The content used for compiling comes entirely from a snapshot and is specific to the delivery mode (whether it will be printed or deployed electronically). The term *compiling* is borrowed from the software development domain and implies that the production process may be partially or fully automated as a transformation of raw content plus assembly information into deliverable format. Production, in the print domain, is the process of converting a final manuscript into its print-ready layout.

Deployment (manufacturing).   This is the manufacturing step where a tangible product is created (for example, a book is printed or content is uploaded to a production Web server). This takes the output of compilation/production.

Delivery/consumption.   This is the step where a user receives or otherwise gains access to content. Delivery may be in the form of a printed book, email (Internet, PDA, cell phone), or a Web page. Syndication and subscription are related to the delivery activity.

Each step is a transformation of sorts that takes one representation as input and produces another representation as output. The output of a step is the input of the next adjacent step. Authoring/assembly takes as input real-world representations of information (conversations, handwritten documents, and so on) and outputs an electronic version (for example, XML) that can be stored in a file system or database. Creating a snapshot produces an immutable versioned collection of electronic content. Compiling changes the immutable snapshot representation into another representation that is specific to a deployment target (for example, converts XML to HTML or Java Server Page [JSP] files, or to SQL code).

Deployment is the act of creating something tangible or updating a live server with the compiled product. The deployment representation may be a printed book, HTML, or data in a database. There may not be an actual transformation at this step, such as in the case of HTML. Delivery is the transformation of deployed data to a particular medium. In the case of printed material, there is no physical transformation. For electronic data, this is the sending of data (either proactively or by request) to some device such as a browser or PDA. The data undergoes another transformation (for example JSPs are invoked, which generates HTML). Some Web content publishing models combine publishing and deployment.

Content Collaboration Reference Model

In this section, we look at an example of a reference model for content collaboration that is within the domain of content management and publishing. The content collaboration metamodel is also known as the work area/staging area/edition model (WSE) (Nakano, 2002). This is a model for the collaboration of Web content creation that uses multiple work areas, a single common staging area, and editions (labeled versions of a collection of assets such as text files and images). This model is very similar to well-known software development models that use a version control system with branching support for configuration management and to support parallel development. The branches in a source code control system are examples of work areas, where individuals or groups can work on a particular private view of the system before integrating changes back into the global branch where others can see the changes.

The components of the WSE are:

Managed asset.   An atomic unit of version-controlled data such as a file or database entity (for example, a record).

Work area.   A branch (collection of managed assets) that has a separate life cycle from its corresponding staging area but is periodically merged back into the staging area. A managed asset may belong to more than one work area.

Staging area.   A collection of managed assets. A staging area may have zero or more associated work areas. A staging area may also be a work area for another staging area (that is, staging areas may form a hierarchy).

Editions.   A versioned collection of specific versions of managed assets that can be retrieved at an arbitrary point in time. An edition is immutable. An edition is a snapshot of a subset of a staging area.

These components are represented in Figure 11.16. They are all *resources* in the OPR model.

The WSE model does not specify the implementation of branching or merging, nor does it define what a managed asset is or how it is persisted. A managed asset may be an XML document that is actually stored as fragments in a database or it may be a set of files on a file system. The model does imply a versioning capability, at least with respect to merging work areas (collections of managed assets) within staging areas. There is nothing in the model that implies that different versions of a file may be retrieved from a given work or staging area (source code control systems do usually support this ability to view the history of a file and retrieve any version of it).

A simple variation of the WSE restricts staging areas from also being work areas. This means that there is only one staging area and one level of work area, which cannot also be a staging area.

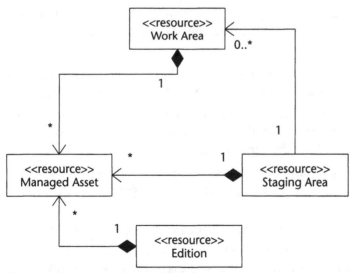

Figure 11.16   WSE reference model.

The operations (usage scenarios) of the WSE are:

Create work area.   Create a branch off of a staging area with current copies of managed assets.

Submit.   Copy assets from work area to staging area.

Compare.   Compare assets in staging area to work area.

Update.   Copy from staging to work area, also known as synchronizing.

Merge.   Combine data in the staging area and work area versions of an asset and resolve conflicts if present (a merge is combined with either a Submit or Update).

Snapshot (edition).   Create an edition (same semantics as the domain model).

The basic WSE model does not specify operations like rollback (removing the most current version or versions like popping a stack). All of these operations are *processes* in the OPR model.

I substituted the term *snapshot* for the original *publish* in this model to remain compatible with the content management and publishing domain model presented. The word means to create an immutable collection of managed assets, but does not necessarily include formatting (for example, transforming XML into HTML).

Content Management Reference Model

The content management metamodel complements the WSE metamodel. Content-based applications typically utilize one or more of the following types of services:

Content storage.   Some low-level services, including data storage and retrieval, indexing and searching, backup, and data import and export.

Version control.   Provides version control semantics including asset versioning, locking, rollback, and file differencing (so that a user may compare different versions of the same asset).

Branching.   Allows an asset to have several simultaneous versions with different histories, yet can be merged with other versions on different branches.

Workflow.   Allows users to manage specific business processes around the creation and management of assets.

Meta data.   Facilitates the classification and searching of assets and can be used to communicate the structure of data from one system to another.

Publish and deployment. Provides capabilities to aggregate assets into sets and to define the presentation of content. Includes features such as formatting/transformation and deployment to external target systems.

Subscription services. Allows users or external systems to subscribe to syndicated subscriptions. May be either push (content delivered when published) or pull (users or system asks for content if it is available).

Syndication services. The ability to syndicate content for other systems to consume: requires managing subscription and notification rules that are activated when an edition is published. Works in conjunction with the publish services. Standards related to subscription and syndication services are the Information and Content Exchange (ICE) protocol, RosettaNet (for example, catalogue subscriptions), and Electronic Business eXtensible Markup Language (ebXML).

The subscription and syndication services may be considered outside of the pure content management model, but they are important for more sophisticated, Business to Business (B2B)-type content applications such as catalogues and are also included for completeness of the model. However, these services can be used to extend or adapt a content application even for internal use. A set of deployment servers can subscribe to content so that they are notified when new content is available and can either receive or retrieve that content based on the subscription agreement. For example, a cluster of Web servers may automatically deploy new content at a predetermined time.

These services may be provided by Content Management System (CMS) vendors or custom built in-house. There is not always a one-to-one mapping of services to software components. A given component may provide several services (either fully or partially) with no clean separation or integration point in which to plug other products that supply those services. However, the reference model does suggest a logical decomposition of a system. If CMS vendors were able to agree on a common reference model and standards for combining the various modules, it would be straightforward to define reference architectures using combinations of vendors' components. (A reference architecture is a projection of a reference model to particular technologies.) Many popular file version control systems support storage, version control, and branching. A workflow engine that is integrated with this version control system would be used to manage various content creation processes such as content review processes.

Summary

Metamodels are useful tools for describing, understanding, and evaluating architectures. Metamodels are models for describing other models and can be thought of as a grammar for a class of models. Reference models are a type of metamodel that capture domain knowledge such as HCI and enterprise applications. The arch/slinky reference model describes the components of an interactive application. The fundamental metamodel for describing software components is composed of a set of primitive building blocks for software components. The workflow/staging area/edition and content management models are useful reference models for describing content management systems.

This chapter completes our treatment of models and their uses in the software architecting process. In the next chapter, we learn about architectural descriptions and viewpoint specifications and look at a specific standard for architectural descriptions.

CHAPTER 12

Creating Architectural Descriptions

We will now learn how to choose the right kinds of models to build and how to create an architectural description. An architectural description is a set of representation models grouped into views (see Chapter 6). Views represent certain aspects of the software system, each addressing a set of related concerns. Views are specified by viewpoints. A viewpoint identifies system stakeholders and the concerns addressed, as well as modeling languages and modeling techniques used to create views.

In this chapter, I provide an introduction to the Institute of Electrical and Electronics Engineers (IEEE) Recommended Practice for the Description of Software Intensive Systems (IEEE, 2000). This is becoming the predominant standard for architectural descriptions.

The topics of this chapter are:

Standardizing architectural descriptions.   The IEEE published its Recommended Practice for Architectural Description of Software-Intensive Systems (IEEE, 2000), also known as IEEE Std 1471-2000, or IEEE 1471 for short. IEEE 1471 does not specify what views an architectural description should have, but rather how those views should be specified.

Creating an architectural description.   The architectural description of a system or application is not the only document for specifying it. An architectural description is composed of views that each addresses a set of stakeholders and their concerns, and which contain a model of some aspect of the system. An information view is a common view.

Applying the architectural description. An architectural description can be used to describe a system that does not yet exist or one that already exists. The architectural description is necessary in order to perform an architectural assessment.

Standardizing Architectural Descriptions

The specification of a software application's architecture is called an architectural description (See Figure 12.1). In the terminology of the IEEE 1471, a *system* has an *architecture*, which is described by an *architectural description*. An architectural description is organized by one or more *views*, each of which consists of one or more *models* and conforms to a *viewpoint*. An architectural description selects one or more viewpoints, each of which covers one or more *stakeholder concerns*. A viewpoint establishes methods for one or more models. The IEEE 1471 definition of an architecture description is "a collection of products to document an architecture."

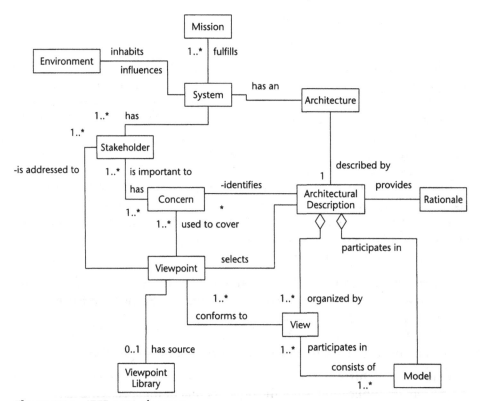

Figure 12.1 IEEE 1471 elements.

IEEE 1471 is intended to encompass all the products or artifacts of system development that capture architectural information. Such specifications are used for representing or modeling the system, specifying how it should evolve, communication among stakeholders, and planning software development.

The IEEE 1471 standard may seem like overkill to some software architects, especially those who work on small projects or with small teams. In my experience, most software development-related standards target large software corporations and government contractors, where conformance to standards is a way to bring some audit capability to the process of software acquisition. (One may argue that this really results in a paper trail that doesn't necessarily improve the acquisition process or quality of the system, but may in fact hide problems.)

The IEEE 1471 can be used effectively on projects of any size. The standard's biggest contribution to software development, I feel, is in defining the concepts and terminology of the specification of software architectures precisely and unambiguously. The standard does not attempt to recommend methodologies, modeling languages, or architectural styles. It is a generalization of architectural descriptions and can be thought of as an architecture specification metamodel.

There is a huge gap between the client's requirements and the implementation-oriented models that prevent many stakeholders from reviewing or understanding the design. This has an impact on the architect, who must make the mental leap from requirements to design. By applying the IEEE 1471, you can reduce this semantic gap and improve the architecting process in general. The standard doesn't prescribe how to architect, but rather recommends the kind of practices you can perform and the kind of information you should maintain in order to make meaningful and useful specifications. All too often I see software developers create specifications, at the request of project managers, that are unclear, unfocused, and that do not have an obvious purpose or target audience. Yet some managers feel that by having the developer go through this exercise, the quality of their code will somehow improve. An effective specification identifies a target audience (the stakeholders) and their concerns. Identifying stakeholders is one of the first and most important steps in creating effective specifications. The stakeholders and their concerns define the scope and purpose for what software developers specify and a clear context in which to write them.

Creating an Architectural Description

The IEEE 1471 specifies a minimum amount of information that an architectural description must contain in order to *conform* to the standard. You should consider your project needs and the role that the architectural description plays in your project before adopting this or any software development standard to the letter. The initial activities for creating an architectural description follow:

1. Identify the architectural description, including version and overview information.
2. Identify stakeholders, their roles, and their architectural concerns.
3. Select viewpoints.
4. Specify viewpoints.
5. Specify views.
6. Record known inconsistencies among the views.
7. Create a rationale for the architecture.

Remember that architecting is a continuous and iterative activity, so these basic steps occur more than once in a system's life cycle. Specifying views is the heart of most architecting and is the step where design activities occur.

Identify the Architectural Description

IEEE 1471 recommends that the architectural description contain the following information as it relates to all of the architectural description products as a whole:

- Date of issue and status
- Issuing organization
- Change history
- Summary
- Scope
- Context
- Glossary
- References

The actual form and content of these elements are determined by the using organization and not the standard. The definitions of these elements should be self-evident, but the interested reader should consult IEEE/EIA Standard 12207.0-1996. I have included this section to be consistent with the IEEE 1471 standard. Identification information doesn't affect the actual architecture, so I won't pursue this section in any more detail other than to say that this is a good practice for technical documentation in general.

Identify Stakeholders

A stakeholder is a person, group of persons, or organization that has a vested interest in the application and that share a common set of concerns and interests in the application. The creation and refinement of the architectural description are the center of all software architecting activities; therefore, the architectural description serves as the medium for communication design decisions among stakeholders. This communication is through the actual models that comprise the architectural description.

Not all stakeholders are interested in all models. Most nonengineering stakeholders won't understand most of the design models. In order to select the appropriate views and models to create, we must first identify who the stakeholders are and what their primary concerns about the application are. IEEE 1471 states that the minimum stakeholders identified must include the following:

- Users of the system
- Acquirers of the system
- Developers of the system
- Maintainers of the system

Sometimes the user and acquirers are the same group. The users are, of course, those people who will use the system to perform some work or who will administer it for others. They are specifically interested in functionality. The acquirers are those people or organizations that fund the project and are primarily concerned with the purpose of the system to solve some business or other problem, the feasibility of the solution, and the cost of developing the application. Developers are primarily concerned with the functionality and the technology that is to be used to implement the functionality. Maintainers are primarily concerned with how to adapt, extend, or otherwise modify the system after it is in production.

Many concerns are similar to system quality attributes, such as usability, buildability, testability, and maintainability. Therefore, the different stakeholder perspectives drive the quality concerns of the product, as well as how to represent the architecture.

When identifying stakeholders for your architectural description, think about the roles assumed by various people and organizations. The developers may include employees of the building organization as well as outside contractors. Will you need to identify them separately? You may not need to identify every stakeholder in the application. Minimally, include those who will actively participate in revising and assessing the architecture.

IEEE 1471 states that the minimum concerns identified should include the following:

- The purpose of the application
- The appropriateness of the application for use in fulfilling its purpose
- The feasibility of developing the application
- The risks of application development and operation to the stakeholders
- Maintainability, deployability, and evolvability of the application

A single concern can be shared by more than one stakeholder and can also be covered by more than one viewpoint.

Select Viewpoints

A viewpoint is a specification for the techniques and models of constructing views. An architectural description is composed of views, which conform to viewpoints. You can think of a viewpoint as a metamodel and a view as a set of models and diagrams that conform to the viewpoint. An information viewpoint describes a system in terms of information semantics and processing. Such a viewpoint can specify the use of UML class diagram notation from which an information view is constructed. Such a view would consist of object models in terms of classes and their associations.

Viewpoints specify the rules and practices for creating, representing, and analyzing views. A viewpoint specifies the modeling languages to be used for describing or representing a view together with the modeling methods or analysis techniques to be used in creating the models of a view. In this way, a view is able to address the concerns specified by the viewpoint. Each view conforms to a viewpoint that specifies the types of models a view may contain, the methods for generating those models, and associated semantics for interpreting the models. Viewpoints separate concerns into smaller sets of design forces that can be resolved in a more local manner. Most software design methodologies utilize multiple viewpoints. Object-oriented methods utilize at least two viewpoints: a static view of classes and objects and a dynamic view of the system's behavior.

In the language of the IEEE 1471, an architecture description *selects* one or more viewpoints, which are used to create its views. This selection is based on the stakeholders to be targeted by the architectural description and their concerns. The selection of architecture viewpoints is important because they form the basis for attaining and eventually representing systems knowledge. The selection of viewpoints may also be prescribed by the choice of design methodology or architecture framework.

In the absence of a standard or prescribed methodology or architecture framework, the architect is left to create viewpoint specifications by determining which types of models can be used to address the target stakeholder concerns. You may define your own viewpoint specification or you may use predefined ones. In the IEEE 1471, an externally defined viewpoint is referred to as a *library viewpoint*. We will see several examples of such library viewpoints in the next chapter on architecture frameworks.

Views are instances of viewpoints. A view can be thought of as a representation of a dimension of an application's architecture. It is important to understand that we cannot have full knowledge of a system so we must divide the system's representation into more easily understood pieces or abstractions. Views give us the first level of decomposition where the abstractions within the view are consistent with respect to a set of stakeholders.

Specify Viewpoints

The standard recommends specifying the following for each viewpoint:

- The viewpoint name
- The stakeholders addressed by the viewpoint
- The concerns addressed by the viewpoint
- The methodology for constructing a view based on the viewpoint
- The source of a library viewpoint, if applicable

If the viewpoint comes from a library of viewpoints, from an architecture framework, or methodology, then its name is the name as it appears in the source. For example, the *enterprise viewpoint* is the name of a viewpoint from the Reference Model for Open Distributed Processing (RM-ODP) architecture framework. In this example, you would also identify the RM-ODP framework as the source of the viewpoint. In the case where the specification for a library viewpoint is readily available and easy to retrieve, you may simply reference the existing viewpoint specification. Several common viewpoints correspond to the types of models identified in Figure 3.1.

Of all the stakeholders identified previously, specify those that are specifically addressed by the viewpoint. Also specify which concerns the viewpoint covers. No single viewpoint will cover all of the concerns of a stakeholder. Each stakeholder will need to see multiple views to complete its picture of the system. However, each type of stakeholder will most likely require a different set of views.

Viewpoint Rationale

The IEEE 1471 states that a rationale should be included for each viewpoint selected. In particular, the rationale should describe to what extent the stakeholders and concerns are covered by the viewpoints. In practice it is not always possible to create a view that entirely covers a concern.

For example, the feasibility of constructing a system can be determined in part by the information in the corresponding view, but also requires evaluating information external to the view and the architectural description itself. Viewpoints that cover specific quality attributes such as maintainability are also difficult to specify entirely and precisely, and therefore the extent to which they can be addressed should be stated in the rationale.

Functional views that are comprised of behavioral models (Chapter 6) can be used in evaluating the appropriateness of the application for use in fulfilling its intended purpose. Use cases are an example of such a behavioral model.

Structural models can be used in evaluating the feasibility of developing the application. Stakeholders with this concern can reason about the feasibility by seeing what needs to be built and what can be created using commercial off-the-shelf components. Furthermore, a work breakdown structure gives them information such as effort involved in developing the application. A viewpoint that covers this concern might be composed of managerial models and could include some initial version of a project plan with work breakdown structures and a bill of materials (for commercial software components). There is another side to feasibility and that is technical feasibility. If the application requires some unproven technology, then a viewpoint that expresses this information may be necessary. The application may rely on technology that is not fully developed or may be risky to adopt.

The exact intention of the term feasibility must be determined by the organization. This intention will drive the selection of the appropriate viewpoint to cover the feasibility concern. Determining feasibility may involve analyzing cost and scheduling of the development effort, or it may involve analyzing the technological approach of the architecture, as described above.

Application development and operation risks, like feasibility, must be defined by the organization before the appropriate viewpoints can be selected. Risks to development include missing marketing windows, delivering late and losing important customers, going over budget, not meeting specified requirements, or developing an unsuitable (invalid) solution. Risks to operation include potential loss of information, productivity, revenue, or even human life. If these risks exist, they should (or some would argue, must) be documented, especially when human safety is a risk.

Quality attributes in general can be expressed as system concerns. By casting qualities as concerns, we explicitly select viewpoints that can be used to reason about the qualities. As we will see, one of the uses of the architectural description is in architectural assessments, where we reason about a design or design alternatives for suitability in achieving the desired qualities. This assessment cannot be done if there are no models specified in a language that explicitly covers the qualities. Not every quality cleanly maps to some viewpoint language or elements of some language. Like a properly structured requirements statement, quality attributes need to be defined explicitly if they are to be considered system concerns.

Viewpoints and Systems Knowledge

The lowest level of systems knowledge (the source level) is the knowledge of which variables or *dimensions* of a system we wish to observe. In systems design these dimensions can be equated with some architectural *viewpoints*, in particular, those viewpoints specifically designed for organizing and expressing system requirements. The views created based on these viewpoints are commonly referred to as analysis models (as in object-oriented analysis or use case analysis). These views represent knowledge at the data level of systems knowledge. Viewpoints and views that represent the solution are at the generative level of systems knowledge, commonly referred to as the design models.

Interdependence of Views

Architectural descriptions should be consistent. An architectural description that has this quality promotes system understanding and knowledge transference. The views of the architectural description have an obvious and harmonious relationship. The knowledge in models doesn't contradict other models, and knowledge is easy to trace between models. A consistent architectural description enables stakeholders to navigate and find information and to trace concepts across multiple views.

No single aspect can capture or represent a system; they must all be considered together. For example, an information view of the system does not adequately address concerns of modifiability. However, by isolating certain aspects of the system design, we can reason about related aspects of the problem we are trying to solve in an easier way than if we attempted to reason about the system in its entirety. Looking at the information view and component view in a single diagram would be confusing and would not help us understand these two aspects of the system simultaneously. However, we must realize that all of the aspects are interdependent and affect one another. A change to the information aspect of the system may require a change in the component aspect as well.

We can perform some reasoning about the system without having to consider the system as a whole. A characteristic of a good viewpoint is the ability to reason about an aspect of the system within the confines of a view without necessarily considering the other views simultaneously. In other words, the content of the view is highly coherent but the views are loosely coupled. A view that only represents the data structures but not the flow of information through the system is not as coherent as a view that represents both models together. We can talk about the data or information that is stored or created in a system, and we can talk about the way the system behaves over time separately, but we know that the behavior and the data are interdependent. It should be possible to reason about what the system does without necessarily knowing how it does it. Reasoning in isolation about the system does not mean that we can alter models in isolation, however. Changing something in the behavioral view of an application may affect the information model, and therefore we need to modify that model and any other model that may have traces to or from the changed model.

Traceability

Traceability is the capability to semantically relate design elements or concepts across models and views. Traces are very important to effective architecture modeling and are a means toward achieving consistency in an architectural description. Without traces it is difficult to determine the relationships between elements in different models and the overall relationship between models in different views.

In Unified Modeling Language (UML), a *trace* is a dependency relationship between two modeling elements in different models that represent the same element or concept but at different semantic levels within and across views. UML traces do not have specific semantics themselves except as a notational reminder for the modeler that such a dependency exists. In practice, managing diagrammatic traces can be difficult, especially if you are managing them manually. An automated design tool that correctly handles traces should be able to notify the user if changes in one model affect the other models, and which elements are affected. In small-scale design, traces are implicit and are usually inherent in the naming convention of elements in models. For example, the names of programming language classes, eXtensible Markup Language (XML) schema elements, database tables, and analysis classes may be the same or derived from each other in a consistent manner.

Methodologies and Viewpoints

If you've used any methodology such as Object Modeling Technique (OMT) or the Rational Unified Process, then you are already familiar with the concept of multiple viewpoints. Methodologies typically specify viewpoints along with the methods for generating the models that form the design views. OMT (Rumbaugh, 1991) specifies three viewpoints: the object, dynamic, and functional views together with a modeling notation for each. OMT, like many methodologies, doesn't distinguish between the concepts of viewpoints, views, and models; the concepts are implicit.

OMT object models specify the static structure of a system in terms of objects and their relationships. An *object diagram* (which is similar to a UML class diagram) represents the object model in terms of class relationships such as aggregation and inheritance. Dynamic models specify the behavior aspects of the system with respect to how the system's state changes over time. Dynamic models include *event trace diagrams* (similar to UML sequence diagrams), *event flow diagrams* (similar to UML object collaboration diagrams), and *state diagrams*. Functional models represent the data transformations within a system. *Data flow diagrams*, which express process and data flows, comprise the functional model. The OMT authors considered these three views as orthogonal yet interdependent, with the object model being the fundamental model and the starting point of design activities.

In OMT, the three views are used for both analysis models and design models so effectively that there are six viewpoints. An object model starts as an analysis model capturing domain knowledge and problem statements. This model is then transformed into a design model that incorporates solution concepts. As each model is refined, it becomes a solution space model. The recommended alternative is to keep the analysis models intact and apply operations to them to produce separate design models. Thus, there is a logical object model (and associated set of diagrams) that reflects the results of object-oriented analysis, and there is a solution-oriented object model (and associated set of diagrams) that reflects the results of object-oriented design. This is common in most object-oriented methodologies, where the intention is to represent the problem using the same modeling language (for example, objects) as the solution, thus making the transformation from analysis to design nearly transparent and maintaining a smaller set of diagrams.

Booch's methodology is very similar to OMT (Booch, 1994). In this methodology there are four views, which are the products of logic and physical models together with static and dynamic models. Booch describes these as two dimensions: the logical/physical dimension and the static/dynamic dimension. The logical models use the language of objects and classes and the physical models use the language of module architecture and process architecture. Like OMT, the views are overloaded to include both analysis and design models. The logical models of a system serve to represent the problem space or the system's architecture. The product of analysis is a logical model that is composed of static models that capture the key problem abstractions and their relationships and dynamic models that capture the intended behavior or scenarios of the system. The products of design are refined static and dynamic models in the same language as the analysis models.

Other methodologies, object-oriented or otherwise, have similar concepts of multiple views of a system that represent the problem and solution expressed in modeling notations and specified in diagrams. These methodologies are sometimes referred to as integrated methodologies because they bring together many different views and methods for generating those views, as well as methods for maintaining consistency across views.

Specify Views

The architectural description will have one view per selected viewpoint. The view contains the actual models of the system. The views will evolve the most frequently of any architectural description products. The IEEE 1471 states that a view shall include identification and introductory information, a representation of the system constructed in accordance with the viewpoint specification, and configuration information. The second point, creating the representation of the system, is the primary focus of this book.

Part of selecting viewpoints is selecting the types of models that are necessary and sufficient for representing an application's architecture. Some architectural models may not have a written specification, but rather exist in the mind of the architect only to be occasionally rendered on a whiteboard. However, for anything but the most trivial systems, it is necessary to relieve the architect of the mental burden of memorizing complex models, as well as to make them available for others to review.

An effective architecture model is one that is necessary and sufficient. By necessary, I mean that the model is needed in order to perform additional architecting or implementation activities and without the model, such further activities are difficult or impossible. We all know that in reality we often operate without necessary models. This situation can be characterized as ineffective architecting or lack of architecting. Ineffective architecting doesn't mean you are guaranteed to fail, but your chances become diminished. By unsuccessful, I don't mean to imply that a running system is never created; rather some aspect of the system didn't meet expectations, such as cost, functionality, or delivery schedule. These are all difficult parameters to control in the software development process because software development is mostly a pure design activity. Design is very open-ended and therefore difficult to predict.

Record View Inconsistencies

While consistency is a desired property of an architectural description, it is frequently unachievable or undesirable. The architectural description should record known inconsistencies among the views (for example, if you have an element in one view that doesn't have an obvious representation in another). Suppose you have several classes of objects represented in an object model, but these classes are not directly represented in the database schema. Instead a simple table is used to record a class name (such as a Java class name) and a block of parameters to be passed to the object's constructor (the parameters may be stored as a small XML string). This mapping of concepts from the object model view to the implementation view cannot be managed alone with simple traces, and in this example you would have to describe the relationship between the two models.

Another example of inconsistency is when relationships between elements that are modeled at one level of abstraction disappear in another level. If the object model specifies a strict relationship with complex constraints between classes and this relationship is not modeled directly in the implementation class model or database schema, then this is an inconsistency that should be specified. It is common practice to elevate many constraints outside of the database and to instead implement them in code.

Create Architectural Rationale

The IEEE 1471 states that an architectural description should include a rationale for selected architectural concepts as well as some description for why particular design choices were made. You may provide a rationale for selecting one architectural style over another. If you've performed an architectural assessment on multiple styles, the results of that assessment should be part of the architectural rationale. Architectural styles were covered in Chapter 10 and architectural assessment will be covered in Chapter 14.

The rationale should attempt to answer the questions that stakeholders may typically ask the architect. If you find that the same kinds of questions are asked frequently, then you may want to include them in the rationale.

Applying the Architectural Description

The amount of information necessary to create an IEEE 1471-compliant architectural description may seem formidable but the standard is grounded in practices that bring a lot of value to the architecting process. The goal is not to produce paperwork that looks like it follows the standard; rather, the goal is to apply the recommended practice in order to guide the development of an effective architectural specification. Some people may dismiss the standard as being too prescriptive or normative for an activity that is fundamentally based in creative problem solving. But even creative problem solving requires some order to the approach and can benefit from leveraging best practices that others have used effectively.

All of the steps of the recommended practice may seem overbearing. But if you were to go through the process of thinking about the rationale of a particular view in your architectural specification and to whom the view addresses, wouldn't you produce a more effective and purposeful model than if you create something ad hoc and without clear purpose? We will see a real example of an architectural specification that was not thought through later in this chapter.

The IEEE 1471 practice can be thought of as a pattern or heuristic approach to figuring out what you should actually write down. Many good software architects go through these same steps intuitively because they've been practicing software design for a long time. Remember that this is the art of software architecting and art means practice, and practice means repeating something.

There are two kinds of design situations in which you may find yourself. The first is the situation where an organization wants to incorporate a standard methodology and the second is the type that already has some practices in place (either using a standard methodology or an ad-hoc one). In the second case, you may not be able to adopt a particular methodology because the organization's practices are already set. In this situation, you must incorporate ideas into the existing methodology. Either situation affects the kinds of models you create and how you create them.

In practice it takes a lot of good judgment on the part of the architect to find a balance between what to specify and how much to specify. Too little specification and a project will suffer from the lack of a consistent and coherent direction. Too much specification and either no one will read the documents or no one will maintain them, and they may fall out of date quickly. The former is most often the case with architects who commonly resort to whiteboard sessions as the primary means of communicating the architecture to other stakeholders. For all but the simplest of systems and the most well-known architectural styles, this practice is not very effective. Too much esoteric knowledge is in the minds of too few individuals, and other developers must rely on the architect's already overloaded time.

At this point you know that an architectural description is a specification of a system that represents the problem space and the solution space in terms of models. These models are the medium for making design decisions and representing design decisions within particular modeling languages. You have learned that a modeling language affects the style of the design as well as the kinds of concepts you can and cannot express. You have also learned that architectural frameworks are meta-architectural descriptions that serve as templates for architectural descriptions by specifying the stakeholders, the architectural description, the concerns addressed, and the viewpoints used to specify the architecture. In the next section, we look briefly at how you start to create an architectural description.

Creating an Architectural Description for an Existing System

You may find yourself hired on to take over a system that has already been under development for some time or to modify a system that is already in operation. In this case, you may need to reverse-engineer the system in order to create an architectural specification for the system, if one does not already exist. This can be difficult because many of the design decisions may have been forgotten. Yet this rationale is very important in order to understand why certain approaches were taken. The previous architect may have already gone down some paths only to encounter hidden issues that made the particular approach unfeasible. This information is valuable to anyone who takes over a system.

Knowing what approaches were not attempted or pursued can be just as important. I was in a situation where the previous architect had gone down a particular path that didn't make sense to me. There was a more viable and simpler solution, and I didn't understand why this approach hadn't been taken. I thought that there might have been some hidden problem to that approach that must not have been obvious and I hesitated to venture down a path that had already been traveled. But there was no architectural description to guide me. I eventually discovered that the second approach hadn't even been considered. If an architectural rationale had existed, I would have had a better idea of whether to even consider the alternative approach.

Performing an Architectural Assessment

An architectural assessment is important in determining the quality of an architecture as represented in an architectural description and to help predict the quality of the application that will be developed according to the description. Assessment is concerned with the design itself. However, if the architectural description is not very easily understood, is inconsistent, or is incomplete, then an assessment may be difficult or impossible to conduct. Architecture assessment is discussed in Chapter 14.

Specification Pragmatics

Implementing the architectural description is difficult because there are too many ways to do it. As software architecting tools become more powerful, they will manage more of the information automatically. For the simplest systems, the architectural description may be a couple of pages of text in a single document, together with diagrams created using an appropriate modeling tool. For a more complex system, you may use several documents or a powerful UML modeling application.

You could also use XML together with a publishing application to manage the information in finer chunks and to selectively deliver or publish Web views of that data. The possibilities are limitless, and you should consider an approach that balances the management of information with other factors like readability and searchability. You can be creative and use software development tools, like a bug-tracking database to manage individual view inconsistencies and architectural rationales. Keep in mind that the biggest hurdle in creating an architectural description is getting the necessary people to read it.

Summary

The architectural description is a tangible set of products that comprise the architectural models and all other information necessary for the proper interpretation of the models. This additional nonmodel information contributes the *pragmatic interpretation* of the architectural description. Without it, interpretation is difficult.

The IEEE 1471-recommended practice, like any development standard, may seem excessive, but I suggest that you think of it as a set of practical guidelines that have been assembled from years of observing best practices. I find that the form actually helps me write more focused specifications, allowing me to concentrate on necessary information and avoid unnecessary information. It logically groups coherent information, making it easier to find exactly what you're looking for.

CHAPTER
13

Using Architecture Frameworks

In Chapter 12, we learned about the architectural description and the importance of multiple views for representing a software system's architecture. In this chapter, we look at two software architecture frameworks: the 4+1 View Model and the Reference Model for Open Distributed Processing. Architecture frameworks are templates for architectural descriptions that are composed of multiple viewpoint specifications and the specification of the relationships between views that conform to these viewpoints.

Software architecture frameworks specify viewpoints necessary to create an architectural description for a certain class of software systems. For example, the Reference Model for Open Distributed Processing (RM-ODP) is a framework for creating architectural descriptions of open distributed systems and the 4+1 View Model is a framework for specifying object-oriented systems.

The topics of this chapter are:

Software architecture frameworks.   An architectural framework is a set of viewpoint specifications and their relationships. A framework is used for describing a certain class of systems, such as open distributed processing systems or object-oriented systems.

The 4+1 View Model of architecture.   Rational Corporation developed a framework for describing systems using object-oriented notations. The 4+1 framework is composed of logical, process, development, and physical viewpoints that revolve around a scenario viewpoint.

Reference Model for Open Distributed Processing.   The International Organization of Standardization/ International Electrotechnical Commission (ISO/IEC) standard for describing open distributed processing systems is composed of five viewpoint specifications: enterprise, information, computational, engineering, and technology.

Software Architecture Frameworks

The term *framework* is used in many contexts in software development. A framework, in general, is a structure composed of parts that together support a structure. Examples of programming frameworks for constructing object-oriented graphical user interfaces (GUIs) are the Microsoft Foundation Classes (MFC) for building C++ GUIs and Swing for building Java GUIs.

Object-oriented application frameworks are class libraries, but rather than writing your own main routine and calling library functions, the framework manages the event dispatching and you supply classes that the framework calls. This is sometimes referred to as the Hollywood pattern (don't call us, we'll call you). The application framework is a partially complete application, a skeleton that needs to be extended or fleshed-out.

Architecture frameworks are frameworks for architecture specifications. Unlike a runtime application framework, you don't extend a partially written architecture framework. Rather, you use it as a template for creating an architecture specification. It is possible, however, to reuse portions of architecture specifications, but we don't refer to those reusable specifications as part of the framework.

Frameworks typically include the following types of viewpoints:

- *Processing* (for example, functional or behavioral requirements and use cases)

- *Information* (for example, object models, entity relationship diagrams, and data flow diagrams)

- *Structure* (for example, component diagrams depicting clients, servers, applications, and databases and their interconnections)

An architect determines if a viewpoint is necessary in a given software development project. A physical viewpoint may not be necessary if the physical structure is trivial and does not require more than a short textual description or if the mapping between the other models to the physical model is trivial and does not need to be specified. If the system is a simple client server with one client application and one server, such as the database, then this model is really trivial. The database technology prescribes what can and what cannot be physically a part of the database. The only mapping you may need is a description of what logic may be written as a stored procedure on the database versus application logic in the client. A simple block-style diagram showing the client, the server, and the interface that the client uses to communicate with the server such as Java Data Base Connectivity (JDBC) or Open Data Base Connectivity (ODBC) may be sufficient. For complex modular or distributed systems, the structural view becomes more important.

Philosophies of Architecture Frameworks

The differences between the various architecture frameworks and methodologies revolve around terminology, representation completeness, and selection of viewpoints.

Differences in terminology affect knowledge transference and reuse (of design artifacts such as standards, patterns, or specifications). Without effective knowledge transference, you will have communication problems among stakeholders, which can run the gamut from just annoying and time-consuming to completely disruptive to the progress of development. (This is why groups like the Institute of Electrical and Electronics Engineers (IEEE) publish standard domain-specific definitions of terms.) If stakeholders have used different methodologies that use different terms for the same concepts, it may be hard for each to sort out what the other is saying. When an architect is researching a methodology or framework to use, it can be difficult to compare them without a common terminology basis. The IEEE 1471 helps out in this area as long as architecture framework working groups adopt the language of the IEEE 1471 or publish a mapping between their terminology and concepts and those of the IEEE 1471.

Frameworks differ in their notion of completeness. Classic object-oriented methodologies such as Object Modeling Technique (OMT) and methodologists such as Booch (Booch, 1994) promote the use of models that are representative of the design at multiple phases of development, for example, models of requirements and conceptual design, down to detailed design and implementation. Some methodologists claim that multiple models are not maintainable and are counterproductive. Certainly you shouldn't use a set of viewpoints because a particular methodology prescribes them. You should select them based on stakeholder concerns and system quality requirements. Some methodologies, like OMT and the Unified Process, promote the notion that only architecturally significant features should be modeled. For example, in the Unified Process the architectural description contains subsets of models such as a set of architecturally significant use cases or classes. In practice, what this means is that models are created that address architectural qualities, and that these models are the architectural description, as opposed to detailed models that represent solutions to particular functional requirements, which are not considered part of the architectural description.

A framework that prescribes necessary viewpoints has advantages as well. You don't need to customize it, which takes some experience and solid judgment on the part of the architecture team. Such a framework would have a specific methodology and set of practices for generating the views and maintaining consistency across those views. It is easier for an architecting tool to support such a framework than it would be to support a highly configurable and customizable framework.

Architecture Framework Goals

No software architecture framework currently satisfies the IEEE 1471 recommendations, which makes comparing them difficult. I will present two framework standards, the 4+1 View Model of Architecture and the Reference Model for Open Distributed Processing. I'll compare them with the IEEE 1471 terminology and show where they conform and where they don't. I will also outline the basic goals of each framework using five general categories identified by Maier and Rechtin (Maier, 2000). The general goals are:

- Codify best practices for architectural description (to improve the state of the practice).

- Ensure that the framework sponsors receive architectural information in the format they want.

- Facilitate architecture assessment.

- Improve the productivity of software development teams by using standardized means for design representation.

- Improve interoperability of information systems.

Besides these general goals, each framework has specific goals that cannot necessarily be compared.

Methodologies and Architecture Frameworks

A software development methodology may incorporate an architecture framework, but a framework is not a methodology. A *methodology* is a collection of practices, processes, methods, techniques, and diagram notations for designing a system. Most software development methodologies do not formally distinguish between architecture representation models and other models (such as detailed object models). Methodologies typically include viewpoint specifications, although they do not fully conform to the IEEE 1471 standard for viewpoint specifications. Methodologies typically focus on detailed design addressing the functional requirements of the system.

Methodologies like OMT or the Unified Process (which is based on the 4+1 View Model) do not formally distinguish between views and viewpoints. This is sufficient for the methodology, but does not make the methodology *open* in the sense that its viewpoint specifications can be reused as library viewpoints (without some additional work on the part of the architect). If the viewpoints of a methodology conform to the IEEE 1471 recommended practice, it makes comparing methodologies easier and even reusing viewpoint specifications possible.

The 4+1 View Model of Architecture

The 4+1 View Model of Architecture (Kruchten, 1995) is a design methodology developed by Rational Software Corporation (and later subsumed by the Rational Unified Process [RUP] and modified, as described in the section *Architecting with the Unified Process*). The goal of this model is to provide a multiviewpoint framework for specifying object-oriented software systems, although the original version of this model did attempt to separate itself from a strictly object-oriented architecture style.

In terms of the original 4+1 View Model (prior to RUP), an architectural description consists of the following four views: logical, process, physical, and development. A fifth redundant view provides scenarios that tie the other four views together. The relationship between these views is represented in the Unified Modeling Language (UML) diagram in Figure 13.1.

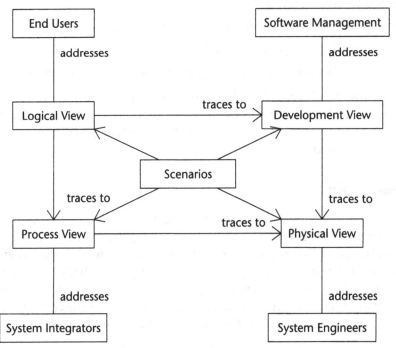

Figure 13.1   4+1 View Model for architectural description.

The 4+1 View Model does not prescribe particular modeling notations for each view, although the author suggests using the Booch notation, which was a popular object modeling notation in the mid-1990s (and is a predecessor of UML). Each view does have a metalanguage. For example, the logical view uses object metalanguage where concepts are described in terms of objects, classes, and their relationships. The process view's metalanguage consists of processes, tasks, and threads. The development view's metalanguage consists of software modules (subsystems) and layers. The physical view's metalanguage consists of hardware nodes, software modules, and processes.

Relationship to IEEE 1471

The definition of a *view* in the 4+1 View Model is loosely defined and, depending on the context in which it is used, may correspond with that of an IEEE 1471 viewpoint or view. Each view in the 4+1 View Model addresses a specific set of concerns of interest to system stakeholders and specifies a metalanguage for the models (diagrams) that make up the view. Also, each view is composed of models. I will retain the original language of the 4+1 View Model but will include the IEEE 1471 terminology as well so that you may see how these 4+1 views map onto the IEEE 1471 viewpoint definition. I will refer to 4+1 views as viewpoints when appropriate and restrict the term *view* to its IEEE 1471 denotation.

The IEEE 1471 specifies a minimal set of concerns that must be addressed by the viewpoints selected in an architectural description. The 4+1 View Model does not address three of these concerns:

- The appropriateness of the application for use in fulfilling its purpose
- The feasibility of developing the application
- The risks of application development and operation to the stakeholders

For a 4+1 View Model-based architectural description, these concerns would have to be addressed by additional viewpoints. For some systems it may be possible to address these concerns with basic textual descriptions and a semiformal project plan.

Logical Viewpoint

The *logical viewpoint* is a viewpoint for representing functional requirements. The key abstractions in this view are taken from the problem domain. Logical views are intentionally platform independent, although the models may map quite easily to an object-oriented programming language. (Recall the problems associated with such seamless development methods in Chapter 4.) Logical views typically represent the problem domain concepts, sometimes called the object model or the business objects. The view should specify how functional requirements are mapped onto classes and realized in their interrelationships. The logical view does not address threads of control. In the logical view, objects are thought of as discrete entities that interact by passing messages among themselves.

Stakeholders and Concerns Addressed

The logical view targets the acquirers, end users, developers, and maintainers of the system. It addresses the functional requirements of the system. Acquirers need assurance that the design will address the intended purpose of the system. The logical view models explicitly show how the functions of the system are decomposed in terms of classes. Developers use these models to actually write code in an object-oriented programming language. Maintainers use these models to understand the system in order to change existing functions, remove functions, or add functions. By using the logical view models, the maintainers can locate the classes involved in a given functional area and understand the intentions of the original designers so that modifications fit with the original design.

The logical view models can also address evolvability of the application. If evolvability is a required quality, then the means for evolving the design should be represented in the logical view.

View Construction

The models for a logical view may be class diagrams or entity relationship diagrams. An object-oriented architectural style is recommended for this view because of its extensiveness in representing functional capabilities and information requirements. These class diagrams are created using object-oriented analysis.

Process Viewpoint

The *process viewpoint* is a viewpoint for representing the processing model of the system. Process views capture the concurrency, synchronization, and distribution aspects of the design.

Stakeholders and Concerns Addressed

The process viewpoint addresses acquirers, developers, maintainers, and system integrators. This view represents the design solution to some nonfunctional requirements such as performance, availability, and fault tolerance. Acquirers need assurance that the design will satisfy nonfunctional requirements. Developers use these models together with the logical model to write the application logic. Maintainers use these models together with the logical models to understand the system and the intentions of the original designers in order to make modifications without compromising the integrity of the system. System integrators use these models in order to understand how this system can interoperate with other systems, both existing and perceived.

View Construction

The process view is described at several levels of abstraction, each addressing a different set of concerns. The highest level of description is in terms of communicating processes. Processes are described in terms of tasks that form an executable unit. Processes are components that can be tactically controlled, meaning that they can be individually started, recovered, reconfigured, and shut down, for example. Examples of architectural styles used in this view are pipes and filters or client/server.

The process view addresses how logical objects interact in order to produce required system behaviors. There are several attributes of classes as represented in the process view:

- *Autonomy* is the characteristic that identifies objects as active, passive, or protected. An *active object* can invoke its own methods and the methods of other objects, and has full control over objects invoking its methods. An active object may react to external stimuli or it may spontaneously invoke methods on other objects. For example, an active object may have a request queue for incoming method invocations and may also have some internal event mechanism like a timer that wakes the object up periodically so that it may do some work. A *passive object* never spontaneously invokes other object's methods and has no control over an object invoking its own methods. A *protected object* never spontaneously invokes other object methods but does monitor the invocation of its own methods. A protected object may use synchronization primitives to serialize method invocations or it may use a queue of requests much like an active object.

- *Persistence* is the characteristic that identifies objects as either transient or permanent. Transient objects only exist within a process life cycle and do not survive restarts. Permanent objects exist beyond the process life cycle and do survive restarts.

- *Subordination* is the characteristic that identifies whether an object's existence or persistence is dependent on another object.

- *Distribution* is the characteristic that identifies if an object in the logical view is accessible on more than one node in the physical view or accessible from multiple processes from the process view.

The process view can be comprised of class diagrams and collaboration diagrams that focus on the active objects that represent the threads and processes of a system. The collaboration diagrams can be supplemented with activity and state diagrams as well that represent the object as a finite state machine (FSM).

Development Viewpoint

The *development viewpoint* is a viewpoint for representing the static organization of the software with respect to the software development environment.

Stakeholders and Concerns Addressed

The development viewpoint addresses software configuration management and concerns such as buildability, maintainability, reusability, and the configuration management of the system's releases. The development view also addresses the partitioning of functionality across subsystems in support of development.

View Construction

Subsystems are organized internally in hierarchical layers where each layer provides a narrow interface to the next layer up in the hierarchy. The components of a development view are modules or subsystems that compose the system. A layers architectural style can be used in a development view. The layers style is similar to the layers pattern. The purpose of using layers in the development view is to minimize dependencies on modules so that they can be implemented and compiled with minimal coupling and dependencies.

Physical Viewpoint

The *physical viewpoint* specifies a means for capturing the mapping of the software onto hardware and specifying its distribution.

Stakeholders and Concerns Addressed

The physical viewpoint addresses acquirers and systems engineers. This viewpoint addresses nonfunctional requirements such as availability, reliability, performance, and scalability. Acquirers need assurance that the implementation and deployment configurations will address performance-related requirements. Systems engineers need to understand how the system may be deployed.

View Construction

There can be several physical configurations of the system to support different operational situations, including testing the system. All of the components from the three prior views map onto this view. The most obvious is the mapping of processes to hardware nodes.

Scenario Viewpoint

The *scenario view* ties all of the other views together. Scenarios are instances of use cases. This view is considered to be redundant with respect to the other four views and hence the "+1" in the name of the framework.

Stakeholders and Concerns Addressed

The scenario viewpoint addresses users of the system, acquirers, developers, maintainers, and testers. The use cases represent key functional requirements of the system. The purpose of the use cases is to act as a sort of script that ties the elements in the different views together.

View Construction

The author suggests using only an architecturally significant subset of scenarios and representing them with object-scenario (UML sequence) diagrams and object-interaction (UML collaboration) diagrams (use case diagrams were not part of the original framework).

Model Overloading

In 4+1, the same types of models are used in different views. Class diagrams and object collaboration diagrams are used in the logical and process views. Object collaboration diagrams in the logical model may represent key application objects passing messages and in the process view may show more than just business objects. Instead of passing general messages, explicit types of method invocations are represented (such as synchronous, asynchronous, and balking). The same type of model can have different interpretations depending on the view in which it is interpreted (recall the pragmatics of model interpretation from Chapter 6).

Many of the 4+1 View Model viewpoints address developer and acquirer concerns simultaneously. While this is useful in reducing the number of models that need to be maintained, it puts a burden on the acquirer to understand low-level models. This is not always practical and can have adverse effects because less technical people are trying to understand the system in an unfamiliar language, such as classes and objects.

Another drawback to model overloading is in the ease in which designers can prematurely commit to implementations, since the same class diagrams used to represent the analysis models (the logical view) eventually evolve into the design models and source code.

Architecting with the Unified Process

The Unified Process, developed by Rational Corporation, is a full-scale software development methodology that extends the 4+1 View Model and incorporates more of the work of OMT and Jacobson's Object Oriented Software Engineering (OOSE) and uses the Unified Modeling Language. In the context of this chapter, we are only interested in those aspects of the Unified Process that most closely match our general notion of an architectural framework. See Kruchten (Kruchten, 2000) and Jacobson (Jacobson, 1999) for a full treatment of the Unified Process.

The original 4+1 View Model suggested using the Booch object notation (UML had not yet been created). However, since UML has subsumed the Booch notation, the 4+1 View Model has changed (Booch, 1998). The new model has renamed the original viewpoints. The new viewpoints are:

- Design view (was the logical view)
- Process view
- Implementation view (was the development view)
- Deployment view (was the physical view)
- Use case view (was the scenario)

The design view is fundamentally the same as the original logical view, although the static aspect of the view may be realized using class diagrams and object diagrams and the dynamic aspect captured using interaction diagrams, statechart diagrams, and activity diagrams. The process view addresses the same concerns as its predecessor and the model types used are the same as in the design view. The implementation view is represented using component diagrams, interaction diagrams, statechart diagrams, and activity diagrams. The deployment view is composed of interaction diagrams, statechart diagrams, and activity diagrams. Like those of their predecessor, the diagram types are overloaded.

The UML by itself does not prescribe any particular viewpoints or modeling practices. Therefore the UML is not an architecture framework, although it is possible to create a framework based on the UML.

The Unified Process use of the term *view* is very different from that of IEEE 1471. In IEEE 1471, a model is contained in a view and is realized or expressed using a modeling notation (and therefore is some sort of specification such as a textual specification or diagram). The term *model* in the Unified Process is more in line with the IEEE 1471 term *view*. The Unified Process defines an architectural view for each model. This definition of an architectural description is sort of inside out when compared to other frameworks. The Unified Process architectural description is a set of architectural views of each of the five engineering models:

- Architectural view of the analysis model
- Architectural view of the deployment model
- Architectural view of the design model
- Architectural view of the implementation model
- Architectural view of the use-case model

The Unified Process models are considered supersets of the architectural view. This doesn't really conflict with the 1471 definition; rather, the methodology can be thought of as extending those definitions by introducing views (and models) that are not part of the architectural description.

Reference Model for Open Distributed Processing

The main goal of RM-ODP is to provide mechanisms for architecting distributed processing and information systems and to support enterprise application integration. RM-ODP supports these goals through five viewpoints, each of which has a precise viewpoint language and rules for mapping models across views. The views of a system form a succession of models from the abstract function and purpose of the system to the concrete implementation of the system. RM-ODP viewpoints separate the distributed nature of an application from its implementation, allowing the application to be designed without prematurely restricting the design to a particular middleware platform. Each of the five viewpoints addresses specific aspects of a distributed system. Views are semantically self-contained, yet interrelated.

The five viewpoints of RM-ODP are:

- Enterprise
- Information
- Computational
- Engineering
- Technology

Each viewpoint has a semantically rich metamodel or viewpoint language for creating views. The viewpoint languages specify rules for mapping objects among other viewpoints as appropriate. I provide an overview of each of these metamodels, but the interested reader should read *Architecting with RM-ODP* (Putman, 2001) or the RM-OPD specifications (ISO/IEC, 1995) for details concerning the full semantics of these languages.

Enterprise Viewpoint

The enterprise viewpoint focuses on the purpose, scope, and policies of the system and provides a means of capturing system requirements. The enterprise viewpoint language is very expressive and can be used for creating business specifications as well as expressing software requirements.

Stakeholders and Concerns Addressed

The enterprise viewpoint addresses all stakeholders but primarily addresses the acquirers and users of the system. It does so by specifying a metamodel that is based on the language of the enterprise. An enterprise view represents the requirements and gives a larger picture of the system within the context of an enterprise. This means capturing all of the external systems, people, artifacts, and business processes that, together with the system, satisfy some particular enterprise objective. The viewpoint addresses the purpose, missions, and appropriateness of the system. The architect needs to develop this model with the help of the system acquirers.

For in-house development, this model captures the objectives that the system is to fulfill for the benefit of the organization. For example, this could be to create online revenue-generating products or to automate some time-consuming, error-prone, hard-to-manage, manual information-intensive tasks, the effectiveness of which affects an organization's productivity and revenues. For a commercial system, the objectives may be more generally stated in terms of customer objectives. Commercial software development can sometimes be based on more vague objectives since each customer has different objectives, but they should still be expressed as much as possible.

View Construction

The enterprise viewpoint language concepts represent a system in the context of the enterprise in which it operates. The system as represented in an enterprise view consists of the following types of elements:

- Enterprise objects
- Communities
- Roles
- Contracts

Communities are formed to meet specific objectives of the enterprise and are composed of enterprise objects. An enterprise object may belong to more than one community. Within a given community, an enterprise object fulfills a specific role that describes its behavior within that community and how it supports the community's objectives. The set of enterprise objects therefore fulfills the community objectives. One or more enterprise objects within a community represent the system itself, while other enterprise objects represent external systems, people, artifacts (for example, documents and records), and business processes.

Enterprise objects assume one or more roles within a community. The roles may be used to represent users, owners, and providers of information within and/or processed by the system. A contract is used to express an objective in terms of enterprise object collaborations and constraints. It may also specify quality of service (QoS) properties such as timeframes in which transactions must be conducted, system performance requirements, and safety and security requirements. Contracts are dynamic and temporal and may be invalidated when objects behave outside of their constraints. A particular type of contract is the environment contract, which is a contract between an enterprise object and its environment and is used to represent QoS requirements.

A community specification consists of the following:

- The specification of enterprise objects that comprise the community
- The specification of the roles assumed by those objects
- The policies governing interactions between enterprise objects in the assumed roles
- The policies governing the life-cycle management of resources used by enterprise objects in the assumed roles
- The policies governing the structuring of enterprise objects and their role assignments
- The policies relating to the environment contracts governing the system

The enterprise view may be composed of use case models. Putman (Putman, 2001) provides a treatment of using UML as the modeling notation for representing an enterprise view. UML use case models do not provide the full semantics of the enterprise viewpoint language, but through some manipulation of the UML syntax, a reasonable approximation can be achieved.

Information Viewpoint

The information viewpoint focuses on the semantics of information and information processing within the system but does not represent data flows. This viewpoint specifies a metamodel for representing functional requirements in terms of information objects. It resembles the 4+1 logical viewpoint in that it is used to specify a business information model that is implementation independent.

An *information view* defines the universe of discourse of the system: the information content and the information about the processing of the system, a logical representation of the data in the system, and the rules to be followed in the system, such as policies specified by the stakeholders. The information viewpoint is central to all the other viewpoints. Changes in an information view necessarily ripple through the other views. An information view refines an enterprise view by providing semantics for policies, community contracts, and environment contracts. An information view together with a computational view represents the information and processes of the functional requirements.

Stakeholders and Concerns Addressed

The information viewpoint addresses the acquirers, end users, developers, and maintainers of the system. Architects use this view to organize and communicate system semantics with other stakeholders. Acquirers need assurance that the design addresses the intended purpose of the system. The information view explicitly shows how the functions of the system are decomposed in terms of information objects. Developers and maintainers use this view to understand the object model of the system. The information view can also address qualities such as evolvability and adaptability.

View Construction

The information view contains the information object model and environmental contracts for the objects. The information viewpoint specifies three schemata for representing the information objects: invariant, static, and dynamic.

The *invariant schema* specifies predicates that must always be true for a set of information objects within a given time period. These predicates constrain the possible set of states in which an information object may exist. The *static schema* specifies the state and structure of a set of information objects at a specific point in time. The *dynamic schema* specifies all the actions that permit a change in state or structure of a set of information objects such as how an object is created and destroyed. This schema is constrained by the invariant schema.

The information view may be composed of UML class models together with Object Constraint Language (OCL) predicates. Putman (Putman, 2001) provides a treatment of using UML as the modeling notation for representing an information view. UML does not provide the full semantics of the information viewpoint language.

Computational Viewpoint

The computational viewpoint specifies a metamodel for representing the functional decomposition of the system as platform-independent distributed objects that interact at interfaces. A computational view specifies the system in terms of computational objects and their interactions. A computational view partitions the system into logical objects that perform the capabilities of the system and are capable of being distributed throughout the enterprise but does not specify how they are distributed.

Stakeholders and Concerns Addressed

This viewpoint addresses the same stakeholders as the information viewpoint. A computational view addresses the structure of the application as distributed objects without specifying particular distribution configurations.

View Construction

A computational view is a type of object model. The elements of the computational viewpoint language are computational objects, computational interfaces, binding objects, interaction types, and interface types. The three types of interactions are signals, operations, and flows. The three types of interface are signal, operation, and stream. Operation interfaces are further subtyped as announcement and interrogation. Actions between two computational objects are represented by interactions. Interfaces and bindings are the mechanisms for interacting. An interface is composed of a set of interactions, which are all of the same type.

A *signal interaction* is a one-way interaction between an initiating object, called a client, and a responding object, called a server. An *operation interaction* is an interaction between a client object and server object that is either an interrogation or an announcement. An *interrogation* is composed of two one-way interactions: a request and a response. An *announcement* is a one-way request from a client object to a server object in which the client object expects no response, and the server object does not respond. A *flow* interaction is an ordered set of one or more one-way communications from a *producer* object to a *consumer* object. These interactions are a generalized metamodel for describing communication styles between objects that can be implemented using a variety of middleware such as Remote Procedure Call (RPC) and Remote Method Invocation (RMI) and message queues (as selected and specified in the technology view).

Engineering Viewpoint

The engineering viewpoint addresses the mechanisms and functions for supporting distributed object interactions and distribution transparency. An engineering view specifies the mechanisms for physical distribution to support the logical processing model of the computational view without specifying a particular technology or middleware platform.

Stakeholders and Concerns Addressed

The engineering viewpoint primarily addresses developers and maintainers of the system. It addresses nonfunctional requirements such as portability and extensibility (the ability to take advantage of new technologies). It supports extensibility by representing the system in a platform-independent manner.

View Construction

The engineering viewpoint language consists of engineering objects, nodes, clusters, and capsules. There are engineering objects and basic engineering objects. *Basic engineering objects* correspond to computational objects that specifically provide application services. *Engineering objects* support the distribution mechanisms, infrastructure, binding, and transparency functions. A *node* is a computer, and it has a *nucleus* that manages system resources and communications for objects on that node. A nucleus is an abstraction for an operating system or application server (object operational) platform. A node contains a configuration of basic engineering objects and engineering objects. A *capsule* is a unit of processing and storage. It contains either basic engineering objects or engineering objects. It is an abstraction for a process or application component. A capsule may contain *clusters*, which are configurations of basic engineering objects that act as a single entity with respect to activation, deactivation, and so on.

Technology Viewpoint

The technology viewpoint specifies a language for representing the implementation of a system. Separating the technology and engineering viewpoints allows the architect to focus on distribution aspects without prematurely committing to a particular middleware platform or influencing the architecture of the application by assuming technologies. All of the views prior to the technology view transcend implementation and are reusable even when technologies change.

Stakeholders and Concerns Addressed

The technology view primarily addresses system developers, maintainers, and testers. It addresses qualities such as evolvability, maintainability, testability, buildability, and extensibility.

View Construction

The technology view maps the other views to implementations, technologies, and standards. This view specifies how the engineering view in particular maps to software, hardware, networks, operating systems, and middleware products.

Summary

All of the frameworks presented in this chapter specify a set of viewpoints from which actual views are specified and these views are composed of models that are realized using some modeling language. The RM-ODP viewpoint languages are semantically rich and do not map entirely into existing modeling notations such as UML. These viewpoint languages are fairly complex and take some time to understand.

The frameworks differ in some regards with respect to methodology. The 4+1 View Model is tied to a use case-driven methodology and uses the more general-purpose UML notation and relies on evolving a few models. RM-ODP is a little more agnostic about methodology but is much stricter in its modeling languages and requires more maintenance of models. The 4+1 View Model focuses on describing object-oriented systems. The RM-ODP is not specific to object-oriented systems and is useful for describing open distributed systems.

CHAPTER 14

Software Architecture Quality

Software quality, product delivery schedules, and development costs must be carefully balanced. You can never hold all three of these variables constant. If you want higher-quality software, then it will take longer to build to account for more rigorous design and testing. This increase in development time also causes the development cost to increase. Nor is it a simple matter of holding the schedule constant and adding more personnel to the project. The relationship between these three variables is not linear. Software quality is commonly sacrificed in order to keep the development cost down and the schedule from slipping. There is a common but incorrect attitude that the system can be made better later.

Software quality is a subject of much research and debate in the academic and industrial realms due to the lack of consensus and formalism in defining quality. There are two basic areas of focus with respect to software quality: software product evaluation and software process evaluation. Software product evaluation consists of validation and verification. Validation tests that we are solving the right problems, while verification tests that the system as built conforms to its specification. Software architecture evaluation is a form of verification; it serves as a predictor of quality before we build the system.

Since the subject of this book is software architecture design, we will look at a subset of software product evaluation. We are not evaluating the software product itself (for example, the executable system or its source code), but rather the architectural design description of the system. The architectural design represented by the architectural description, while not part of the product proper, is a key artifact in the design and implementation of the product.

In this chapter, we look at what it means to evaluate a software system's architecture and survey a few practical evaluation methods and techniques. We evaluate an architectural description in order to verify that the system it describes will possess certain required or desired quality attributes. One of the motivations for creating an architectural design prior to more detailed design and coding is to improve the quality of the system while addressing risks and identifying potential defects earlier in the development life cycle where they are faster, easier, and cheaper to fix. While it is not entirely possible to verify that the system or application will, in fact, possess certain qualities, we can assess the architectural description for a system to see if a system based on the design is likely to possess some specific qualities. We cannot predict every system quality such as validity, usability, and some performance qualities, but we can get a reasonable amount of assurance as to some specific quality attributes, such as specific types of modifications to the system and some aspects of performance and reliability. Of course, nothing can prevent a development team from departing from the architectural description.

This chapter addresses the following topics:

Importance of assessing software architecture.   The software architect and the development teams start by assessing a design based on quality attributes in order to better predict the quality of the system that is described by the design. An architectural design can be assessed for some, but not all, quality attributes.

How to improve quality.   There are many techniques that we can use to improve the quality of a system as well as improve productivity of the development team. Systematic design processes help the software architect discover the best solution. Focusing on developing a solid understanding of the problem to be solved greatly reduces risks to projects while improving the quality of the system by focusing on the right things. Assessing software architecture designs helps us predict whether the system that is to be built will exhibit certain quality attributes. This can be through the use of scenarios.

Architecture evaluation.   A survey of architecture evaluation methods and processes is presented. Evaluation methods are processes for assessing architectures using teams of stakeholders and methods of identifying scenarios against which to assess an architectural design.

Assessing modifiability.   Modifiability is a quality attribute that can be affected by the architecture. Modifiability can be assessed by applying change cases, which are scenarios that describe specific developer tasks for introducing a change to the system.

Assessing performance.   Performance is a quality attribute that can be affected by the architecture. There are some techniques for assessing the performance characteristics of a design before actually constructing the system.

Importance of Assessing Software Architecture

When a complex system is developed without conscious attention to addressing quality attributes, the results can have a profoundly negative impact on an organization. I have joined several projects after the software architecture has been established and the system partially or fully developed. In most cases, the architecture was bad in the sense that there were many unspoken or unarticulated qualities that the system should have exhibited but did not. Some of these qualities were economical business qualities, such as time-to-market and return on investment (ROI). Many of these problems could have been identified earlier in the development life cycle, before any substantial amount of code had been written. The results in many of these situations was that a module or subsystem had to be redesigned and mostly rewritten because the design decisions that needed to be undone permeated a large part of the system.

A key software engineering principle is that quality cannot be tested into the product; it has to be designed into it. Modifying existing code is much more time-intensive and expensive than modifying design specifications. Therefore, as part of a systematic design process, you should perform assessments of the design. These two examples review quality problems discovered *after* the systems had been implemented.

Content Publishing System Example

In this example of a publishing system, the first level of architectural decomposition was well done. The system was separated into three main systems: a content authoring and assembly system, a content publishing and deployment system, and a content delivery system. The basic system architecture is represented in Figure 14.1. The delivery system was well designed; it was a classic client/server Web-based application. The content that was deployed on the system was packaged as individual applications that were constructed of Java Server Pages (JSP), HyperText Markup Language (HTML), media content, and application meta data that ran on a common platform. The common runtime logic interpreted the application meta data to determine the actual behavior of each application. The applications were all instances of a specific type of application. In this case, the applications were learning products such as graduate record examination (GRE) practice tests. Instead of hand-coding each individual practice test application (for example, using JSP) or even building them from common code libraries, the common logic was captured in a runtime platform, which interpreted the application meta data and generated the user interface. In this example, every application was defined as a set of questions and behaviors about how to present and score the questions. Some behaviors defined what question was selected next based on the previous answers.

The authoring and publishing system was not so well designed. The publishing system was plagued with usability and performance issues. There were no tools for creating the applications (also called products) that were eventually deployed on the delivery system. All products had to be hand-coded in eXtensible Markup Language (XML). Programmers were responsible for translating vague application specifications (sometimes written on a notepad) into their XML representation. Had the appropriate product designer tools been available, there would not have been a need to use expensive programmers. A product designer would have been able to assemble an application from the repository of reusable test questions and then specify some parameters for the various behaviors. Since there were no tools, it was very difficult for the organization to deliver applications in a timely manner and deliver applications that could take advantage of advanced features. Furthermore, the cost of hiring a programmer to assemble tests made the system expensive and difficult to use.

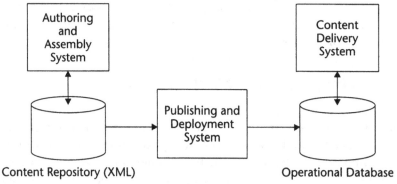

Figure 14.1 Publishing system architecture.

Enterprise Application Example

In the enterprise application example, there was absolutely no decomposition whatsoever. The system was stand-alone and closed. The system was a type of knowledge management system that could not be integrated with other systems, which is the antithesis of a knowledge management system. Human/computer interaction (HCI) logic and data were intermixed with application logic and data. For example, an email notification component was tightly coupled with the other parts of the system because they all had knowledge of the fact that email was used as an HCI mechanism. The system exhibited no information hiding or modularity. It was relatively unstable as changes to features and even bug fixes caused cascading changes. There was no opportunity for parallel development since so many decisions were interdependent.

We'll look at example evaluations of both of these systems in the sections on modifiability and performance, later in this chapter.

How to Improve Quality

What should these development groups have done in order to eliminate these quality problems? In both examples, the architectural design should have been evaluated prior to implementation. This leads to the question: What can we evaluate? Common quality characteristics that can be evaluated (verified) at the level of the architectural description are modifiability, performance, and reliability. Validity can be (partially) evaluated by inspecting the object model and user interface and interaction models (for example, prototypes and mockups).

It is not possible to assess every quality attribute or even every aspect of a given quality characteristic. We can assess some aspects of performance characteristics by evaluating the architectural description, but we cannot actually obtain performance measurements by design inspection alone. However, we can reason about a design and design variations and make some informal assessments of the performance characteristics. This can help us to eliminate some design variations.

As we have learned, a complex system is full of interdependencies, which means that many quality attributes interact with each other. In some cases, a performance quality attribute may conflict with a modifiability quality attribute. We can assess each quality attribute in isolation, but we cannot make design decisions without considering the combined effect of interdependent quality attributes.

How do we assess the quality of a system's architecture? There are two aspects to this question:

- How to evaluate an architectural description (architectural assessment or analysis)?
- How to conduct an architectural assessment (an architectural evaluation)?

An architectural evaluation is the application of an assessment or analysis technique within an organizational context such as a formal architectural review.

We perform assessments of architecture design in order to improve the potential quality of the system before it is implemented. Architecture assessment also facilitates the application of design methods like the method of forward steps of the method of systematic variation. In these techniques several alternative design (variations) are created. Assessment provides us with the tools to compare design variations and eliminate them, thus reducing the potential solution field.

Architecture assessment allows us to measure or observe the quality of a design after the design has been created. There are other complementary activities and methods for helping improve the quality of a system, such as the application of the various design methods and techniques presented throughout this book. Let's recap some of those activities and techniques.

Systematic Design Process

In Chapter 4, we learned about systematic design processes and how they can be used to help facilitate the design process and produce high-quality designs. The application of systematic design processes, design principles, and heuristics helps the designer reason about the problems being solved and how best to solve them. By definition, the design should be of higher quality because it leverages existing design knowledge. Furthermore, the design process runs more effectively since there is less solution searching.

In a systematic design process, a designer is searching for a solution. The designer can go down many paths. Each branch in the path increases the number of potential solutions that may be discovered. These solutions are referred to as a *solution field*. By simultaneously considering multiple design variations, we increase our chances of discovering a suitable solution. However, a solution field can become prohibitively large producing a negative effect on the process. Thus, combining design assessment with solution searching helps a designer manage the size of the solution field.

Christopher Alexander wrote about achieving quality (the quality without a name) by using pattern languages for designing towns and buildings in *The Timeless Way of Building* (Alexander, 1979). According to Alexander, if a pattern language is correctly applied to the design and construction of a town or building, then it will possess the quality without a name. This is a difficult quality to define, but basically it means that the structure is whole; in essence, every quality that should be in a building is present and all competing design forces are in perfect balance. Therefore, there is no need to evaluate or even test the design for quality because the quality is inherent in the process.

We can achieve some of this in our design process even if we cannot achieve the ideal that Alexander describes. Experience has shown us that a system that is constructed piecemeal, without regard for any strategic design or architecture, results in a stovepipe system that is difficult to maintain. Experience has also shown us that if we go through a design process and establish clear design goals and objectives, then we are less likely to build a stovepipe system and we are able to make more informed design trade-offs.

Understand the Right Problem

The quality of the requirements ultimately predetermines the quality of the system. A fast and robust system with a highly intuitive graphical user interface (GUI) is useless if it doesn't solve a real problem. Some companies have managed to develop technologies before understanding what the application of that technology is. However, this is a book about applications, and a good application must have utility. Remember that this is the first element of the Vitruvian triad (*utilitas*).

The software architect, in many cases, performs the role traditionally assumed by a systems analyst. As a software architect, you should not assume that the list of requirements you have been given is the best possible list. Most of the time the requirements are vague, complex, and not stated in a way that identifies the true problem being solved. You must analyze these requirements not only to understand their interdependencies and hidden structures, but also to understand the problems that really need to be solved. In every requirements analysis situation that I've been involved with, there are several requirements that are not what they seem.

Here is an example. In one enterprise system, there was a requirement to allow users to delete some data that was no longer necessary. The requirement specification actually stated that the system would not permanently remove the data from the database but would mark it as hidden so that it no longer showed up in the user interface and therefore could no longer be operated on. The requirement didn't make much sense. There was a need for users to remove data that they no longer wanted or needed, but, on the intended system, behavior was to simply hide the data in the operational database. This was semantically equivalent to removing data from the application perspective; the data was gone but not destroyed. The only difference is that the hidden data could still be retrieved if a database administrator (DBA) accessed the database directly. Of course, this violates the principle of information hiding.

Upon analysis of the requirement, it was revealed that the acquirers were trying to solve several unstated problems with this single "feature." We started over and articulated explicitly each problem that was to be solved and found that the real requirements were different than the original requirements. A summary of the right problems was as follows:

- Allow users to change the state of some data so that it no longer affects the processing of the system but yet is still available for viewing and other operations. (This would not have been possible with the original proposed requirement.)

- Allow users to extract data that is no longer needed in the operational database and place it into some archive or data warehouse.

- Allow users of the system to permanently delete unwanted or unused data from the operational database. If users want to keep the data around for other possibly unknown future purposes, then they can archive it first, as stated above.

Each of the separate problems needed different solutions. The requirements were lumped together because the original writers of the requirements did not fully understand the problems that really needed to be solved. They had aggregated several problems into a single problem and had temporarily forgotten what the original problems were.

System Level View of Requirements

One of the most important things you can do as a software architect is analyze the dependencies between requirements in order to understand the system view of the requirements. Why? Because this helps lead to a better decomposition and understanding of the problem you are solving. Also, by applying Occam's Razor (the principle of stripping away assumptions to find the simplest solution or explanation), you can produce a problem structure that at its most fundamental form begins to suggest a design. If you look at how Christopher Alexander applies patterns in *The Timeless Way of Building* (Alexander, 1979), he is analyzing the problem while simultaneously selecting solution patterns. The process of understanding the problem and solving it is one fluid and recursive process.

Recall from Chapter 5 that a design structure matrix (DSM) can be used to represent the interactions between requirements. I have found that creating a DSM with the team responsible for the software specification helps frame the discussion and facilitate the discovery and documentation of requirement interactions. In one such analysis, it was discovered that based on the current architecture of the system, a set of seemingly unrelated new feature requirements were highly interdependent. If the team had assigned developers to go off and start coding to the initial requirements specification, they would not have discovered these interactions until after a substantial amount of code had been written.

Differentiating Design and Requirements

Recall that design begins earlier than we usually think. Whenever a feature is specified in a requirements document, there is design. Most people don't handle abstraction well, even writers of requirements. The problem is that when these people are writing up requirements, they tend to shift focus from abstract problem statements to concrete features. Once these feature requirements make it into a system, they become hard to eradicate later. I don't mind if I receive requirements that already have design concepts embedded as long as the problem statements are clear. Then if there is a problem with the feature, it can be traced back to the problem statement.

We usually think of design as the set of decisions that map requirements to technology: I have a problem with this because most of the important design decisions have already been made by the time technology-based decisions are being made. There is also an emphasis in most of the literature on software architecture as being the *level of design* involving the internal organization of software in terms of components, their relationships, and guidelines for their composition and construction. This is only half of the story. The other half begins with the actual specification of the system in terms of problems being solved. Requirements are part of the architecture. In other disciplines, it is the role of the architect to solicit and understand the requirements. The architect should be skilled at analyzing requirements.

This is not to say that concrete features are not legitimate requirements. A customer may request a very specific feature such as a modification to the user interface or the addition of some fields in a particular entity. The architect should be able to judge what requirements need to be challenged and which do not.

Assessing Software Architectures

Architecture assessment is the activity of measuring or analyzing a system's architecture in order to understand its quality attributes. Recall the hierarchy of systems knowledge in Chapter 6. Architecture assessment is a form of systems analysis in which we are trying to understand the system's behavioral characteristics given its design structure. This involves moving from the generative layer (the architectural description) to the data layer (the values of certain quality attributes). Of course, we are trying to analyze a system that doesn't yet exist. Our analysis is limited to those quality attributes that we can simulate using an architectural description.

Analyzing a model is more difficult than analyzing a working system. It is not always possible to evaluate a software design to understand a single quality attribute. Some quality attributes interact with each other, such as modifiability and performance. A common technique for making a system modifiable is to introduce layers of modules. However, layers can result in computational overhead. If each layer is responsible for wrapping and unwrapping information structures, then this can result in a lot of additional data creation and parsing. If a layer can be removed, then there are fewer transformations occurring. Some systems allow layers to be bridged in order to provide some performance improvements, but at the expense of modifiability.

The field of software architecture is still relatively immature and there is not a lot of information available on software architecture assessment. The Software Engineering Institute (SEI) at Carnegie Mellon University has contributed a lot toward this area, but the techniques and methods are still not in mainstream use, certainly not by smaller, less mature software development organizations. Research in this area is confounded by the fact that there are no standard ways for describing software architectures using unambiguous and precise languages that facilitate easy analysis.

Architecture assessments should not only be performed by the architects themselves as part of a systematic design process, but they should also be performed by outside committees of stakeholders as part of the development life cycle. No one would allow an architect in any other discipline to work on a design without the stakeholders having some opportunity to see the work. More often than not in software development, this is just the case. Stakeholders wouldn't know what to ask other than questions regarding functional requirements and perhaps a few questions regarding performance. Even then the questions are not designed to probe and analyze the architecture to understand its quality attributes.

There are two basic classes of analysis techniques: questioning and measuring. Questioning techniques involve the generation of qualitative questions that can be asked about the architecture, such as whether a certain class of functions can be added or modified in the system without recompiling or redeploying the system. Another question could be whether such a class of functions can be added without stopping the system at all (a critical real-time system such as an air traffic control system, which can't be offline for maintenance). Measuring techniques are quantitative and address specific qualities or system parameters such as the throughput of the system under a specific user or system load.

Many software quality communities contribute knowledge to the area of software and software architecture analysis. These different communities focus on specific quality attributes and analysis techniques. For example, there is a community that focuses on software system performance software metrics (such as complexity metrics for code execution paths), and scenario-based architecture analysis methods. The software metrics community uses measuring analysis techniques such as module coupling and cohesion measures as predictors of software quality. The performance community uses techniques such as queuing models as described by Smith and Williams (Smith, 2002), which are based on the mathematical theory of queues, to understand the execution and performance characteristics of a design. Scenario-based methods are question-oriented analysis techniques. The performance-related analysis methods include both measuring and questioning techniques. The communities for software modifiability and reusability also include measuring (for example, software metrics) and questioning (for example, system change scenarios).

In the next section, we see how some nonfunctional requirements can be reified, that is, converted into a concrete scenario, which can then be assessed. In the section that follows, we see that the quality architectural description itself can affect the ability to assess the architectural design.

Scenarios: Reifying Nonfunctional Requirements

Recall from Chapter 8 that a single quality attribute can be quantitatively measured or qualitatively observed or reasoned about. Architectural assessment is a technique for verifying nonfunctional requirements or quality attributes. Since the system does not yet exist, it cannot be executed to see if it possesses the right quality attributes. Most architecture assessment methods use scenarios as a way of simulating a system so that it may be reasoned about.

There are three categories of quality attributes: *external stimuli, architectural decisions,* and *responses.* External stimuli are the events that cause the architecture to respond. For example, a user performs a specific operation that must execute within a limited time, or a maintenance engineer adds a new function to the system. Responses are how the system would react to the stimuli. In the performance example, the response is the amount of time it took to satisfy the user request. In the maintenance example, the response is how many code modules needed to be modified and what other tasks the engineer had to perform to add the new function. In order to assess an architecture for adherence to quality attribute requirements, those requirements should be expressed in measurable or observable terms. Architectural decisions are the design elements or design rules that have a direct impact on achieving attribute responses (Clements, 2002).

In order to make nonfunctional quality attributes measurable or observable, they must be reified as concrete tasks or scenarios. A technique developed at SEI is to convert quality attribute requirements into concrete scenarios for users, developers, and maintainers. Scenarios for modifiability, for example, are sometimes called *change cases.* Scenarios can be a very powerful specification technique because they make seemingly vague or abstract requirements into tangible concrete tasks.

Scenarios can be realized through the creation of a *quality attribute utility tree*, which is one of the main steps of SEI's Attribute Trade-off Analysis Method (ATAM). The utility tree is used to translate abstract requirements into concrete scenarios used to analyze a system's architectural design. If we think of the utility tree as having some virtual root, then the nodes immediately below the root represent the quality attributes, such as described in Chapter 8. That is, the quality model that we have chosen to articulate our requirements and use in the utility tree is isomorphic. An example utility tree for the content publishing and deployment system is represented in Figure 14.2. This example contains a few core requirements for the entire system.

The New Products scenario applies to the delivery component. The Reconfigure Repository scenarios apply to the authoring/assembly and publishing/deployment components. If security were a primary concern, then it should show up in the utility tree. If there are requirements for handling hardware failures, then that should be under the availability branch.

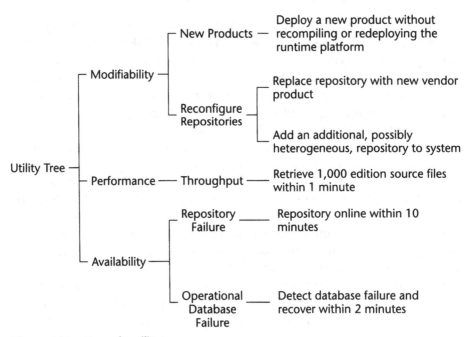

Figure 14.2 Example utility tree.

The Role of the Architectural Description

The architectural design models that comprise the architectural description can have a significant impact on the ability of an architect to analyze an architecture. It is very difficult to analyze an architecture that is not actually written down. The types of models used are relevant in the analysis. In some cases, specific models need to be created for a single quality attribute. For example, in order to assess the architecture for performance, various execution models need to be created. Recall that the architectural description is composed of views that address different concerns. These concerns include specific quality requirements. System maintainers need a view that represents the system from the perspective of maintenance tasks. Different evaluation methods suggest the types of specifications or models needed in order to make the analysis possible.

Architecture Evaluation

Architecture evaluation is a development life-cycle activity whereby several stakeholders analyze the software architecture together in a formal or informal process using an assessment technique such as scenarios. Evaluations can utilize the same architecture assessment techniques described. In some methods, such as ATAM, the stakeholders generate the utility tree and the scenarios as part of the evaluation process.

The characteristics of the development organization affect when and how evaluations are conducted. In small organizations that have a less mature engineering culture, a formal evaluation proceeding may not be appropriate. However, many of the principles and patterns of the evaluation techniques can still be applied. The architect may document a handful of critical scenarios that are used to guide the software design and that serve as input into the testing process.

Formal evaluations should be done as soon as the architectural design concept is stable enough to be assessed, but before any real commitment to development has been taken. This allows the team to discover problems with the architecture at a time when such problems are easier and cheaper to address. However, evaluations *can* be performed after the system is under development or even when it is complete. In some cases I've had to reverse-analyze a system's architecture to determine why some undocumented design decisions were made when no one else on the team had any recollection of why. Although these were not formal evaluation proceedings, I used the same techniques of generating scenarios based on what stakeholders believed characterized the critical quality attributes and evaluated the existing system against them. Quite often the system that was built had quite different characteristics than what the stakeholders believed. In one case, the stakeholders believed that the system was flexible and could easily adapt to end-user information architecture and business process needs. The original designers, who were no longer on the project, had assured the other stakeholders that the system was flexible and adaptable. Because these qualities were not articulated specifically, there was no way to assess that the system satisfied the acquirers' concepts of flexible and adaptable.

This situation is very common and is not a deliberate attempt to build something other than what the stakeholders are asking for. However, in the context of an *ad hoc* development process and without proper specification of the system, acquirers are not able to articulate their specific needs and the developers are not capturing these specific quality requirements in any useful way. You can probably think of at least one such characteristic of the system that you have worked on. The acquirers want the user interface to have an acceptable response time or the system must be flexible enough to integrate into a customer's existing information architecture and Information Technology (IT) architecture. But these desires, if left at this level of specification, can rarely be satisfied completely or accurately. Remember, understand the right problem and solve the right problem. This is our imperative as software architects.

There are several software architecture evaluation methods:

Scenario-based Architecture Analysis Method (SAAM). This was probably the first documented software architecture analysis method and was originally developed to analyze an architecture for modifiability. However, it is useful for analyzing any nonfunctional aspect of an architecture. It is founded on the use of stakeholder-generated scenarios to assess an architecture.

Architecture Trade-off Analysis Method (ATAM). This is a successor of SAAM and is also gaining widespread use. This method incorporates quality attribute utility trees and quality attribute categories in the analysis of an architecture. Whereas SAAM does not explicitly address the interactions between quality attributes, ATAM does. Thus, the trade-offs are with respect to competing quality attributes. ATAM is a specialization of SAAM, specifically focusing on modifiability, performance, availability, and security.

SAAM Founded on Complex Scenarios (SAAMCS). This method considers the complexity of evaluation scenarios as the most important risk assessment factor.

Extending SAAM by Integration in the Domain (ESAAMI). This method integrates SAAM with domain-specific and reuse-based software development processes.

Software Architecture Analysis Method for Evolution and Reusability (SAAMER).   This method focuses specifically on the quality attributes of evolution and reusability.

Scenario-Based Architecture Reengineering (SBAR).   This method utilizes scenarios, simulation, mathematical modeling, and experience-based reasoning for assessing quality attributes. This method also incorporates an architecture design method.

Architecture Level Prediction of Software Maintenance (ALPSM).   This is another method for analyzing maintainability using scenarios, called change scenarios, which represent maintenance tasks.

Software Architecture Evaluation Model (SAEM).   This method is based on formal and rigorous quality requirements.

Different quality attributes can be evaluated using different techniques. Many of these methods share several principles in common and differ in how they characterize specific quality attributes. See Clements (Clements, 2002) for detailed descriptions and case studies for SAAM and ATAM. A good survey of architecture analysis methods can be found in Dobrica (Dobrica, 2002).

Assessing Modifiability

Modifiability is a general quality attribute for specifying a change to a system. The change may be part of a maintenance task, a development task, or an end-user configuration task. Modifiability requirements should be articulated as specific scenarios, also referred to as a *change case* (like a use case but for modeling nonfunctional attributes). In practice it may not be feasible to document every conceivable change case. However, you should identify the most critical change cases.

Let's look at some example modifiability requirements from the publishing system example. Not all of these requirements were explicitly stated in the requirements specification and therefore were not implemented. Had an architectural evaluation or walkthrough been performed, it is quite possible that someone on the team would have asked about these qualities since they were brought up after the system had been developed. Recall the modifiability scenarios from Figure 14.2:

- Deploy a new product without recompiling or redeploying the runtime platform
- Replace repository with new vendor product
- Add an additional, possibly heterogeneous, repository to system

The first requirement was made explicit in the requirements specification and was satisfied. In some cases a new product required a behavior that was not part of the core system. Each behavior was written in a separate Java class that implemented a particular interface. The behavior class had an arbitrary set of initialization parameters that needed to be stored in an operational database. This was achieved by using XML to represent the arbitrary parameters. A product referenced a behavior, which was represented by a behavior class table that identified the actual class to load and instantiate. The XML parameters were passed to an initialized method. Adding new behavior classes, therefore, did not require changing any existing code or database schemas.

The ability to reconfigure the repository subsystem or change repository vendors without affecting the product data itself was a tacit requirement. It was not articulated until after the system had been implemented. In particular, it must be possible to replace a particular vendor's repository with another one as well as introduce additional instances of the repository for performance reasons. Each product had a product definition file, which contained parameters for all of the behaviors used and links to all of the reusable content files that made up the core content of the product. Unfortunately, the product definition file contained repository information for each file. This meant that the location of the content files could not be changed without having to edit the product definition file. There were dozens of product files and eventually there would have been hundreds and potentially thousands as the company branched into other test preparation areas.

Had this been discovered during an architectural design review, a new design such as that represented in Figure 14.3 could have been proposed. In this design a database of file meta data is stored in a file broker system that would allow both the authoring/assembly and publishing subsystems to store location transparent identifiers, yet be able to retrieve the files. If a file's location changed, then only the meta data would need to be updated. The meta data could be stored in a central server or even a local (business unit) mirror server. The other subsystems would not be aware of the actual configuration of meta data servers. In addition to abstracting the location of files, the broker would also abstract the particular repository access methods so that client subsystems only needed to know the broker's access methods. If a new vendor's repository was added, then the appropriate access functions would have to be written once and installed on the broker server, perhaps following the same design pattern as the behavior class above. This design would have satisfied both the ability to change repository vendors and reconfigure the repository system by possibly using heterogeneous repositories.

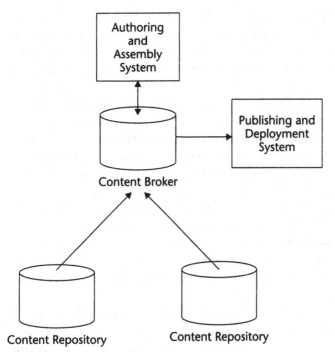

Figure 14.3   Content broker architecture.

The client/server-based knowledge management system mentioned earlier also suffered from a modifiability defect. In this case, the problem was not the failure to satisfy specific modifiability requirements but rather the failure to be maintainable in general. There were no specific modifiability requirements, but we could identify two practical scenarios:

■ As part of the system's evolution, add new objects and allow the client application to invoke operations on these new objects within the same transaction when operating on existing objects, for example, the ability to delete two objects from the system as a single transaction.

■ Developers can modify the application program interface (API) of a particular business object to allow for a variety of access and operation options. For example, some methods may return all of the object's data while some may return specific fields. The developer of a client should have the option to use the most suitable methods.

The API for the middle tier was designed to pass XML documents as data objects between the client and server. The client would create a request as an XML document and invoke a general-purpose server method to accept the request. The server would respond with another XML document. The intention was to make a very flexible server that could handle new types of requests without having to modify the APIs. The problem, however, was that the architecture was actually more rigid because of this decision, not more flexible. Each XML document was associated with a code module that could parse the particular XML document and then map the data fields to the database. Effectively, it was invoking the middle-tier API on behalf of the client. The business logic was no less complex than if it had been invoked from a distributed object like an Enterprise Java Bean (EJB). Furthermore, the client interaction was much more complex. If an error occurred, an XML response had to be parsed and interpreted in the client. The client had to figure out what exactly was the error.

Since all data was returned as a single response, it made the system slow and even occasionally crash when the results of a particular request were long. If the system had been written using EJBs that utilized Java Data Base Connectivity (JDBC) to access the database, then the system could have taken advantage of various platform and database capabilities such as temp tables and cursors to handle large lists of query results.

This single design decision resulted in several compensating decisions. In an attempt to improve performance, a proprietary caching mechanism was written. Now resources that could have otherwise been devoted to solving business problems and adding functionality to the system were instead focusing on solving technology problems. This resulted in the system being delivered later than planned, suffering from several quality issues, and having fewer capabilities than it could have had. If an architectural evaluation had been performed, these problems could have been identified and an alternative architecture proposed. In this case, the proposal would have been to follow common Java 2 Enterprise Edition (J2EE) design practices and EJB patterns and idioms.

If the general scenarios above were used to assess the architecture, then it is possible that the problems with the XML approach would have been identified before committing to this architectural decision. One benefit of using an EJB-based architecture is that a developer can create a session EJB that operates on more than one entity EJB within a single transaction. The entity EJBs are written without any knowledge of the other entity EJBs, the session EJB, or the fact that they may operate within a transaction. This allows new objects to be designed and implemented and for new business-related rules to be defined without rewriting the existing objects. Each XML-based operation could not be invoked within a shared transaction, so it would be very difficult to extend a transaction to include new XML-based operations. One way may be to create a new combined-XML document for the new transaction. In any case, the system is just too difficult to modify or extend.

The second scenario would also require the creation of new XML documents and code for mapping them to the database. If a finer-grained operation is desired, then a new XML document needs to be defined and new code for mapping it to the database is required. This change case is much more complex than using distributed objects.

There is a related problem in design called *subjectivity*. This is the principle that no single interface can satisfy the needs of all client systems. The original intention of the XML-based API and middle-tier design was an indirect attempt to solve the subjectivity problem.

Assessing Performance

There are two conflicting views about performance: the "make-it-work-then-make-it-fast" community and the "filter-every-decision-through-a-performance-analysis" group. Both views are typically considered to be extreme.

A better approach is shown in Figure 14.4. When considering architecture, you may emphasize performance measurement because that really is part of "make it work" in terms of the architecture. This is performing activities in quadrants II and III (the order doesn't matter because the design work is done in iterations). During detailed design (coding), design decisions are theoretically localized and you can move from quadrant I to IV. In this case, the "make-it-work" emphasis in detailed design is less risky because performance tests can be performed against a smaller component area, since global performance issues should have been addressed earlier in the development life cycle (quadrant III).

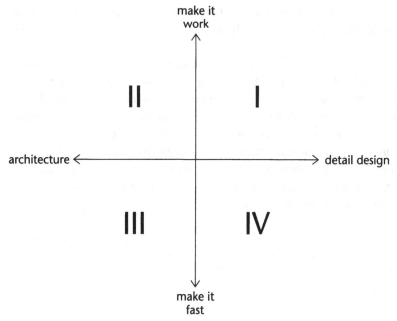

Figure 14.4 Function versus performance.

One performance myth (Smith, 2002) is that you have to have something to execute in order to performance-test it. In fact some aspects of system performance can be predicted by analyzing the architecture. Many performance problems, as we have seen in the examples, stem from the architectural design decisions. A performance bottleneck that can be traced to a single code routine or that is isolated to a few areas in code can be easily fixed, for example, an inefficient algorithm or memory allocation strategy. But an architectural change means that the design decision is somehow fundamental to the whole system organization. Perhaps it is the design of the protocol between several components.

Design rules are shared assumptions across a set of components. When you decompose a system, look at those design rules to see what the characteristics are of the communication between the components. You don't always have to perform an extensive performance analysis. You can get some idea of the potential areas where performance can be a problem. At the architectural level, performance is characterized by the interaction between components. If these components are different software processes, then analyze the communication characteristics between the components.

Smith and Williams present a software process engineering (SPE) method based on creating performance models for critical use case scenarios. For each critical use case, select the key performance scenarios, establish performance objectives, construct the performance models, add software resource requirements, add computer resource requirements, and evaluate the performance model. If the results are not acceptable and it is feasible, then modify the product concept (architecture), modify or create scenarios, and repeat the process. If the results are not acceptable and it is not feasible to modify the architecture, then the performance objectives must be revised. This may require negotiations with the system acquirers.

The key scenarios for a critical use case are those normal scenarios that are performed frequently. Abnormal scenarios (for example, error situations) may not necessarily have the same performance requirements. Recall that a sequence diagram can be used to represent a use case scenario. The performance objectives and workload criteria are specified. Performance objectives specify the quantitative criteria. These may be specified as response time, throughput, or resource usage constraints. Workload intensities can be specified as an arrival rate such as the number of Uniform Resource Locator (URL) requests or as the number of concurrent users.

The performance models of Smith and Williams are represented using execution graphs, which are created from the performance scenario sequence diagrams. Recall our content publishing system example. In Figure 14.5 is the *compile edition* use case. One scenario of this use case is represented in Figure 14.6. This is the normal use case (in which there are no errors in fetching the edition source). The content server A may need to get additional content from another content server B. In fact, it may need to get additional content from multiple sources. Content server A may be a central server that retrieves XML data from an XML repository and media files from a media server. The content deployer may invoke the `compileEdition()` function multiple times, for example, if he or she discovers an error in a source file and corrects it. Any changes are eventually committed back to the content broker.

In Figure 14.6, I use a UML sequence diagram embellishment developed by Smith and Williams. The sequence within the box labeled *loop* indicates that the section of the sequence diagram is repeated. The portion of the sequence within the box labeled *alt* indicates that these sequences may be executed or they may not. Since the alt box is in the loop box, this indicates that within each loop or iteration of the indicated sequence, the alt sequence may or may not be executed.

Suppose our performance objective is a typical edition that has 2,000 source files that should take 17 minutes to retrieve and compile. Retrieving should be within 2 minutes and compiling within 15 minutes (recall our throughput scenario in Figure 14.2 that states that 1,000 files shall be retrieved within 1 minute). The original system took over 9 hours to fetch 2,000 files and 45 minutes to compile. These numbers are based on how many editions a content deployer can deploy in a single day. The original system had to be started the night before and then the edition was deployed the next morning, assuming all went well. A 17-minute overall performance objective would provide ample time to deploy several editions a day and fix errors when they occur with less risk to delaying their deployment.

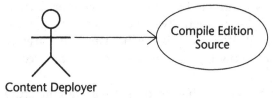

Content Deployer

Figure 14.5   Compile edition use case.

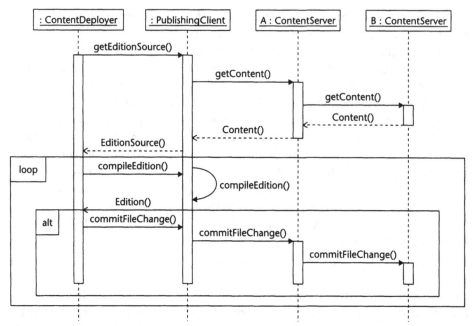

Figure 14.6 Compile edition use case sequence diagram.

Summary

Architecture assessment allows the software development team to observe or measure the architecture of a system before it has been constructed in order to better predict the quality of the eventual system. This helps lower the risks associated with developing complex software systems. Architecture assessment can be part of a formal evaluation process conducted by many system stakeholders or an informal activity conducted by the design team as part of their everyday design work. Regardless, the activity serves as a quality control mechanism in software development. Without this mechanism, the software development organization may not know if a design has achieved an acceptable balance of quality attributes.

It is appropriate to end this book with a chapter on software architecture quality. The subject of this book is improving the quality of software through architectural design. Through architecting we can create models of the software system that we intend to construct. These models help us to manage the complexity inherent in specifying requirements and searching for a design. The more complex a system is, the more important architectural design becomes. The best way to improve the quality of a system is to actively address complexity and continually check design decisions against the system's required quality attributes early in the development cycle. Many of these quality attributes compete, and therefore a design must balance them. Quite often we are forced to make design trade-offs when we cannot find a solution that balances these competing forces entirely. Architecture assessment gives us the knowledge we need in order to make the best architectural design decisions.

APPENDIX

Bibliography

Alexander, C. 1964. *Notes on the Synthesis of Form*. Cambridge, MA: Harvard University Press.

Alexander, C. 1979. *The Timeless Way of Building*. New York: Oxford University Press.

Baldwin, C., Clark, K. 2000. *Design Rules: Volume 1. The Power of Modularity*. Cambridge, MA: The MIT Press.

Bass, L., Coutaz, J. 1991. *Developing Software for the User Interface*. Reading, MA: Addison-Wesley.

Bass, L., Clements, P., Kazman, R. 1998. *Software Architecture in Practice*. Reading, MA: Addison-Wesley.

Best, L. 1990. *Application Architecture: Modern Large-Scale Information Processing*. New York: John Wiley and Sons.

Booch, G. 1994. *Object-Oriented Analysis and Design with Applications*, 2d ed. Menlo Park, CA: Addison-Wesley.

Booch, G. 1998. *The Unified Modeling Language User Guide*. Reading, MA: Addison-Wesley.

Bosch, J. 2000. *Design and Use of Software Architectures: Adopting and Evolving a Product-Line Approach*. Harlow, England: Addison-Wesley.

Brooks, F. 1975. *The Mythical Man-Month: Essays on Software Engineering*. Reading, MA: Addison-Wesley.

Buhrer, K. 2001. "From Craft to Science: Rules for Software Design—Part II." *The Rational Edge.* January, 2001. http://www.therationaledge.com/content/jan_01/f_craftsci_kb.html.

Buschmann, F., Meunier, R., Rohnert, H., Sommerlad, P., Stal, M. 1996. *Pattern-Oriented Software Architecture: A System of Patterns.* Chichester: John Wiley and Sons.

Carroll, J. 2002. *Human-Computer Interaction in the New Millennium.* New York: Addison-Wesley.

Clements, P., Kazman, R., Klein, M. 2002. *Evaluating Software Architectures: Methods and Case Studies.* Boston, MA: Addison-Wesley.

Cooper, A. 1999. *The Inmates Are Running the Asylum.* Indianapolis, IN: SAMS.

DeGrace, P., Stahl, L. 1993. *The Olduvai Imperative: CASE and the State of Software Engineering Practice.* Englewood Cliffs, NJ: Yourdon Press.

Dijkstra, E. W. 1968. "The Structure of the 'THE' Multiprogramming System." *Communications of the ACM* 11, no. 5: 341-346.

Dikel, D., Kane, D., Wilson, J. 2001. *Software Architecture: Organizational Principles and Patterns.* Upper Saddle River, NJ: Prentice Hall PTR.

Dobrica, L., Niemelä, E. 2002. "A Survey on Software Architecture Analysis Methods." *IEEE Transactions on Software Engineering* 28, no. 7 (July): 638-653.

Gamma, E., Helm, R., Johnson, R., Vlissides, J. 1995. *Design Patterns: Elements of Reusable Object-Oriented Software.* Reading, MA: Addison-Wesley.

Gell-Mann, M. 1994. *The Quark and the Jaguar: Adventures in the Simple and the Complex.* New York: W.H. Freeman and Company.

Hofmeister, C., Nord, R., Soni, D. 2000. *Applied Software Architecture.* Reading, MA: Addison-Wesley.

Hubert, R. 2002. *Convergent Architecture: Building Model-Driven J2EE Systems with UML.* New York: John Wiley and Sons.

Humphrey, W. S. 1989. *Managing the Software Process.* Reading, MA: Addison-Wesley.

Humphrey, W. S. 1994. *A Discipline for Software Engineering.* Reading, MA: Addison-Wesley.

IEEE 1990. "IEEE Standard Glossary of Software Engineering Terminology." *IEEE Std 610.12-1990.* New York, NY: Institute of Electrical and Electronics Engineers.

IEEE 2000. "IEEE Recommended Practice for Architectural Descriptions of Software Intensive Systems." *IEEE Std 1471-2000.* New York, NY: Institute of Electrical and Electronics Engineers.

ISO/IEC 1995. "Basic Reference Model of Open Distributed Processing." *ITU-T X.900 services and ISO/IEC RM-ODP 10746 services.* Geneva, Switzerland: International Organization for Standardization.

ISO/IEC 2001. "Software Engineering—Product Quality—Part 1: Quality Model." *ISO/IEC 9126-1:2001.* Geneva, Switzerland: International Organization for Standardization.

Jackson, M. 1995. *Software Requirements and Specifications*. Harlow, England: Addison-Wesley.

Jacobson, I., Griss, M., Jonsson, P. 1997. *Software Reuse: Architecture, Process, and Organization for Business Success*. Harlow, England: Addison-Wesley.

Jacobson, I., Booch, G., Rumbaugh, J. 1999. *The Unified Software Development Process*. Reading, MA: Addison-Wesley.

Kruchten, P. B. 1995. "The 4+1 View Model of architecture." *IEEE Software* 12 no. 6.

Kruchten, P. B. 2000. *The Rational Unified Process: An Introduction*, 2d ed. Reading, MA: Addison-Wesley.

Maier, M., Rechtin, E. 2000. *The Art of Systems Architecting*, 2d ed. Boca Raton: CRC Press.

Mowbray, T., Malveau, R. 1997. *CORBA Design Patterns*. New York: John Wiley and Sons.

Nakano, R. 2002. *Web Content Management: A Collaborative Approach*. Boston, MA: Addison-Wesley.

Norman, D. 2002. *The Design of Everyday Things*. New York: Basic Books.

Pahl, G., Beitz, W. 1996. *Engineering Design: A Systematic Approach*, 2d ed. London: Springer.

Parnas, D. 1972. "On the Criteria to Be Used in Decomposing Systems into Modules." *Communications of the ACM* 15, no. 12: 1,053-1,058.

Perry, D. E., Wolf, A. L. 1992. "Foundations for the Study of Software Architecture." *ACM SIGSOFT Software Engineering Notes* 17, no. 4: 40-52.

Putman, J. 2001. *Architecting with RM-ODP*. Upper Saddle River, NJ: Prentice Hall PTR.

Rayside, D., Campbell, G. T. "An Aristotelian understanding of object-oriented programming." In *Proceedings of OOPSLA 2000* (Minneapolis, Minnesota, United States): 337-353.

Rechtin, E. 1991. *Systems Architecting: Creating and Building Complex Systems*. Upper Saddle River, NJ: Prentice Hall PTR.

Riel, A. J. 1996. *Object-Oriented Design Heuristics*, Reading, MA: Addison-Wesley.

Rowland, I., Howe, T. N., editors. 2001. *Vitruvius: Ten Books on Architecture*. Cambridge, England: Cambridge University Press.

Rumbaugh, J., Blaha, M., Premerlani, W., Eddy, F., Lorensen, W. 1991. *Object-Oriented Modeling and Design*. Englewood Cliffs, NJ: Prentice Hall.

Rumbaugh, J., Jacobson, I., Booch, G. 1999. *The Unified Modeling Language Reference Manual*. Reading, MA: Addison-Wesley.

Schmidt, D., Stal, M., Rohnert, H., Buschmann, F. 2000. *Pattern-Oriented Software Architecture, Volume 2: Patterns for Concurrent and Networked Objects*. Chichester: John Wiley and Sons.

Sewell, M., Sewell, L. 2002. *The Software Architect's Profession: An Introduction*. Upper Saddle River, NJ: Prentice Hall PTR.

Shaw, M., Garlan, D. 1996. *Software Architecture: Perspectives on an Emerging Discipline*. Upper Saddle River, NJ: Prentice-Hall.

Smith, C., Williams, L. 2002. *Performance Solutions: A Practical Guide to Creating Responsive, Scalable Software*. Boston, MA: Addison-Wesley.

Taylor, R. N., Medvidovic, N., Anderson, K. M., Whitehead, Jr., E. J., Robbins, J. E., Nies, K. A., Oreizy, P., Dubrow, D. L. 1996. "A Component- and Message-Based Architectural Style for GUI Software." *IEEE Transactions on Software Engineering* 22, no.6: 390-406.

Whitehead, A. N. 1948. *An Introduction to Mathematics*. London: Oxford University Press.

Winograd, T. 1996. *Bringing Design to Software*. Reading, MA: Addison-Wesley.

Zeigler, B., Preahofer, H., Kim, T. 2000. *Theory of Modeling and Simulation: Integrating Discrete Event and Continuous Complex Dynamic Systems*, 2d. ed. San Diego, CA: Academic Press.

Index